W9-BSK-096

# Knowing Moral Truth

# Knowing Moral Truth

*A Theory of Metaethics
and Moral Knowledge*

Christopher B. Kulp

LEXINGTON BOOKS
Lanham • Boulder • New York • London

Published by Lexington Books
An imprint of The Rowman & Littlefield Publishing Group, Inc.
4501 Forbes Boulevard, Suite 200, Lanham, Maryland 20706
www.rowman.com

Unit A, Whitacre Mews, 26-34 Stannary Street, London SE11 4AB, United Kingdom

Copyright © 2017 Lexington Books

*All rights reserved.* No part of this book may be reproduced in any form or by any
electronic or mechanical means, including information storage and retrieval systems,
without written permission from the publisher, except by a reviewer who may quote
passages in a review.

British Library Cataloguing in Publication Information Available

**Library of Congress Cataloging-in-Publication Data**

Names: Kulp, Christopher B., author.
Title: Knowing moral truth : a theory of metaethics and moral knowledge /
    Christopher B. Kulp.
Description: Lanham : Lexington Books, 2017. | Includes bibliographical
    references and index.
Identifiers: LCCN 2017006782 (print) | LCCN 2017015146 (ebook) | ISBN
    9781498547031 (Electronic) | ISBN 9781498547024 (cloth : alk. paper)
Subjects: LCSH: Ethics. | Knowledge, Theory of.
Classification: LCC BJ1031 (ebook) | LCC BJ1031 .K85 2017 (print) | DDC
    170/.42--dc23
LC record available at https://lccn.loc.gov/2017006782

∞ ™ The paper used in this publication meets the minimum requirements of American
National Standard for Information Sciences Permanence of Paper for Printed Library
Materials, ANSI/NISO Z39.48-1992.

Printed in the United States of America

To my wife, Akemi Odomo

# Contents

# Acknowledgments

There are many people over the years with whom I have discussed matters dealt with in this book; I have profited greatly from their insights. The following stand out as especially meriting my appreciation: Mane Hajdin, Michael Hickson, William Parent, William Prior, Robert Shanklin, and Artur Szutta. In particular, I want to thank Robert Audi for his inspiration and for his penetrating commentary on various parts of the book in earlier forms. I also wish to thank audiences at the University of Texas–San Antonio, the University of Gdansk, Poland, and Santa Clara University for helpful commentary on presented papers which bear on many parts of this book.

In addition, I wish to thank Santa Clara University's Markkula Center for Applied Ethics for their generosity in awarding me a Hackworth Faculty Research Grant for work on this book. I also wish to thank Santa Clara University's Office of the Provost, for awarding me both sabbatical leave and for a course release under the Santa Clara University Faculty Research Course Release Program. The university's assistance has been invaluable to this project.

I also gratefully acknowledge permission to quote from several of my previous publications. My thanks to *International Philosophical Quarterly*, for permission to quote from my article, "Disagreement and the Defensibility of Moral Intuitionism," *International Philosophical Quarterly* Vol. 56, issue 224 (December 2016): 487–502. Also, for quotations which are here used by permission of Bloomsbury Publishing, Plc, I wish to thank both Jill Graper Hernandez and the Continuum International Publishing Group for allowing me to quote from my article "Moral Facts and the Centrality of Intuitions," in *The New Intuitionism*, edited by Jill Graper Hernandez (New York and London: Continuum, 2011): 48–66. And finally, I wish to thank Springer Pub-

lishing Company for permission to quote from my article, "The Pre-Theoreticality of Moral Intuitions," *Synthese* Vol. 191 (October 2014): 3759–778.

Last but hardly least, I wish to thank my wife, Akemi Odomo, whose
constant support was the sine qua non of writing this book.

# Chapter One

# The Epistemic Starting Point

## 1.1. OUTLINE OF A METHODOLOGY:
## THE SPIRIT OF G. E. MOORE

On the morning of December 14, 2012, twenty-year-old Adam Peter Lanza entered Sandy Hook Elementary School in Newtown, Connecticut, and began shooting the school's occupants. By the time Lanza died at the scene of a self-inflicted gunshot wound to the head, twenty-six people lay dead or dying. In addition to Lanza's death, six of the school's staff members, most of them teachers, were killed. Their names are:

| | |
|---|---|
| Rachel D'avino | Lauren Rousseau |
| Dawn Hochsprung | Mary Sherlach |
| Anne Marie Murphy | Victoria Soto |

Twenty of the school's children were also shot to death. Their names and ages are as follows:

| | |
|---|---|
| Charlotte Bacon, 6 | James Mattioli, 6 |
| Daniel Barden, 7 | Grace McDonnell, 7 |
| Olivia Engel, 6 | Emilie Parker, 6 |
| Josephine Gay, 7 | Jack Pinto, 6 |
| Ana M. Marquez-Greene, 6 | Noah Pozner, 6 |
| Dylan Hockley, 6 | Caroline Previdi, 6 |
| Madeleine F. Hsu, 6 | Jessica Rekos, 6 |
| Catherine V. Hubbard, 6 | Avielle Richman, 6 |
| Chase Kowalski, 7 | Benjamin Wheeler, 6 |
| Jesse Lewis, 6 | Allison N. Wyatt, 6 |

Nancy Lanza, mother of Adam Lanza, was the twenty-seventh victim. She was found dead at the family home, with four gunshot wounds to the head. The police believe that she had been shot while sleeping.

As of this writing, this incident remains the third largest mass-killing of its kind in US history.[1] It has become widely known as the "Sandy Hook Shootings." Perhaps a more appropriate reference would be the "Sandy Hook Massacre." The *Oxford English Dictionary* defines (the noun form of) 'massacre' as "a general slaughter of human beings." This incident certainly qualifies; and the term 'massacre' aptly underscores how horrifying, repulsive, despicable, and utterly outrageous we think it is. But in the interest of familiarity, I will stick with the now standard reference. I especially draw attention to the killing of the small children; for it is hard to conceive of any category of persons[2] that could be less deserving of such treatment. These children are as close as we can readily come to being purely innocent victims.[3]

There are many ways to think about these killings. We might look at it psychologically: What psychopathy might have induced Lanza to murder these people, in particular the small children? We might look at it sociologically: Were there any especially strong societal stressors that conduced to Lanza behaving this way? Legal issues: Should the shooter be judged criminally insane? Political issues: Would a change in gun laws have prevented this event from happening? And we can certainly look at it *morally.*

Let's assume that Lanza was in possession of his senses when he committed this slaughter—an assumption admittedly difficult to confirm because Lanza killed himself before a psychiatric examination could be performed. That is, let's suppose that Lanza *chose* to do what he did, and therefore was responsible for his actions. At first blush, there could scarcely be anything more straightforward than that what Lanza did was morally wrong in the extreme.[4] Similar moral judgments seem applicable: impermissible, unjustifiable, contemptible, abhorrent, cruel, vicious, perverse . . . the list is long. *A central thesis of this book is that what appears to us at first blush is in the end, after rigorous analysis, quite correct: Lanza's behavior is a paradigm case of moral wrongness.*

Who in the world could think otherwise? Well, there are a lot of people who, officially at any rate, think otherwise: thoughtful people, in fact. But these people assuredly don't represent the views of the proverbial "man in the street." The average person would find the Sandy Hook Shootings not only deeply upsetting, but profoundly morally wrong—and would point to the immorality of the event as (at least part of) the *cause* of their upset. Indeed, they would consider this act wrong no matter *where* it occurred, *when* it occurred, or *who* performed it. *It is wrong, period.* And I emphasize that this judgment is enshrined in the criminal law of any nation with which I am familiar. But it is at this juncture that our average person parts company with some of the intellectual cognoscenti. For some of these "experts" would find the act morally wrong only in some restricted, qualified respect, not "wrong, *period*," as does the average person. They think, for example, that it is only wrong "from our perspective." Other experts would for a variety of different reasons find the very concept of "moral wrongness" and its cognates misguided or ill conceived—perhaps even lacking in meaning. For all of these folks, it can't be true simpliciter that the Sandy Hook killings were morally wrong. But certainly, this is in stark contrast to our ordinary thinking.

There are many variations on the theme that our ordinary, common sense moral thinking is systematically wrong. Later we will look at these matters in some detail. But the point to be taken here is that, surprising though it may be, many morally informed people would not consider the Sandy Hook Shootings, or any other such act, to be morally wrong in the straightforward, robust sense of "morally wrong" that the average person thinks it is, and around which we construct our very lives. But in all fairness, it is important to emphasize that many of these "moral dissidents" are anything but crazed sociopaths. Many are people of genuine good will and deep erudition.

To anyone unfamiliar with the history of Western philosophy, especially with academic discussion of the nature of ethics, of metaethics, during the last hundred years or so, this is a shocking result. Such folks are apt to exclaim, "If *anything* is morally wrong, the Sandy Hook Shootings were wrong. To deny this is simply unthinkable!" And some of the philosophical cognoscenti would agree. A case in point would be G. E. Moore,[5] one of the founders of contemporary analytic philosophy, and the philosopher most responsible, with the publication of *Principia Ethica* in 1903, for the preeminence of metaethics in the first half of the twentieth century. Moore would be appalled not only by the murders, but by any view inconsistent with thinking it wrong in (roughly speaking) our ordinary sense of the term.[6] Indeed, Moore's reaction to doubts about the moral wrongness of the Sandy Hook Shootings would be of the same ilk as those he expressed regarding broad skeptical doubts about the existence of the external world.

In his famous article "Proof of an External World," Moore sets out to respond to Kant's remark that, "It still remains a scandal to philosophy . . . that the existence of things outside of us . . . must be accepted merely on *faith*, and that, if anyone thinks good to doubt their existence, we are unable to counter his doubts by any satisfactory proof."[7] Moore answers Kant's challenge by holding up one hand, holding up another, and then claiming to know "with certainty" that two hands exist, and that therefore at least two things exist "outside of us" in the sense of not being a mere product of our own minds—that is to say, exist in an external world independent of our own making.[8] He further claims that he could give an indefinitely large number of

such proofs, as could anyone else. Moore thinks it utterly clear that an external world exists, and that he has provided a fully satisfactory proof that it
does, for it meets the three conditions requisite for any such proof: (i) The
premiss from which he deduced the proof was different from the conclusion
reached; (ii) he knew the premiss of the argument to be true (i.e., he knew
that these were his hands); and (iii) he knew that the conclusion follows from
the premiss (i.e., it is a valid argument). [9] But Moore acknowledged that "I
am perfectly well aware that in spite of all I have said, many philosophers
will still feel that I have not given any satisfactory proof of the point in
question [viz., that an external world exists]." [10] For these philosophers require that he prove his premiss against any possible doubt, and this Moore
admits not only that he cannot do, but that he sees no possible way of doing.
He cannot, for example, *prove* that he is not dreaming when he asserts that
these are his hands, even though he has not the slightest reason to believe that
he *is* dreaming, and that indeed he has conclusive reason to believe that he is
not dreaming. [11]

Moore's approach, and his dilemma, if you will, bears on our project. For
along with common-sensists like Moore and the mid-eighteenth-century
Scottish philosopher Thomas Reid, and along with American pragmatists
like John Dewey and Charles S. Peirce, I believe that we must "begin where
we are"—that it is futile to first search for some sort of indubitable Cartesian
starting point, immune to challenge, before beginning philosophical inquiry. [12] And where we are with regard to morality is, I submit, well represented by our reaction to the Sandy Hook Shootings. We are horrified; we
condemn it as atrocity; we consider it morally wrong no matter who perpetrated it, when or where. This is of signal importance; for it is the moral and
epistemic "loadstar" that properly guides development of our abstract moral
theories. I would even go so far as to say that, if a conception of the nature of
morality entails that the killing of the Sandy Hook Elementary School children and staff members is other than egregiously wrong, *so much the worse
for that conception of morality*. The metaethical theory of this book will seek
to provide explicatory depth and rigor for our ordinary moral judgments like
this. It is in this fashion that we will proceed.

I do not, however, take any of our moral judgments to be infallible—
although in some cases they approach this limit of epistemic credibility. The
metaethical and epistemological perspective of this book is fallibilist to the
core. If we find that we cannot construct a credible conception of morality
which supports our ordinary moral judgments—if we find that our opponents
can meet our arguments with responses more cogent than ours—then our
only recourse may be to abandon our ordinary, tutored conception of morality. The alternative is irrationality. I am, confident, however, that it won't
come to this.

## 1.2. "WHAT WE REALLY THINK": THE UBIQUITY
## OF FIRST-ORDER MORAL KNOWLEDGE

G. E. Moore famously remarked that, "I do not think that the world or the sciences would ever have suggested to me any philosophical problems. What has suggested philosophical problems to me is things which other philosophers have said about the world or the sciences."[13]

There is reason not to take Moore strictly at his word here,[14] but there can be no doubt that he was especially motivated to pursue philosophical inquiry by other philosophers, especially those whose views he considered outrageous. Beginning with his Cambridge undergraduate days in the early 1890s as a member of the secret discussion society known as "The Apostles" (obviously not a thoroughgoing secret), Moore became famous for pressing hard on views he thought lacked credibility, in particular those he considered fundamentally incompatible with sound common sense.[15] And what, we might ask, could be more prima facie incredible than that the Sandy Hook Shootings were not morally wrong, plain and simple? Our commonsense thinking is crystal clear: "Of course they were!"

The clarity we have on the moral status of the Sandy Hook killings is hardly unique. Who now wants to defend the Confederate State's endorsement of chattel slavery? Who thinks the Union wrong to have abolished it? Who would not condemn the massacre of the Jews in the Holocaust? Who thinks that Pol Pot's Kymer Rouge should have murdered some two million Cambodians? No one reading this, I am sure.

Nor is our clarity of judgment limited to the negative: we all salute the New York City Fire Department's bravery during the 9/11 terror attack. We all admire the selflessness of those who donate a kidney to a friend who would otherwise die or be forever tethered to a dialysis machine. We all think that we owe kindness to our dear and devoted friends, respect for hard-won achievement, and praise for discharging our duty in the face of adversity. None of this is really controversial—at least not as we ordinarily think of things.

But many philosophers think that all of this is fundamentally misconceived. The Confederacy's endorsement of the chattel slavery of black people? Well, it all depends on your perspective: *relative to* the Confederacy, it was morally fine; *relative to* the Union, very bad. The French didn't like it either, nor did the British; but it would appear that the African slave traders had little objection to it. Soon we will have to put these matters much more carefully, but the general point is that the moral rightness or wrongness, permissibility or impermissibility, praiseworthiness or condemnability of chattel slavery or the Holocaust or of whatever act or policy or set of social mores is at issue, *is perspectively relative*, that is, relative to a standard of judgment. If we don't share that standard, then of course we are not going to agree with the judgment, *nor need we*. But again, we certainly don't ordinarily think that way. We think that the Confederacy was dead wrong about slavery. We think the Nazi's inexcusably mistaken for perpetrating the Holocaust. Perhaps some benighted members of the Ku Klux Klan or virulent anti-Semites do not agree with us, but who takes these views seriously?[16] If we ask ourselves, in the spirit of Mary Midgley's simple but wise question,[17] "What do we *really* think about this?" we would surely reply, "It is horribly wrong—and it is outrageous to think otherwise." Indeed, I suspect that many of us would be sympathetic to the sentiments of Wittgenstein's student and an important philosopher in her own right, G. E. M. Anscombe when she tells us, "if someone really thinks, *in advance*, that it is open to question whether such an action as procuring the judicial execution of the innocent should be quite excluded from consideration—I do not want to argue with him; he shows a corrupt mind."[18]

The fact is we are exceedingly confident about many moral judgments. Actually, we think that we possess a great deal of moral *knowledge*. But we now need to get a bit clearer on what moral knowledge is, and why some well-informed people have doubts that we have any.

There are different types of knowledge.[19] For example, there is knowledge "how"— knowledge how to ride a bike, for instance. Perhaps you can't really tell someone else how to ride a bike—surely a five-year-old child could not provide much of an explanation—but you (and the five year old) may nevertheless ride with aplomb: you know *how* to ride a bike. And there is "objectual knowledge," that is, knowledge of an object. Although you may not be able to provide a description of the low-hanging doorway, because you haven't really focused your attention on it, you know *of* the low doorway's presence, and ducked your head accordingly.[20] And there is "propositional knowledge," that is, knowledge that a proposition is true. Thus, if I know that the leaves of an oak tree are green, or that the sum of two and three equals five, then I know that the proposition 'The leaves of an oak tree are green', or that the proposition 'Two plus three equals five' is *true*. This is often referred to as "knowledge that," because it is knowledge that such-and-such is the case.

In subsequent chapters we will have to get much clearer on propositional knowledge, but the point to be taken is that much if not all of our moral knowledge is propositional. Thus, if we know something to be true or to be false regarding morality, we know the truth or falsity of a moral proposition. Take the following propositions:

P1: Chattel slavery, such as was practiced in the southern states of the United States prior to the American Civil War, is morally wrong.
P2: It is prima facie morally praiseworthy to return kindness with kindness.

If we know that chattel slavery as practiced in the antebellum South is wrong, then we know the *truth* of the moral proposition expressing it. And if we know that it is morally praiseworthy, unless there is specific reason to the contrary, to return kindness with kindness, then we know the *truth* of the proposition expressing this. Similarly for the following propositions:

> P3: A normative ethical theory is defective if it entails the falsehood of the principle that, ceteris paribus, like cases should be treated alike.
>
> P4: Kant's deontological ethics has greater explanatory power regarding the indefensibility of chattel slavery than does Mill's utilitarianism.

If we know the truth, or the falsity, that a normative ethical theory is defective if it entails the falsehood of the principle that like cases should be treated alike, absent specific reason to the contrary, then we know the truth, or the falsity, of the proposition expressing this. And similarly regarding the explanatory power of Kant's deontology vs. Mill's utilitarianism.

P1–P4 are all examples of what in the contemporary literature are called "first-order" moral propositions. They are first-order because they are propositions the subject matter of which is "within" morality, that is, within the conceptual domain typically designated "the moral."[21] It will be convenient, however, to distinguish between propositions like P1 and P2, in contrast to propositions like P3 and P4. The former have to do with judgments about specific acts, policies, etc.; the latter have to do with normative principles or criteria applicable to the judgment of particular acts, policies, etc. Let's call propositions like P1 and P2 "Class A" first-order moral propositions, and propositions like P3 and P4 "Class B" first-order moral propositions. Class A propositions will be of special importance for us.[22]

There is, however, another type of moral proposition, which are commonly called "second-order" moral propositions. These are propositions *about* morality, that is, propositions about the nature and status of morality itself. Here are several examples:

> P5: Moral judgments are true or false only relative to a specific society or culture.
>
> P6: There are no first-order moral truths, nor are there any first-order moral falsehoods.

These are propositions not about the moral defensibility, permissibility, rightness, etc., of a particular act, policy, or attitude, as are P1 and P2; nor are they about the defensibility, appropriateness, etc., of particular normative theories or principles, as are P3 and P4. They are, rather, propositions having to do with the *nature* of morality—its general features, its conceptual status, etc.

The subject matter of what is often termed "applied ethics" is exemplified by propositions like P1 and P2. It asks questions such as: Is capital punishment morally permissible? What is a morally just distribution of wealth in nations such as the United States? What are our obligations to friends? The subject matter of what is often termed "normative ethics" is exemplified by propositions like P3 and P4. It asks questions such as, Is Kant's deontology preferable to W. D. Ross's deontology? Is act-utilitarianism more defensible than rule-utilitarianism? Is Aristotelian virtue ethics applicable to adjudicating claims about the permissible limits of political freedom? And the subject matter of what is often termed "metaethics" is exemplified by propositions like P5 and P6. Metaethics asks questions such as: Is all first-order moral truth and falsity relative to what the majority of people believe? Are there non-natural moral properties? What is the relationship of moral properties to the physical world?

One of this book's principal concerns is metaethics, so we will take very seriously issues regarding the truth or falsity of second-order moral propositions like P5 and P6. But this book is also concerned with first-order moral matters, such as those expressed by propositions like P1–P4. In fact, the first-order moral will play a very important role for us, because I will argue that *we can best obtain a proper understanding of the nature of morality by first getting a firm grasp on the meaning and the truth or falsity of first-order moral propositions.* In fact, first-order moral propositions, of the sort typified by P1 and P2, will be especially important for us in order to lay the foundation for understanding not only morality's nature and status, but also our epistemic access to moral truth—the second principal concern of this book. But *do* we have any moral knowledge?

What we *really* think, we may say to Professor Midgley, is that we know all kinds of (Class A) first-order moral truths.[23] I know that this proposition is true:

> P7: It is morally wrong for anyone to walk into my office and (intentionally) shoot me to death as I sit here writing this book.

Indeed, if I know the truth of any moral proposition, I know this one. *I am sure you know it is true as well.* If anyone were seriously to say to my family, to my friends or colleagues, to the investigating police officers, "No, I don't *at all* know that shooting Kulp to death as he sat there writing his book was really morally wrong," they would be appalled, incredulous, morally scandalized.[24] You would be, too, especially were the victim not me, whom you have likely never met, but your own brother or friend or spouse. You would certainly know *that* was wrong. And here is something else we know: we know that the following generalization is *false:*

P8: It is always morally permissible for adults to have coercive sexual intercourse with young children.

Our normal thinking is that anyone asserting P8's truth would be asserting an outrage, and not just because he or she is asserting a (completely) untenable generalization. For we surely know that any instantiation of this generalization is at the very least prima facie false. For example, we all know, not least of all you the reader, that it is *false* that it is morally permissible for an adult to have coercive sexual intercourse with *your* young child.[25] All doubts and qualifications about moral wrongness evaporate here. Raping *your* child? Are you mad!? Pedophiles may obfuscate, psychopaths may balk, *but let us hear their defense.*

The fact is that, taken on a case by case basis, "what we really think" is that we know an indefinitely large number of moral truths. We not only know (P7) that it's wrong to walk into my office and shoot me, we also know that it is morally wrong for anyone to walk into *your* office and shoot *you* to death as you sit there writing *your* book; and we know that it is morally wrong for anyone to walk into your *brother's* office and shoot *him* to death as he sits there writing *his* book. By the same token, we not only know that P8 is false, we also know that it is *false* that it is morally permissible for an adult to have coercive sexual intercourse with your *sister's* young child, or your *cousin's* young child, or *neighbor's* young child, or for that matter *Adolf Hitler's* young child.

We could go on ad nauseum listing first-order moral propositions like this, the truth or falsity of which we are perfectly convinced we know. In fact, what we *really* think is that first-order moral knowledge, of the sort we are looking at here, is ubiquitous. Everybody knows a lot of things, morally speaking: the stability of society, in fact the very integrity of our moral lives, requires it. To merely "believe" that your young child shouldn't be raped seems epistemically anemic at best. Were you to claim, after such brutalization of your own young son or daughter, that you believe, *but don't know* that the rape was genuinely morally wrong, would leave people aghast—and not only because they would think your attitude reflects a dearth of parental love. They would think that you lacked any real understanding of morality.[26] There are important lessons in this regarding how we should frame a philosophical conception of the nature of morality.

## 1.3. THE RELEVANCE OF CASE SPECIFICS

Our list of first-order moral truths and falsehoods has stressed specific cases. The reason for this is that our confidence in our beliefs about specific cases of moral rightness and wrongness, permissibility and impermissibility, praiseworthiness and blameworthiness, etc., is often remarkably high. For example, my confidence in the truth of P7 (i.e., it is wrong for anyone to shoot me as I sit here writing this book) is exceptionally strong: in fact it could scarcely be stronger. Similarly, I am sure that your confidence that it is *false* that it is morally permissible for an adult to have coercive sexual intercourse with *your* young child (i.e., an instantiation of P8) could scarcely be stronger. There are many reasons for this. One is that there is a concreteness about cases like this that makes them easily grasped: the implications of such action are vividly clear. Such cases lack the abstractness that often decenters us from focusing on what we really think is important. A second reason is that, especially in the cases just specified, one's own welfare, or someone's about whom one cares greatly, is directly involved. This tends to sharpen our moral perceptions. A third reason is that, unlike moral generalizations such as:

P9: Kidnapping is always, under any circumstances, morally indefensible,

one is not challenged to consider whether there may be unusual situations that would justify an exception to such a normally odious practice—a relevant concern for, say, utilitarians—or whether there may be a defensible moral principle, for example, Kant's second version the Categorical Imperative (often called the "Humanity Formula"), prohibiting treating people as mere means,[27] which may nevertheless be overridden by an even more general principle, say, a principle mandating the preservation of innocent human life. The point is that individual cases are often more easily grasped than moral generalization. But not always:

P8: It is always morally permissible for adults to have coercive intercourse with young children,

is, to our normal way of thinking, clearly false. But it seems that much of the vividness with which we are aware of its falsehood stems from our negative epistemic reaction to some of its instantiations—instantiations such as that it is morally permissible for an adult to have coercive sexual intercourse with *your* young child. The falsehood of this will be vividly apparent to *you*, and for that matter, to anyone else with any powers of empathy whatever. And a fourth reason, embodied in most of the exemplar first-order propositions we have looked at so far, is that the moral features of specific cases involving *harm* tend to be especially clear to us.[28] Moral generalizations, and moral abstractions generally, often lack this kind of psychological and epistemic urgency. When they do not lack it, it is frequently because of the urgency we associate with some or all of their instantiations—that is, with the particular cases that are generalized over or alluded to.

The point of bringing out these features of particular first-order moral cases is to illustrate two important facts. First, such cases provide a foundation upon which to construct abstract moral theory, whether normative or metaethical. Second, as I have already alluded to in §1.2, if an abstract moral theory, whether normative or metaethical, is substantially incompatible[29] with our ordinary responses to specific cases, we have prima facie reason—often strong prima facie reason—to reject the abstract theory. But admittedly only prima facie reason; for as I have already stressed, our ordinary moral thinking is certainly not exempt from error: we do make mistakes, we can raise legitimate doubts about our judgments, and we may have to revise our views. Still, in many cases our moral judgments are amazingly resistant to revocation. This deserves to be taken with the utmost seriousness. Moral skeptics, in my view, do not.

## 1.4. SKEPTICISM AND MORALITY

There are many forms of moral skepticism, and indeed, the very term 'moral skepticism' means different things to different people. I will use the term atypically, indeed provocatively, and in a way that covers a lot of territory. What I shall mean by moral skepticism is, roughly speaking, *any conception of morality that is substantially at odds with our normal, broadly common-sensist way of understanding morality.* But this is much too rough. More precisely, what I mean is this:

> Moral skepticism = *df.* Any conception of morality that systematically denies either (i) non-relative truth or falsity to first-order moral discourse on the grounds that there are no non-relative first-order moral facts; and/or (ii) that such moral truth and falsity is often known to us.

This is at once very narrow—some philosophers would agree that there are non-relative moral truths, but balk at objective moral facts—and very wide; for some philosophers would argue, for example, that a "genuine" moral skeptic denies the very possibility of morality, however conceived, not just non-relative moral truth.[30] I mean to reject any view that is skeptical that our ordinary conception of morality is fundamentally correct. It is important to see here that "ordinary morality" has both *metaethical* commitments and *epistemological* commitments: we think that there are first-order moral truths—this is the metaethical side of things—and we think that we often know these truths—this is the epistemological side of things. Moral skepticism, as I conceive it here, is at odds with both of these commitments.

Let's look a bit more closely at the first part of this definition of moral skepticism—part (i), which deals with moral truth and facts. I need to be clear that I am not terming a view "moral skepticism" if it entails the simple

falsehood of a proposition that our ordinary, tutored moral thinking considers
true, such as:

> P7: It is morally wrong for anyone to walk into my office and shoot me to
> death as I sit here writing this book.

By "simple falsehood," I mean that the proposition, understood in the normal
way,[31] is false on its own terms, not that it is false because, for example, it
suffers some kind of presupposition failure owing to the fact that, say, its
meaning presupposes that there is such a thing as moral wrongness, but there
isn't. In other words, a person could say that it is *false* that nobody should
shoot me while sitting here writing this book, or that it is *false* that slavery is
wrong, etc., and still not be a moral skeptic in my sense of the term. It is,
rather, the *systematic* nature of the objector's disagreement with our ordinary
moral thinking that makes her a moral skeptic. When she thinks that there is
something globally wrong with our ordinary first-order moral thinking, then
we have a skeptic.

A non-moral analogy may make things clearer. Consider a proposition
such as 'Ghosts are invariably friendly'. Let's stipulate that there are no
ghosts, that is to say, that the actual world, not some merely possible world,
contains no ghosts. Now we may deny the truth of this proposition on two
different grounds: one is because there are no such things as ghosts; a second
is because ghosts are on occasion, or frequently, or always (pace Casper of
American cartoon fame) *un*friendly. The second ground would not be a skeptical claim in my sense of "skeptical," but the first would be. For the second
type of denial of 'Ghosts are invariably friendly' is a denial of the proposition "on its own terms," while the first type of denial is on the ground that the
subject term of the proposition fails to denote (i.e., does not refer), or alternatively, that the proposition suffers from presupposition failure—either type
of failure owing to the non-existence of ghosts: we may analyze the specifics
of this type denial of our ghost proposition in several ways, the details of
which are not of concern to us at the moment.

Now back to our moral proposition,

> P7: It is morally wrong for anyone to walk into my office and shoot me to
> death as I sit here writing this book.

The simple falsehood of this proposition would consist in its being false "on
its own terms," meaning that it is *not the case* that it is morally wrong for
someone to walk into my office and shoot me to death as I sit here writing
this book; perhaps it is in fact morally right, or morally permissible, or
morally praiseworthy (perish the thought!) to kill me like this. According to
this type of denial of P7, P7 is false not because its terms fail to denote—for

example, because there is no such thing as "me," or that there is no such activity as "writing a book"—and it is not false because there is no such thing as "moral wrongness." On the other hand, a *skeptical denial* of the truth of P7 would be because of the latter sort of reason: P7 is simply off the mark, not "on its own terms," but because there is something *in principle* amiss with what the proposition is purported to asset. [32]

Moral skeptics, then, think that there is something fundamentally wrong with our ordinary thinking about moral truth. There are several broad reasons they think this. One is familiar even to non-philosophers, and in a loose way believed by many people, although I think that in fact they don't fully believe it, or do so only inconsistently with other beliefs that they hold. This is *moral relativism.* Moral relativism comes in several versions, all of which deny the non-relative truth of first-order moral propositions like P7. We will look at moral relativism(s) very carefully in chapter 5, but for now it will suffice to get the general idea before us. Probably the most widely known version, what I shall call "*sociocultural moral relativism*,"[33] well illustrates the broad perspective. According to this version of relativism, although propositions like P7 are either true or false,[34] *whether* they are true or false depends on the sociocultural context out of which they arise. So such relativists may say that they cannot tell whether P7 is true, because as rendered here it is inadequately expressed. In order to know whether P7 is true or false, one would have to specify in which sociocultural context the proposition is embedded, which may well require including specification of the temporal spread within that context. Why all this? Because such propositions are only true or false relative to a sociocultural context. Thus, P7 may be true relative to one sociocultural perspective, but false relative to another.

Let this sink in: P7-type propositions are true or false only relative to the values of a particular society/culture at a specific time. And so the truth or falsity of propositions such as

> P1: Chattel slavery, such as was practiced in the southern states of the United States prior to the American Civil War, is morally wrong.

and,

> P8: It is always morally permissible for adults to have coercive sexual intercourse with young children,

is radically dependent upon, determined by, the values of society/culture. This is not merely a descriptive claim of the sort that social scientists are especially qualified to make. It is not, for example, like the sociological claim that as a matter of fact the people of the United States at time *t* believe that killing me as I sit here writing my book is morally wrong, or disapprove of slavery, or approve of coercive sexual intercourse with children. It has to do, rather, that what the term 'morally wrong' *means*. That is to say, for $X$ to be morally wrong just means for $X$ to be contrary to the moral values of a particular society/culture. If that society/culture considers $X$ morally wrong, then it *is* morally wrong—in that society/culture. If they believe $X$ to be morally right, then $X$ *is* morally right. Each society/culture is sovereign over their moral valuation: there is no higher principle(s) of judgment to appeal to in order to resolve moral disagreement.[35]

But this is not how we normally think of things. Perhaps some things genuinely are wrong in one society but not in another—perhaps modes of dress, public expressions of affection, conventions of address, things of this sort—but not *everything*. Again, as Midgley would press, what do we *really* think about a society that considered P7 false—a society which held that it isn't morally wrong to go and just shoot somebody for no apparent reason, or a society that approves of chattel slavery or child rape? Well, we disagree, and *strongly*. We think that any society/culture which permits these sorts of things is benighted, profoundly mistaken, and that they should change their views posthaste—perhaps forced to change their views, or at least their behavior, but this is a separate matter.[36] We could multiply examples ad nauseum: we simply do not think that the correctness of *all* moral values is simply a product of society. Some, maybe, but certainly not all.

And this judgment of tutored, ordinary moral thinking applies to any proffered source of morally relative valuation, whether it be society/culture, as we have just been discussing, or some other source of historically conditioned moral metric. *We just don't think that everything is relative, morally speaking.* On the contrary, we think that it is a *fact* that some things— slavery, murder, child molestation, courage, magnanimity, for example—are right or wrong, permissible or impermissible, praiseworthy or condemnable, quite independent of what people think. On this view, moral facts simply aren't the same as social facts, or historically optional conceptual facts, or facts about agreements, or anything like this. To believe otherwise, to believe with the moral relativist, makes one a moral skeptic, in our sense of the term.

There are other versions of moral skepticism than relativism. A more radical metaethical view, one quite prominent in twentieth-century philosophical circles, is moral non-cognitivism. Moral relativists believe that first-order moral discourse, locutions like

> P1: Chattel slavery, such as was practiced in the southern states of the United States prior to the American Civil War, is morally wrong,

are true or false. They just disagree with us on what makes such discourse true or false. Relativism is a version of moral *cognitivism*—there are many others—which is, roughly speaking (we will be much more precise about this later), the metaethical view that first-order moral discourse is "fact stating"—true if it succeeds in stating the relevant fact, false otherwise. But moral *non*-cognitivists deny this: locutions like P1 are *neither* true *nor* false. For P1-like locutions are not a type of discourse that is fact-stating—at least not in the primary, moral sense of the term. There are several types of view that come under this general heading, for example, emotivism, prescriptivism, and expressivism—we will sort through this latter—but for our purposes here the central point of all of them is that first-order moral discourse, in particular locutions like P1 and P7, express some kind of non-cognitive attitude about some kind of putative moral judgment. A. J. Ayer's version of emotivism is a good example.[37]

As Ayer sees it, we are fooled into thinking that locutions like P1 and P7 are fact-stating discourse—that chattel slavery is morally wrong, that I shouldn't be shot—and we are fooled into thinking this because such locutions are expressed in essentially the same grammatical form as propositions such as 'All bachelors are unmarried males', or 'That oak tree has green leaves'. On Ayer's view, all propositions are of the same general type as the two just expressed. The former is an analytic proposition—a proposition such that its truth or falsity is (roughly) a matter of the meaning of its constituent terms—and the latter is a synthetic proposition, the truth or falsity of which is (roughly) a matter of the what the world is like, which is in turn to be ascertained through empirical observation. Which type, then are P1 and P7? Ayer says neither: they aren't analytic—neither is true simply by virtue of the meaning of terms—but neither are they synthetic, because no conceivable observation can tell you whether or not slavery or shooting me dead while writing my book are wrong. P1 and P7, and other locutions like them, really aren't propositions at all; they are expressions that just *look like* they are propositional. P1 and P7 are actually locutions which, when asserted, are expressions of a negative emotion about slavery and shooting me, conjoined with the intention of inducing our hearers to have a similar emotion.

This is not the place to pursue in detail non-cognitivist metaethical views. But it is clear that they differ radically from our normal thinking about first-order moral claims. We certainly think that locutions like P1 and P7 are true or false, that they at least purport to state a fact about what is morally right or wrong, permissible or impermissible. And in fact we think that P1 and P7 are true. They both seem quite clear, both are readily comprehended, and for that matter both seem beyond reasonable dispute: we shouldn't treat people as mere property, and you shouldn't just walk in and kill someone for no reason. *It is simply a moral fact that you shouldn't.* But the moral non-cognitivist will have none of this, at least not in a way that genuinely comports with our ordinary moral thinking. This is to be a moral skeptic.

There are still other forms of moral skepticism. Moral nihilists certainly qualify. They think that there is no (first-order) moral truth. J. L. Mackie, a moral "error theorist," is a good example.[38] Mackie agrees that first-order moral discourse is cognitively meaningful—and to that extent his skepticism is not as radical as non-cognitivists like Ayer; but the problem, he thinks, is that propositions like P1 and P7 are all *false.* Why? Because such propositions attribute moral properties like wrongness or goodness to some appropriate subject, that is, to a person, a policy, an act, etc. But there is no good reason to suppose that there are any such things as moral properties—properties like "rightness" or "goodness." And why this? Because such properties would be, as Mackie puts it, metaphysically "queer": there just isn't any empirical evidence to support belief in their existence. So moral discourse suffers from massive presupposition failure: propositions like P1 and P7 presuppose that there are moral properties, but there are none: they are all false, there are no moral facts. *Morality is an illusion.* Needless to say, we do not ordinarily think this way. Many moral propositions, like P1 and P7, seem obviously true. Thus, moral nihilists are skeptics.

In subsequent chapters we will examine the moral skepticisms just sketched, and others broadly like them, quite carefully. Note, however, that the moral skepticisms considered so far have concentrated on the *metaethical* side of things—on calling into question the existence of non-relative first-order truth and falsity, and non-relative first-order moral facts. Other versions of moral skepticism, however, concentrate on the e*pistemological* side of things. They cast doubt on our ability to know such moral truths, even if there were any. These doubts may originate from a variety of sources—some from general epistemological concerns about the very possibility of human knowledge (or even justified belief) in any of a broad spectrum of human inquiry, including *moral inquiry*; and some raise doubts about the possibility of moral knowledge in particular. Any of these skepticisms, however, just like the various metaethical skepticisms discussed above, challenge common-sense morality's conviction that many moral truths and falsehoods are known to us, not merely believed. We think that we *know* that chattel slavery is wrong, that coercive sex with children is wrong, that returning kindness with kindness is prima facie praiseworthy, *that Adam Lanza shouldn't have shot those children* at *Sandy Hook Elementary School.*

There is much more to say about moral skepticism, but I have said enough to make it clear that many thoughtful people, philosophers in particular, believe that the fundamental commitments of our ordinary, tutored, common-sense moral thinking are systematically, even radically mistaken. I am out to defeat these views. The vindication of ordinary morality is my aim. But first it would be helpful to lay out how I shall attempt to do this.

## 1.5 PRÉCIS OF WHAT WE MUST DO

This is a book on metaethics and moral epistemology.[39] *Its basic thesis is that our ordinary, tutored moral thinking is correct at its core.* By "ordinary, tutored, moral thinking," I mean the way that intelligent, informed people, who come from any of a vast array of sociocultural backgrounds, typically think about first-order moral matters. It is not possible to put too fine a point on this, but it is well illustrated by the near global consensus we share over such issues as the wrongness of chattel slavery or the praiseworthiness of loyalty to one's friends, by our abhorrence of unprovoked aggressive war or sadistic cruelty inflicted upon people against their consent. It is my contention, then, that we are fundamentally correct to think that some things—some acts, policies, attitudes, inclinations, moral beliefs, etc.—are genuinely right and others genuinely wrong, or that they may manifest any of a variety of other moral predicates: permissible, impermissible, praiseworthy, condemnable, etc. I emphasize that this is not to say that we are never mistaken: that would be ludicrous. We are in fact often mistaken, and this is one of the things that has served to undermine the status of ordinary moral thinking in the eyes of many. *In some moral matters, however, we rightly have a very high degree of confidence.* This will be the foundation upon which we shall argue that in its deepest essentials, our ordinary moral thinking is not off the mark.

We are indeed often convinced that we are right in our moral judgments, and remain so. But by the same token, we often become convinced that what we once believed is wrong. In other words, we sometimes firmly believe that we possess moral truth, but come to see that we were in the thrall of falsehood. But what do we mean by "truth"? Philosophers have meant many things by this, many quite at odds with our ordinary notion of truth. But if we fail to get straight at the outset of our inquiry on how to understand truth, our entire undertaking will be hobbled by unclarity or error. I will defend a *realist* conception of truth, that is, a conception of truth that takes it to be fundamentally a matter of the way the world is. It will reject any conception of truth that makes it depend on our knowledge, our ideas, our purposes, our language, etc. On the contrary, I will argue that truth is intimately connected with mind-independent *facts.* But this in turn will require that I provide an account of facts—in particular, an account of *moral facts*—because on my view, and in accordance with our ordinary, tutored moral thinking, when we know a truth, what we possess is knowledge of a fact. To know a (first-order) moral truth, then, is to know a (first-order) moral fact. These matters are the subject of chapter 2.

Providing a deep account of moral facts, however, will require us to inquire into their constitution. And one of the constituents of facts of whatever kind is properties. In particular, we will need to get a clear understanding of the nature of *moral properties*—properties such as rightness, permissibility, praiseworthiness, and so forth. Many have argued, however, that there are no such things as moral properties. Others, that there are at least no sui generis moral properties—that any putative "moral" property is in fact reducible to some other type of property—to a "natural" or "physical" property such as a neurological state, for example. I will argue that moral properties do indeed exist—that they are universals, some instantiated, others not—and that they are irreducible to any other type of property. Neither, however, do moral properties swing free of non-moral properties. My argument will be that moral properties supervene on physical properties. When we get a firm grip on the nature of moral properties, we can get a firm grip on the nature of moral facts and moral truth. All of this is the subject of chapter 3.

When we have a firm grip on moral properties, moral facts, and moral truth, we are in a position to say some important things about moral knowledge. The kind of moral knowledge that will be especially important to us is knowledge of the truth or falsity of Class A first-order moral propositions like

> P7: It is morally wrong for anyone to walk into my office and shoot me to death as I sit here writing this book;

and

> P8: It is always morally permissible for adults to have coercive sexual intercourse with young children—

or especially, instantiations of propositions like P8, such as 'It is morally permissible for an adult to have coercive sexual intercourse with *your* young child'. For it is knowledge of the truth or falsity of propositions like these that form the epistemic core of our ordinary moral thinking. If we don't know them to be true (P7) or to be false (P8, and the instantiation of it just given), it looks like we don't have any moral knowledge at all. But surely you *do* know that it is not acceptable for an adult to have sex with your young child. I certainly do. But in order to make these claims stick, we need to get clear on exactly what it means when one asserts, 'I know that *p*', where *p* is any Class A first-order moral proposition, such as P7 or P8. In other words, we will need an "explication" of 'I know that *p*'. Providing such an explication will draw heavily on our notions of moral truth, moral facts, and moral properties—the subjects of chapters 2 and 3. It will put us in a position to reject any version of moral relativism, moral nihilism, moral non-cognitivism, and other such views. Our position will be a robust version of *moral realism*, roughly, the metaethical view that there are non-relative first-order moral truths—

truths like P7—which are what we know when we possess first-order moral knowledge. All of this will be the subject of chapter 4.

After getting clear on what it is to know first-order moral truths, we will address the fundamental epistemological question: How do we come into epistemic contact with such truths? Among those who think that there are moral truths, some take them to be at base empirical; to possess firsthand moral knowledge, we must obtain them in broadly the same way we do other empirical knowledge. I will argue, however, that moral propositions like

> P7: It is morally wrong for anyone to walk into my office and shoot me to death as I sit here writing this book,

are not empirical in an "observational" sense of the term, in contrast to synthetic propositions like 'That building over there is made of brick'. But neither is it analytic, like propositions such as 'All bachelors are unmarried males'. Analytic propositions are, roughly speaking (there are various analyses of this), necessarily true or false in virtue of the meaning of their terms or the conceptual relations they assert, and can in principal be known without appeal to experience, that is, known a priori. Synthetic propositions, like 'That building over there is made of brick', are contingently true or false, and can only be known through appeal to experience, that is, known a posteriori. I will argue that some first-order moral propositions are analytic, hence knowable a priori, and that others are synthetic, and knowable only a posteriori. However, I will also argue that there are some synthetic first-order propositions that are knowable a priori. They are in this respect like propositions such as 'A house cannot be painted green and blue all over'; the proposition it is true, but not true merely in virtue of the meaning of its constituent terms. We can know it to be true just by understanding it: no observational test is required. Synthetic moral propositions will be fundamental for us, and synthetic a priori propositions especially so. Yet our belief in any first-order moral propositions is certainly fallible—our skeptical opponents are to that extent correct—even though in some cases we can legitimately be very sure we are not in error. The skeptic, however, requires too much of us if she demands infallibility. Some well-justified moral beliefs are inferential—we infer them from other secure moral beliefs—but not all of them are inferred, or we would face a vicious infinite regress epistemic justification. Some moral beliefs, that is to say, are *non*-inferential, and come to us in the form of *moral intuitions*. Indeed, moral intuitions often play a pivotal grounding role, and serve as a basis for some of our most secure moral knowledge. Moral theory, however, is also important, but moral intuition can serve an important role in guiding moral theory, both in terms of theory motivation and in terms of providing a check on theory acceptability. But by the same token, moral theory can play an important role as a check on moral intuition. In the ideal, what we should seek is a kind of *reflective equilibrium,* where the full range of our epistemic resources—intuition, theory, the testimony of others, etc.— is brought to bear. All of this is the subject of chapter 5.

There is of course an important distinction between first-order moral knowledge and second-order moral knowledge. One can possess a lot of the former, but little of the latter. One can know a lot about the truth or falsity of things like

> P1: Chattel slavery, such as was practiced in the southern states of the United States prior to the American Civil War, is morally wrong;

but know precious little about things like,

> P5: Moral judgments are true or false only relative to a specific society or culture,

or

> P6: There are no first-order moral truths, nor are there any first-order moral falsehoods.

This happens all the time. Indeed, perhaps few but philosophers know much about second-order moral matters, but we would hardly want to say that few but philosophers are morally informed—if by that one means that one knows little about the difference between what is right to do or wrong to do. Up to this point in our inquiry, the focus has largely been on first-order moral knowledge, which is as it should be; for on the view developed here, the first-order, in particular the Class A first-order, is primary. That is where we should start in order to understand aright second-order moral knowledge— that is, metaethical knowledge, knowledge *about* morality. It provides the foundation on which to develop a cogent rejection of a panoply of moral skepticisms, such as moral relativism, moral non-cognitivism, moral nihilism, et al. A robust regard for first-order moral knowledge motivates commitment to the second-order thesis of moral realism. But with the outlines of a defensible moral realism in hand, we are able to explain why our ordinary moral thinking is fundamentally correct. All of this is the subject of chapter 6.

The vicious murders that Adam Lanza committed at Sandy Hook Elementary School were very, very wrong; no ifs, ands, or buts.[40] Our ordinary, tutored moral thinking is crystal clear on this. And even if most cases of moral wrongness lack the urgency and outrageousness of this paradigm of perversity, our ordinary moral thinking is fundamentally on the right track in thinking that there are definite answers, even if sometimes hard to discern, to questions of the form, "Was that act wrong?" Now to get started on giving teeth to this claim.

## NOTES

1. For an authoritative report, see the *Report of the State's Attorney for the Judicial District of Danbury on the Shootings at the Sandy Hook Elementary School and 36 Yogananda Street, Newtown, Connecticut on December 14, 2012,* by the Office of the State's Attorney, Judicial District of Danbury, Stephen J. Sedensky III, State's Attorney, November 25, 2013.

2. I will bypass Kantian concerns that these children, being in their nonage and thus less than full rational agents, would not qualify as full-fledged persons. This is a complex issue, but surely everyone would grant, including Kant, that their status as moral agents is in this case relevantly comparable to that of adults.

3. Apparently Adam Lanza had an altercation with several school personnel the day before the shootings. Whatever grudge he may have borne against the school's teachers (or his mother), it seems hard to conceive how this could extend to the children—certainly not en masse.

4. If Lanza was incapable of choosing what he did—if he was psychotic, for example, in such degree that he was incapable of controlling himself, or was uncomprehending of what he was doing—then we would only dubiously apply the designation of "morally wrong" to his actions. Lanza's behavior would be, roughly speaking, morally analogous to that of a tornado: the tornado and the violent psychotic are destructive of innocent human life, but neither is morally blameworthy.

5. George Edward Moore (1873–1958) was born in England, and spent virtually his entire career at Cambridge University. He, along with Bertrand Russell (1872–1970), is generally credited with founding analytic philosophy, broadly speaking, the now dominate form of academic philosophy in the English-speaking world. (The great German mathematician and logi cian Gottlieb Frege [1848–1925] is considered by many to be a third.)

6. In *Principia Ethica* (Cambridge: Cambridge University Press, 1903), Moore endorsed a version of utilitarianism, a common enough normative ethical theory. The *meaning* of moral terms, however, is a more subtle matter, more about which in later chapters.

7. Immanuel Kant, *The Critique of Pure Reason,* translated by Norman Kemp Smith, B xxxix n., page 34; quoted by Moore, in "Proof of an External World," in G. E. Moore, *Philosophical Papers* (New York: Collier, 1959), 126.

8. See Moore, "Proof of an External World." Quite a lot of preparatory discussion preceded this proof, most of it disregarded in the plethora of examinations of Moore's famous argument.

9. Ibid., 145.

10. Ibid., 147; my insertion.

11. Ibid., 147–48; the kind of thing that Descartes thought it necessary to prove, but found so difficult to do.

12. The path that Descartes initiated in his famous *Meditations on First Philosophy Meditations on First Philosophy*, translated by Donald A. Cress (Indianapolis, IN: Hackett Publishing Co., 1993 [1641 in Latin; 1647 in French]). But I see intimations of this approach going back to Plato's Theory of the Forms in, for example, *The Republic*, translated by Francis MacDonald Cornford (Oxford: Oxford University Press, 1945). Alfred North Whitehead famously remarked that European philosophy is a series of footnotes to Plato. See his *Process and Reality* (New York: Free Press, 1979), 39.

13. G. E. Moore, "An Autobiography," in *The Philosophy of G. E. Moore*, edited by Paul Arthur Schilpp (Chicago: Open Court, 1942), 14.

14. See Tom Regan, *Bloomsbury's Prophet: G. E. Moore and the Development of His Moral Philosophy* (Eugene, OR: Wipf and Stock, 1986).

15. In Vol. 1 of his autobiography, Bertrand Russell describes Moore as a Cambridge undergraduate burning holes in his pants as he fiddled with lighting his pipe during heated discussion. The effect of Moore's philosophical passion on his fellow Apostles—whose mem-

bership reads like a "Who's Who" of late Victorian British intellectuals—was electrifying. *The Autobiography of Bertrand Russell*, Vol. 1 (London: George Allen & Unwin, 1967).

16. To the extent that either group is taken seriously in enlightened circles, it is because of the harm that may be wrought by acting on these odious beliefs. These views are not taken seriously on their merits.

17. Mary Midgley, "Trying Out One's New Sword," excerpted from *Heart and Mind* (UK: Harvester Press, 1981) in *Morality and Moral Controversies*, 8th ed., edited by John Arthur and Steven Scalet (Upper Saddle River, NJ: Pearson, 2009), 34–37 (35); my emphasis. Midgley is discussing the plausibility of "moral isolationism," the thesis that members of one culture cannot understand a different culture adequately to judge it morally. Midgley rejects moral isolationism, in part basing her claim on an examination of concrete cases. She calls upon us to seriously consider what we really think about these cases—"really think" in the sense of not allowing ourselves to get caught up in a theory which perverts sound judgment. This is an important point which will have major bearing throughout this book.

18. G. E. M. Anscombe, "Modern Moral Philosophy," *Philosophy*, 33 (1958), 1–19 (17); her italics.

19. I assume here of course that the extreme skeptic is wrong—that knowledge is in fact possible. And even if it weren't possible, these are among the forms that knowledge *would* take *if* it were possible. More about this in chapter 5.

20. See Robert Audi, *Epistemology*, 3rd edition (New York and London: Routledge, 2011) for useful discussion of objectual knowledge and belief.

21. See, for example, David Brink, *Moral Realism and the Foundations of Ethics* (Cambridge: Cambridge University Press, 1989), 1.

22. I do not mean to imply that this is an exhaustive classification of first-order moral propositions. It is, however, a distinction that will be of importance, implicitly or explicitly, to much discussion throughout this book.

23. Professor Midgley would agree completely.

24. And you may thereby suddenly become a "person of interest" to the police.

25. You don't have a child? Use your imagination.

26. Compare: under normal lighting conditions, etc., you say, "What I am now looking at is my right hand—at least I believe it is my right hand, but I don't *know* that it is." Our normal response to this is, "Of course you know that is your right hand! Why are you saying that you only 'believe' it? You are implying that there are doubts where none belong." Wittgenstein's work in, for example, *On Certainty*, eds. G. E. M. Anscombe and G. H. von Wright (New York: Harper & Row: 1969), and *Philosophical Investigations,* 3rd edition, trans. G. E. M. Anscombe (New York: Macmillan, 1958) makes clear how unusual, even epistemically inappropriate, such expressions are. I don't just believe that $2 + 2 = 4$, I *know* it. So do you.

27. Immanuel Kant, "So act as to treat humanity, whether in thine own person or in that of any other, in every case as an end withal, never as means only," *Fundamental Principles of the Metaphysics of Morals*, translated by T. K. Abbott (New York: Prometheus Books, [1785] 1987), 58.

28. There are clear sociological and psychological reasons for this, in some respects partially explicable in evolutionary terms.

29. "Substantially incompatible" is of course imprecise. In the next section I will make clearer the kind of deviations from ordinary moral thinking that should worry us.

30. See Walter Sinnott-Armstrong, "Moral Skepticism and Justification," in *Moral Knowledge?* (Oxford: Oxford University Press, 1996), 3–48.

31. This is a bit misleading, because the meaning of a proposition—however 'meaning' is construed—determines what proposition it is. Thus, if $x$ and $y$ are propositions with different meanings, then $x \neq y$. True, we can misunderstand a proposition, but this is in effect to believe wrongly that one proposition is actually another. The point of the example here is that understanding P7 as we normally do, it is a "simple falsehood" if the proposition isn't true because it expresses a falsehood.

32. *If* P7 is even a proposition. More about this below.

33. I mean to be neutral here on whether it is a society or a culture that determines moral truth.

34. Bi-valence is generally, but not universally, accepted by both relativists and non-relativists.

35. All of this, and its implications, will receive much closer analysis in subsequent chapters.

36. That is, $X$ could be wrong, but there may be no adequate justification to coerce people to refrain from doing $X$, for example, lying about their height or weight, at least in normal circumstances.

37. A. J. Ayer, *Language, Truth, and Logic* (New York: Dover, 1952).

38. See J. L. Mackie, *Ethics: Inventing Right and Wrong* (New York: Viking Press, 1977).

39. Some take the latter to fall under the general heading of the former: moral epistemology is a part of metaethics. I will treat them as separate although closely connected. On the view developed here, one's account of moral knowledge first requires that one say a lot about the nature of morality—about metaethics.

40. Again, assuming that Lanza possessed moral agency at the time of commission of the killings.

## Chapter Two

# Truth and Moral Facts

## 2.1. TRUTH: REALIST AND ANTIREALIST

If we are going to defend the correctness of our ordinary moral thinking, the first thing we must do is get clear on the nature of truth. For truth does not mean the same to everybody, certainly not to all philosophers—and philosophers are the principal ones calling into question our ordinary conception of morality. More specifically, as we saw in chapter 1, those I am terming "moral skeptics" raise systematic doubts about the truth of our ordinary first-order moral claims, claims such as

> P7: It is morally wrong for anyone to walk into my office and shoot me to death as I sit here writing this book.

A major goal of this book is not to merely identify and describe these objections, but to respond polemically—to rebut the skeptics, and to provide a positive account of moral truth. That will require specifying what we mean by truth.[1]

Assume for the sake of argument that P7 is true. Well, what does it *mean* for P7 to be true? This is actually a rather complicated issue, but we can get a good start by first saying what truth itself is. I will divide the range of responses into two broad camps: realist and antirealist.[2] It will be useful to begin by saying a bit about what I mean by the term 'realism'.[3]

Some philosophers have thought that there is something specific that makes a proposition, a theory, a concept, or what have you "realist." Others disagree, holding that there is nothing specific that one can point to as a "realist maker." And among those—the first group—who think that there *is* something specific that bestows realism, there is disagreement over what that something is.

Consider, then, those who consider themselves realists. Some think realism is fundamentally a matter of metaphysics, of ontology. I will call this construal of realism, *ontic realism.* What is common among various versions of realism, on this view, is that something of the relevant type exists, has positive ontic status. Take naïve realism in the theory of perception: the naïve realist holds that ordinary objects of perception—trees, flowers, houses, mountains, etc.—are not ontically dependent on perception. A mountain's existence, for example, is a matter independent of any perceiver: the perceiver, *S*, does not cause the mountain to exist by perceiving it. And the same for a house, even though perceivers may be (and in fact are) responsible for building it. Once built, the house exists, whether perceived or not. Put more generally, all of this is to say that material objects are perceiver-independent entities, or equivalently for our purposes, mind-independent entities.

Contrast *anti*realism in the theory of perception, for example, the version of phenomenalism advocated by John Stuart Mill in *An Examination of Sir William Hamilton's Philosophy.*[4] On Mill's view, when *S* has a visual perception of a "mountain," what is actually occurring is not *S*'s perceiving a material object, but *S*'s having a visual sensation. "Material objects" are not perceiver-independent entities, but what he calls "permanent possibilities of sensation." The "mountain," then, is to be understood as the perceptions that *S would* have *were S* to be subject to certain conditions. Unlike naïve realism, for the Millian phenomenalist, no perceiver, no mountain.

Examples are easily multiplied of this general construal of realism. Thus, in mathematics, realists hold that numbers exist, for example, as timeless platonic entities, while antirealists hold that numbers are mind-dependent constructs. Realists about time hold that time exists as a component of an independently real Einsteinian space-time. Antirealists about time—idealists like McTaggart,[5] for example—hold that time is a mental construct. The general point here is that ontic realists and ontic antirealists alike view the term 'realism' as referring to a metaphysical thesis about *existence*.

The other broad way to understand realism is in terms of a concept having to do with truth. Let's call this *alethic realism.*[6] One prominent way to construe this version of realism is to say that a proposition is "realist" if and only if it purports to say something about the way the world is: the proposition is true if the world is the way the proposition says it is, otherwise it is false. Or to put this a bit more carefully, a proposition (statement, sentence) *p* of the form '*X* is *F* '—where *p* asserts that *X* (a material object, a state of affairs, an event, etc.) has (possesses, manifests, instantiates, etc.) some property *F*—is true because the world is such that *X* is *F*. If the world is such that *X* is not *F*—that is, if *X* does not have property *F*—then *p* is false.[7] According to this view, then, the *false* proposition, 'President Obama weighs nine hundred pounds' is just as "realist" as the *true* proposition, 'President Obama was twice elected to the US presidency'. Both propositions are realist because they both purport to describe the way the world is, the former incorrectly, the latter correctly.

Let's again look at two theories of perception to see the point. The naïve realist believes that propositions asserting a relationship between perceivers and material objects are true or false—true if they correctly assert this relationship, false if they do not. Thus, the proposition '*S* sees snow on the summit of Mont Blanc (in France) at time *t*' is true depending on whether (i) there *is* snow on the summit of Mont Blanc at *t*, and (ii) *S* sees *that* there is snow on the summit of Mont Blanc at *t*. The truth-determinant here is the way the world is, that is to say, *reality*.

Contrast Mill's phenomenalism: this is antirealist because the propositions it countenances are not assertions about the relationship between perceivers and perceiver-independent material objects. Phenomenalism does not endorse the assertion '*S* perceived that the rock is round', *if* by that one means that the term 'rock' means what we ordinarily ("naively") mean, namely, as referring to a perceiver-independent material object, *because Mill's phenomenalism does not countenance the existence of perceiver-independent material objects*. Rocks, leaves, clouds, mountains, or what have you are not perceiver-independent entities, but "permanent possibilities of sensation." Propositions about "material objects" are actually claims about sequences of sensations of the form, 'If *S* were to do *A* in circumstances *B*, then *S* would have sensation *C*'. Thus, propositions about material objects are not about material objects *simpliciter*, but rather about mind-dependent entities.

We can say similar things about alethic realism and antirealism in the philosophy of mathematics. There is debate about whether mathematical truth and falsehood is determined by a mind-independent world of numbers (or some other mind-independent mathematical entity, e.g., sets), or alternatively, is determined by the characteristics of an elaborate conceptual scheme(s) developed by humans for human purposes. We are realist about mathematical propositions if we believe the former, antirealist if we believe the latter. Or take the philosophy of time: a proposition about time, a "temporal" proposition, is realist if it is made true or false according to whether it is correct or incorrect about the mind (or purpose, or conceptualization) *inde*pendent nature of time. It is antirealist if, for example, it is made true or false in virtue of our experience—our "temporally experienced time," one might say.

So there are, then, (at least) two broad ways to understand 'realism': as an *ontic* concept, and as an *alethic* concept. There are proponents of both, and the debate about which is better is long and involved. But we don't need to get into all of that here. I will make use of both ways of thinking about realism. In fact, I think there is a strong connection between ontic realism and alethic realism, a connection which I will make clear shortly. But just now our main concern is *truth*; for we are trying to understand what it is for a proposition to be true. I now need to be explicit about this.

## 2.2. A REALIST CONCEPTION OF TRUTH

I have said repeatedly that I shall argue that there are first-order moral truths. More specifically, I shall argue that not only are first-order moral locutions *propositional*, but (i) that many are *true*, and (ii) that they are true in a *realist* sense of 'true'. But exactly how are we to understand realist truth?

People have meant many things by the term 'true', but what I mean is captured most aptly by William Alston: any plausible conception of the nature (meaning, definition) of (propositional) truth must preserve what he calls the "T-schema," namely, "the proposition that *p* is true *iff* (i.e., if and only if) *p*"[8]. Thus, the proposition 'Mont Blanc has snow on its summit' is true if and only if Mont Blanc has snow on its summit, and false otherwise. This conception of truth is, by both Alston's and my lights, a realist conception of truth, albeit a "minimalist" realist conception. It is *realist* because what it means for *p* to be true is that *p* says *the way the world is*, i.e., *p* comports with the relevant facts about the world. It is *minimalist* because it does not specify the nature of the relation between proposition and world—it doesn't spell out precisely what is often called the "correspondence" between true proposition and world, a task that falls to a full-blown correspondence *theory* of truth. But as Alston cogently points out, "Anyone who sees that any instance of . . . [the T-schema] is analytically true has a firm grasp on the realist conception of truth."[9] If you see that, qua instance of the T-schema, it is analytically true that the proposition 'There is snow on the summit of Mont Blanc' is true if and only if there is snow on the summit of Mont Blanc, then you see, fundamentally, what realist (propositional) truth is. The "truth maker" here is *the way the world is,* which is to say, facts about the world.[10]

Now I want to reject any antirealist version of truth. In particular, I want to reject *epistemic* conceptions of truth. This means that I reject pragmatist notions of truth like William James's, where '*p* is true' means "believing that *p* is good . . . and good for definite assignable reasons."[11] And I want to reject Charles S. Pierce's view, for whom '*p* is true' means "that *p* is fated to be agreed upon by all who investigate *p*."[12] And John Dewey's, too, where '*p* is true' means that which successfully resolves a problem situation.[13] These and other pragmatist conceptions of truth fundamentally regard '*p* is true' as *meaning* that *p* is knowable, or epistemically defensible, or warranted, or justifiable, or some such thing as this. Pragmatist conceptions of truth, then, turn truth into an epistemic concept. This is not realist.

Similarly, I want to reject *coherentist* notions of truth like F. H. Bradley's, for whom '*p* is true' means "that which satisfies the intellect"[14] and is "an ideal expression of the Universe, at once coherent and comprehensive."[15] And Brand Blanchard's, for whom '*p* is true' means that *p* coheres with an "all-comprehensive and fully articulated"[16] whole. These and other coherentist notions of truth regard '*p* is true' as fundamentally meaning that *p* is completely justified owing to its maximal coherence with other fully justified propositions.[17] A primary reason I want to reject any and all epistemic conceptions of truth is that if one takes an epistemic condition to be necessary and/or sufficient for the truth of *p*, one ipso facto denies the necessity and sufficiency of the T-schema. This is because if the T-schema is necessary and sufficient, then asserting (i) the necessity of an epistemic condition for defining truth means that the T-schema isn't sufficient, and (ii) asserting the sufficiency of an epistemic condition for defining truth means that the T-schema isn't necessary.[18]

Still, I want to go a bit further than Alston's minimalist account. Some recent work by John Searle is suggestive.[19] Very briefly, on Searle's view we assess statements as true when we consider them trustworthy, that is, when we think that "the way they represent things as being *is the way that they really are*."[20] Furthermore, "the criterion of reliability is given by disquotation"[21]—disquotation being where a sentence expressing a proposition is replaced with an actual proposition (i.e., with *what* the sentence expresses). Thus, take an instance of (to use Alston's term) the T-schema, say,

T1: 'There is snow on the summit of Mont Blanc' is true *iff* there is snow on the summit of Mont Blanc.

The left-hand side of T1, 'There is snow on the summit of Mont Blanc', is trustworthy just in case the right-hand side of T1, there is snow on the summit of Mont Blanc, is the case. If it isn't true that there is snow on the summit of Mont Blanc, then 'There is snow on the summit of Mont Blanc' is untrue, thus (ultimately) untrustworthy, and similarly mutatis mutandis for any instance of the T-schema. Searle urges that "We need a meta-linguistic predicate for assessing success in achieving the word-to-world direction of fit, and that term is 'true'."[22] This predicate, moreover, is assigned to statements "in virtue of conditions in the world" that are "independent of the statement"; "we need general terms to name these how-things-are-in-the-world, and 'fact' is one such term . . . [another is] 'state of affairs'."[23]

My purpose here is not to develop a detailed realist theory of truth, but to say enough to be clear about what I mean when I say that a proposition is true. Thus, when I claim that '*p* is true', I am (i) making a *realist* claim about the truth of *p* captured most fundamentally by Alston's T-schema, and (ii) claiming that this realist conception of truth is usefully elaborated by Searle's correspondence conception of truth, which explicitly appeals to the notion of extra-linguistic facts—and facts will play a very important role throughout this book.

One other point: central to Alston's and Searle's, as well as to my conception of truth, is the importance of the way the world is. The world is the truth-maker of propositions: truth is not a conceptual or linguistic construct. I am claiming, then, that alethic realism—realism regarding truth—is parasitic on ontic realism: *the world confers truth*.

## 2.3. FIRST-ORDER MORAL TRUTH

The principal reason for getting a realist conception of truth before us is to see how it will help in the explication of what it means for a first-order moral proposition to be true, or for that matter, to be false. Let's go back to a proposition that has done, and will continue to do, a lot of work for us:

> P7: It is morally wrong for anyone to walk into my office and shoot me to death as I sit here writing this book.

This is representative of many of what we called in chapter 1, §1.2 "Class A" first-order moral propositions, such as 'Cruelty to the elderly is wrong', or 'Taking people's personal property without their consent is in most if not all cases impermissible', or even 'It is praiseworthy to cause suffering to one's pets'. I think the first two propositions are clearly true, and the third is clearly false; but whether they are in fact true or false—whether I am correct in my judgment about their truth or falsity—is not our present concern. The issue is, *if* they are true, or *if* they are false, *what is it for them to be true or to be false*? The outlines of an answer to this question are easy to see in light of the discussion of the previous section. For proposition P7 to be true, it must fulfill the T-schema. Thus, the proposition 'It is morally wrong for anyone to walk into my office and shoot me to death as I sit here writing this book' is true if and only if it is morally wrong for anyone to walk into my office and shoot me to death as I sit here writing this book. Similarly, the proposition 'Cruelty to the elderly is wrong' is true if and only if cruelty to the elderly is wrong. Note that the same applies to the proposition 'It is praiseworthy to cause suffering to one's pets'; it, too, is true if and only if it is praiseworthy to cause suffering to one's pets. But it is not the case, or so I claim, that it is praiseworthy to cause suffering to one's pets; so the proposition 'It is praise-worthy to cause suffering to one's pets' is *false*.

And so on for any other proposition, including any other first-order moral proposition (whether Class A or Class B). This, then, is an important part of our answer to the question: What is it for a first-order moral proposition of the form 'that *p*' to be true? Our answer: it fulfills the T-schema, namely, "the proposition that $p$ is true *iff p*." If the proposition fails to fulfill the T-schema, it is false.

At first blush this may not impress, but it should. For it captures the primary thrust of our deeply held intuition that when we make an assertion—when we state something to be the case—*what* we are asserting to be true *is* true just so long as what we assert really is the case. When I assert, 'There is a mailbox in front of my house at time $t$', I am affirming the truth of the proposition, 'There is a mailbox in front of my house at $t$'. Now this proposition is true if and only if it is the case that there is a mailbox in front of my house at $t$, which is to say that there *really is* a mailbox in front of my house at $t$. If there is no such mailbox, what I am asserting, the *proposition*, is false. My wishing that there is a mailbox in front of my house at time $t$, or my being happy about it because it better orders my perceptual experience, or anything else like this does not make it true that there is a mailbox in front of my house at $t$.[24] It is *reality* that makes this proposition true, nothing else. This is what is captured by the T-schema.

Let me flesh this out a bit. Recall that in the §2.2 we saw that what makes the T-schema a realist conception of truth is that what it *means* for 'that $p$' to be true is that it expresses the way the world is—that $p$ comports with the facts. We shall say a good bit about facts shortly, but let's for the moment focus on the realism-maker in this account of truth, viz., the way the world is. Our Searlean correspondence conception of truth emphasized that, "We need a metalinguistic predicate for assessing success in achieving the word-to-world direction of fit, and that term is 'true'."[25] So our mailbox proposition is true because of the relation of the proposition to the way the world is—its relation to reality.

Now contrast this to the antirealist conceptions of truth briefly canvassed in §2.2. The pragmatist analysis of the meaning of the truth of the mailbox proposition, that is, what it *means* for the mailbox proposition to be true, would be some variation on the theme that it is advantageous, given certain purposes, to believe that there is a mailbox in front of my house. And the coherentist analysis would be some variation on the theme that the proposition, 'There is a mailbox in front of my house' is true means that it is completely justified owing to its maximal coherence with other fully justified propositions. These are both epistemic conceptions of truth: they make the truth (or falsity) of the mailbox proposition fundamentally an epistemic matter, not a matter of the way the world is, which is an ontic, or metaphysical matter. On the view I am advocating here, the truth of the mailbox proposition, and indeed of all propositions, is a matter determined by the world, not by our conceptualization of the world,[26] or by any other epistemic relation between us and the world. This distinction is of signal importance.

As plausible as this distinction may be when defining the truth of propositions like the mailbox proposition, matters become much more controversial when it comes to the truth of first-order moral propositions like P7. We will have to do a good bit of explaining to show why we should regard the truth of propositions like P7 as relevantly analogous to the truth of propositions like the mailbox proposition, but at this point let's just get the basic idea before us: I have said that 'It is morally wrong for anyone to walk into my office and shoot me to death as I sit here writing this book' is true if and only if it is morally wrong for anyone to walk into my office and shoot me to death as I sit here writing this book. And this is to say that the truth of this proposition is not determined by—does not *mean*—that it is advantageousness to believe it, as the pragmatists would have it; nor is it determined by its being completely justified owing to its maximal coherence with other fully justified propositions, as the coherentists would have it. Its truth has nothing to do with any epistemic relations. Its truth is an ontic matter, a matter of its relation to *reality*.

Another important way to put these matters is to say that the proposition 'There is a mailbox in front of my house' is true because the proposition expresses a fact or comports with the facts. And similarly with first-order moral propositions like P7: it is true because it is a *fact* that it is morally wrong for anyone to walk into my office and shoot me to death as I sit here writing this book. This is a very important notion when it comes to understanding and justifying the basic contours of our ordinary, tutored moral thinking. We must get clear, then, on the nature of facts.

## 2.4. FACTS

Facts in general seem problematic to many, sufficiently so that they would just as soon do without them.[27] A primary reason that many eschew facts is Occam's razor-type concerns: Do we really need to posit an abstract entity to do the work done by the notion of a "true statement"? After all, 'President Obama was twice elected to the United States presidency' is both a true statement and a fact. The notion of a true statement does not introduce anything metaphysically strange, but the notion of a fact does. So let's just stick with "true statement." Well, I agree that these metaphysical concerns might have merit if what is at issue is the necessity of positing facts as sui generis entities. But what seems clearer still is that the notion of a "true statement" will not do the same work as "facts." Searle seems on target when he argues that,

> Facts are not the same as true statements. There are several ways to demonstrate this. . . . First, it makes sense to speak of facts functioning causally in a way it does not make sense to speak of true statements functioning causally. [For example, says Searle, "'The fact that Napoleon failed to perceive the danger to his left flank caused his defeat' makes good sense, whereas 'The true

statement that Napoleon failed to perceive the danger to his left flank caused his defeat' either makes no sense at all or means something totally different."] Second, the relation of a fact to a statement is one-many since the same fact may be stated by different statements. For example, the same fact is stated by "Cicero was an orator" and "Tully was an orator."[28]

In any event, I am loath to jettison facts, because without them I see no way to account for much of ordinary discourse's ability to do what it certainly at times seems to do, namely, to state how things are—that is, to express the way the world is.

To get clear on the nature of facts, some recent work by Ramon Lemos is quite suggestive.[29] Let's begin by distinguishing between propositions, states of affairs, and facts. We will understand a proposition to be an abstract entity, the sort of thing expressed by declarative sentence-tokens such as 'There is snow on the summit of Mont Blanc'[30]; and we will understand a state of affairs to be, as Lemos puts it, "something's being, doing, or having something."[31]

Let's pause for a moment. The previous paragraph's mention of the term 'abstract entity' in reference to the ontic status of propositions may alarm those who are allergic to positing the existence of anything not empirically observable. This is, alas, an allergy for which I know no cure. I will have more to say about these matters in chapter 3, but for the moment, let me say this: if propositions are in trouble because they are abstract, so are many other purported entities with which we deal constantly and quite comfortably, for example, properties such as "identity" or "roundness" or "being the brother of," and numbers such as the positive integers. Many efforts have been made to avoid positing such entities, some on Occam's razor-type grounds, others on grounds of more or less radical versions of empiricism, such as logical positivism. But logical positivism is dead, and—*pace* contemporary defenders—radical empiricism of pragmatist and Humean varieties are fraught with problems, one being their commitment to antirealism regarding truth, and another being their commitment to antirealism regarding ontology (radical empiricist's think that we "make the world," not the other way round: for them, what *is*, is what it is because of its epistemic relation to cognizers, that is, to what fulfills our purposes, or what is yielded by empirical inquiry).

Certainly, this does not dispose of my opponents. But it does put us in a position to take the modest step of agreeing in good conscience with many if not most contemporary philosophers that it is plausible to posit the ontic permissibility of propositions to serve as truth-bearers.[32]

Understanding propositions and states of affairs in the way specified several paragraphs above, we should note that although propositions are true or false, truth and falsity does not apply to states of affairs: states of affairs either obtain or do not obtain. Thus, utterances or inscriptions of the form '*X* has property *F* '—for example, 'Mont Blanc has snow on its summit'—are propositional, that is, express propositions, and are either true or false. But, the state of affairs of Mont Blanc's having snow on its summit is, qua state of affairs, neither true nor false; rather, the state of affairs either obtains or does not obtain.

What then about facts? There seem to be several senses of the term 'fact'.[33]

> *Sense 1*: Designates a state of affairs that obtains. For example, there being snow on the summit of Mont Blanc, which is a state of affairs that obtains, is a *fact*. (There being a Catholic church on the summit of Mont Blanc, which is a state of affairs that does not obtain, is not a fact.)
>
> *Sense 2*: Designates the obtaining of a state of affairs, as opposed to designating the state of affairs that either does or does not obtain. For example, the obtaining of the state of affairs of my moving my fingers as I type this sentence, is a *fact*.
>
> *Sense 3*: Designates a true proposition. For example, '*p* is true' and '*p* is a *fact*' say the same thing.
>
> *Sense 4*: Designates something (anything) that exists independently of (as Searle might put it) human or other intelligent representations. For example, Mont Blanc is a *fact*: no one's representation made Mont Blanc exist.

Not all of these senses of 'fact' are equally useful for our purposes—for example, *Sense 4* isn't commonly used in philosophical parlance—and some are more philosophically problematic than others, that is, even though 'fact' is certainly *used* in the third sense, in some cases without relevant confusion, Searle seems correct (as I have already noted) that we should not simply identify the two, at least not in any wholesale way. But I agree with Lemos that these distinctions plausibly point us in the direction of maintaining that the term 'fact' does not denote a unique, irreducible ontological category. Yet this is not to say that the concept of a fact is otiose. As Lemos remarks, "If there are real entities, states of affairs that do or do not obtain, and true propositions, then there are also facts."[34] And of course it seems overwhelmingly plausible that there are real entities, that there are states of affairs that do or do not obtain, and that there are true propositions.

The sense of 'fact' that seems particularly relevant for us is *Sense 1*, a state of affairs that obtains. Thus, for example, the proposition, 'There is snow on the summit of Mont Blanc' is true because, as indicated before, it is a *fact* that there is snow on the summit of Mont Blanc, which in this sense of 'fact' is to say that the state of affairs of there being snow on the summit of Mont Blanc obtains. Or take an example more germane to our purposes, say

> P7: It is morally wrong for anyone to walk into my office and shoot me to death as I sit here writing this book.

In the sense of 'fact' in play here, it is a fact that—although this will need to be refined momentarily—the state of affairs of its being morally wrong for anyone to walk into my office and shoot me to death as I sit here writing this book *obtains*.

Still, this won't quite do. Some states of affairs obtain, others do not. Mont Blanc's having snow on its summit obtains; President Barack Obama's being twelve feet tall (*pace* some of his more ardent supporters) does not obtain. These are both examples of what I will call "physical states of affairs." There are other types of states of affairs, for example, mathematical states of affairs—$2 + 2 = 4$ is an instance—and, as I shall soon ague, there are *moral states of affairs*, such as its being morally wrong for anyone to walk into my office and shoot me to death as I sit here writing this book. Some states of affairs obtain temporally, for example, the World Trade Towers being part of the New York City skyline obtained in the year 2000; lamentably, it does not now. Other states of affairs obtain non-temporally, or eternally, for example seven being a prime number.

Sometimes more than one state of affairs may obtain not only simultaneously, but in connection with another state of affairs. For example, if the physical state of affairs of three oranges sitting on a desk at time $t$ obtains, so does (necessarily) the obtaining of the state of affairs of there being a specific cardinality, *three*, which is a non-physical state of affairs. If no such physical state of affairs obtained, there would be no such numerical state of affairs that obtained.

I will have more to say about relations between types of states of affairs in §2.5 below; but right now, let's see how this discussion of propositions, facts, and states of affairs ties together. Take the proposition, 'There is snow on the summit of Mont Blanc': what it means for this proposition to be true is that it fulfills the T-schema, namely, 'There is snow on the summit of Mont Blanc' is true if and only if there is snow on the summit of Mont Blanc. And assuming that there is snow on the summit of Mont Blanc, this proposition expresses the *fact* that there is snow on the summit of Mont Blanc. Further, to say that it is a fact that there is snow on the summit of Mont Blanc is to say that the state of affairs of there being snow on the summit of Mont Blanc *obtains*. Contrast the false proposition, 'President Obama is twelve feet tall'. It does not fulfill the T-schema, because it is *not* the case that President Obama is twelve feet tall, which is to say that it is *not* a fact that President Obama is twelve feet tall, which is further to say that the state of affairs of President Obama being twelve feet tall does *not* obtain.

## 2.5. FIRST-ORDER MORAL FACTS

Our main concern is of course moral facts, and the discussion so far has been primarily aimed at preparing us to understand them. Let's now look at moral facts specifically.

As we saw in chapter 1, §1.2, there are two broad classifications of moral propositions: first-order and second-order. To refresh our memory, here are two examples of second-order moral propositions from §1.2:

> P5: Moral judgments are true or false only relative to a specific society or culture.
>
> P6: There are no first-order moral truths, nor are there first-order moral falsehoods.

And here are three examples of first-order moral propositions, also from §1.2:

> P1: Chattel slavery, such as was practiced in the southern states of the United States prior to the American Civil War, is morally wrong.
>
> P3: A normative ethical theory is defective if it entails the falsehood of the principle that, ceteris paribus, like cases should be treated alike.
>
> P7: It is morally wrong for anyone to walk into my office and shoot me to death as I sit here writing this book.

P5 and P6 are propositions *about* morality. They purport to tell us something about what morality is like. Thus, P5 says in effect that propositions like P1 and P7 are true or false only relative to the norms of a specific society or culture: so 'Chattel slavery, such as was practiced in the southern states of the United States prior to the American Civil War, is morally wrong', *is true* in society $X$ if and only if society $X$ holds it to be true, or false in society $X$ if and only if $X$ holds it to be false.[35] The same applies mutatis mutandis to the truth or the falsity of P7.[36]

In contrast to P5 and P6, the second set of propositions—P1, P3, and P7—are propositions "within" morality: we have termed them first-order moral propositions, and have further subdivided them into Class A and Class B. P1 and P7 are examples of the former, P3 of the latter. Class A positions purport to express moral truths about such things as what is permissible or impermissible, obligatory or supererogatory, praiseworthy or condemnable, etc., while Class B propositions purport to express truths about such things as comparing the defensibility (i.e., the truth) of norms used to determine the permissibility, obligatoriness, praiseworthiness, and so forth, of actions, policies, or what have you. What makes these propositions within morality is that they—their meaning, their truth conditions (i.e., the conditions that must be fulfilled for propositions of this type to be either true or to be false)—

*presuppose* the truth, or the falsity, of second-order moral propositions like P5 and P6. For example, P6, which says that there are neither first-order moral truths nor first-order moral falsehoods, *denies* the propositionality of P1, P3, and P7, and any locution like them. So the *truth* of P1, P3, and P7 presupposes the *falsehood* of P6. In fact, the very cognitive meaningfulness—the very possibility of being either true or false—of P1, P3, and P7 presupposes the falsehood of P6. For if P6 is true, P1, P3, and P7 wouldn't be the kind of thing, viz., moral *propositions*, that they appear, grammatically and otherwise, to be.

Let's concentrate now on Class A propositions like P1 and P7, which will prove of particular importance to us. I want to show not only *that* such first-order moral locutions are propositional, but *how* and *why* they are propositional. The short explanation is, because they express moral facts—or at least are the sort of propositions that may express such facts (not all moral propositions do).

We have seen in §2.3 that for a non-moral proposition to be true is, in brief, for it to express a non-moral fact, which in turn is for the proposition to express a non-moral state of affairs that obtains. The pattern is the same for first-order moral propositions.[37] For it to be *true* that it is morally wrong for anyone to walk into my office and shoot me to death as I sit here writing this book (P7), is for it to be a first-order moral *fact* that it is morally wrong to kill me like this, which is to say that the first-order moral state of affairs of its being wrong to shoot me to death as I sit here writing this book *obtains*. Similarly, for it to be *true* that chattel slavery is wrong (P1) is for it to be a first-order moral *fact* that chattel slavery is wrong, which in turn is for it to be a first-order moral state of affairs that *obtains* that chattel slavery is wrong. Conversely, for it to be *false* that chattel slavery is morally wrong is for P1 not to express a moral fact—or better, for P1 to *fail* to express a moral fact, which in turn is for the moral state of affairs of chattel slavery's being morally wrong *not* to obtain. Thus, falsehood in the case of first-order moral propositions works similarly to falsehood in non-moral propositions: a false first-order moral proposition fails to express a first-order moral fact, which in turn fails to express a first-order moral state of affairs that obtains.

First-order moral locutions certainly seem to be propositional because they seem to meet the conditions requisite for propositionality—or, perhaps we should say, given disputes over the precise conditions of propositionality which we can't get into here, because they meet the general conditions widely considered sufficient for other types of locutions to qualify as propositional. Thus, moral locutions commonly attribute a moral property, or a larger set of moral properties, to some moral subject—to an act, policy, intention, etc. They certainly *appear* to be either true or false[38]; and they are of the form over which we can quantify (e.g., '*All* instances of murder are prima facie impermissible'[39]).

More about the propositionality of first-order moral locutions soon: moral facts are our focus just now, and on our view, moral facts are moral states of affairs that obtain. True first-order moral propositions express these facts, and thus express moral states of affairs that obtain; false first-order moral propositions fail to do this.

First-order moral propositions commonly attribute a moral property to a relevant subject. For example, the proposition 'Smith behaved wrongly' attributes the property of moral wrongness to a specific individual, Smith. The proposition is true if it is a fact that Smith behaved wrongly, and false otherwise. 'The American policy of internment of Japanese-Americans during the Second World War is morally condemnable' is a proposition which attributes the moral property of moral condemnability to a particular policy carried out by the US government. This proposition is true if it is a fact that the US policy was morally condemnable, and false if it is not a fact. Other first-order moral propositions may be generalizations, for example, 'It is always praiseworthy to help a friend'; and still others may be subjunctive conditionals, for example, 'If Nancy were to punch Joe, she would be morally criticizable'. If true, these propositions, too, state facts, the first a general fact—a generalization about the moral praiseworthiness of helping friends; the second, far more controversially, a fact about what *would* be the case regarding Nancy's moral criticizability if she *were* to perform a certain act, namely, punching Joe.[40]

What these cases have in common is that the propositions in question assert some moral fact that actually is the case, or that would be the case if certain conditions were to be fulfilled. I now need to say something more about the nature of these moral facts.

## 2.6. MORAL FACTS AND SUPERVENIENCE

Consider a non-moral expression such as, 'Mont Blanc has snow on its summit'. We of course find this intelligible, but if pressed, we would have to admit that it is not completely clear. Is it expressing the proposition that at all times that Mont Blanc has existed, past and present, it has had snow on its summit? This surely isn't its natural reading: we are much more inclined, I think, to read it as asserting that at the present time there is snow on Mont Blanc's summit. But this isn't precise either; for does 'present time' refer to the time at which the proposition was asserted, or is it to include the time that we are reading it? Probably the former . . . but? Actually, of course, this sentence-token—this inscription—has not fully expressed a proposition: it needs a temporal indexical. So the proposition is better expressed by the sentence-token 'Mont Blanc has snow on its summit at time $t$', where the variable '$t$' would then be instantiated with a temporal constant. Still, one might argue, the term 'summit' is not adequately circumscribed. Precisely what are we to take to be Mont Blanc's summit? Normally the reference of 'summit' in such contexts is not epistemically problematic, but there are contexts in which it could be—for example, given certain scientific purposes involving meteorological observations.

But let's assume that these issues of unclarity are resolved. The truth or falsity of the proposition—whatever the proposition precisely turns out to be—is a matter of whether or not it is a fact that Mont Blanc has snow on its summit, and that in turn is a matter of whether it is a state of affairs that obtains that Mont Blanc has snow on its summit. Now ask, what *kind* of state of affairs obtains when Mont Blanc has snow on its summit? My answer is that it is a *physical* state of affairs that obtains. That is to say, Mont Blanc's having snow on its summit (at *t*) is a way the world is (at *t*), and this "way the world is," is a matter of what the physical world is like. That, in turn, is to say that a certain ordered set of physical entities, exhibiting a certain ordered set of internal and relational physical *properties*, exists at *t*. An exhaustive specification of this set of internal and relational properties would constitute an exhaustive specification of this particular physical state of affairs.[41] And one way to say that this state of affairs obtains is to say that this set of properties is instantiated in toto in *this world*, not in some other (merely) possible world.[42]

Now supplying the specifics of what should be on the list of physical *objects*, and of what should be on the list of physical *properties,* is in the main the province of the empirical sciences— most fundamentally, it would seem, the natural sciences. I say "in the main" because discriminating between the physical and the non-physical, although largely left up to the sciences themselves, also intersects with philosophical interests, as we see in the work of many recent philosophers of science.[43] It is, after all, not clear that it is a scientific question, an *empirical* question, as opposed to a conceptual, philosophical question as to what properly falls under the rubric of "science." For it is possible that a term or concept may receive tacit scientific approval despite its unrecognized non-empiricalness, thus its de facto nonscientific status: concerns in some quarters about contemporary string theory may be an example, owing to doubts that the theory can be observationally tested in any conventional sense of the term. Nevertheless, we rightfully look to the natural sciences to determine what does and what does not deserve admission into our physical lexicon. There is of course an array of scientific subdisciplines—chemistry, astronomy, biology, physiology, etc.—but physics is routinely deemed the most fundamental arbiter of what counts as "physical."[44] Suffice it to say that if, for example, chemistry or biology were to posit an entity that is in principle ruled out by physics, all would agree that there is a problem—for chemistry or for biology, not for physics.[45]

So let us stipulate—in this context a relatively uncontroversial move—that physics has the final word in describing the characteristics of physical states of affairs. And so our exemplar physical proposition, 'Mont Blanc has snow on its summit', is going to be assessed as true or false in terms that ultimately will be determined by the pronouncements of physics. And this in turn will be determined by physics' pronouncements on whether the physical state of affairs of Mont Blanc having snow on its summit (at *t*) obtains or not.

What now about moral states of affairs? Well, first of all, what is a moral state of affairs? As a first approximation, let us understand a first-order moral state of affairs to be a state of affairs that instances at least one first-order moral property. Chapter 3 will discuss moral properties in detail, but at this juncture illustration with relatively uncontroversial examples will suffice. So take a conveniently simple moral proposition such as,

P10: The torture of Syrian civilians, including children, by Syrian military forces is morally wrong.

Let's make several simplifying assumptions: First, let's assume that we have an adequate understanding of the constituent terms of the proposition, such as who does and who does not count as a Syrian civilian, who does and who does not count as a Syrian child, what does and what does not count as torture, what it is to be morally wrong, etc.[46] Second, let us assume that descriptions adequate to our purposes of comprehending what constitutes Syrian military forces, of who counts as a child, and so forth, can be given in broadly physical terms.[47] And third, let us assume that the alleged torture is occurring at the time that P10 was asserted, that is, that the proposition's temporal indexical is the time of its assertion (viz., at the writing of this passage). Now, for P10 to be about a moral state of affairs, it must predicate some moral property of some relevant entity, what I will henceforth call a "moral subject." This P10 does: it predicates the moral wrongness of torturing Syrian civilians, including children, *of* a moral subject, namely, the Syrian military forces (or the Syrian military force's actions), no matter exactly how the concept of "Syrian military forces" is explicated. After all, this alleged torture is *intended* by individuals comprising the membership of the Syrian military forces, and who are the proximate cause of these actions: they are moral agents who bear responsibility. We are clearly in the realm of the moral here, and matters are clear enough for us to proceed.

P10, then, is a (Class A) first-order moral proposition: it is a *moral* proposition because it is about a moral state of affairs; and it is a *first-order* moral proposition because it predicates a first-order moral property, moral wrongness, of a moral subject, the Syrian military forces (or their leadership). I will refine this monetarily, but for now we can say that in order for P10 to be true, the moral state of affairs to which it refers must obtain. And in order for this state of affairs to obtain, it must be the case that there *actually is* a state of affairs such that there are Syrian military forces, that there *actually is* a state of affairs such that there are Syrian civilians (including children), that there *actually is* a state of affairs such that torture is occurring, and that there *actually is* a state of affairs such that the torture is morally wrong. Further, all of this must obtain at some specific time, which we have stipulated as the time of P10's assertion. What we are saying here, then, is that there is a physical state of affairs such as that described that obtains at *t,* and that this physical state of affairs instances the moral property of wrongness.

This needs further explanation, but note first that just as some *non*-moral states of affairs do not obtain, some *moral* states of affairs do not obtain. For example, the moral state of affairs of it being morally wrong for the United States to have dropped nuclear bombs on Great Britain during the Second World War does not obtain and never did, for the simple reason that the United States never engaged in any such act against Great Britain. Of course the subjunctive conditional is true, assuming that such conditionals take truth values, viz., *if* the United States *were* to drop nuclear bombs on Great Britain (under any remotely plausible scenario), then the United States *would* commit a (grievous) moral wrong. Note further that some moral states of affairs once obtained but no longer do. For example, the state of affairs of it being morally wrong for the state of Alabama to enslave black people does not obtain now, although lamentably it once did. (So the state of Alabama is not criticizable for currently enslaving blacks.) Similarly, some moral states of affairs do not obtain now, but will in the future. Thus, there is no currently obtaining state of affairs manifesting wrongness for an act not yet committed.[48]

Let's put these matters a little more carefully:[49] I have said that a state of affairs is "something's being, doing, or having something."[50] I take a state of affairs-*type* to be the *kind* of "something's being, doing, or having something," such that what is had is an ordered set (an *n*-tuple) of properties (in the limiting core, only one) of a specific type. Thus, for example, a physical state of affairs-*type* is a *kind* of state of affairs such that a set of physical properties is instanced if it obtains. Similarly, a *moral* state of affairs-*type* is a *kind* of state of affairs that would instance a moral property were it to obtain. Now, a state of affairs-*type* is instanced if and only if a corresponding state of affairs-*token* obtains: tokens instance types. Thus, a moral state of affairs-*type* is instanced if and only if a moral state of affairs-*token* obtains. To illustrate, if Howard treats his parents with kindness and generosity (at *t*), then this act of kindness and generosity is an instance of a type of state of affairs, a *moral* of state of affairs, owing to the instancing of a particular state of affairs which has (or manifests) a particular set of moral properties, for example, kindness and generosity of Howard's action toward his parents. In brief, then, the instancing of a state of affairs-token is necessary and sufficient for the obtaining of a state of affairs-type, in this case a *moral* state of affairs-type.

Now clearly some kinds of states of affairs do not admit of moral properties, but others do. Mathematical or logical states of affairs, for example, do not seem to be of the sort that permit moral properties to be directly associated with them. What, for example, would it mean to say that the numerical state of affairs of three being a prime number greater than the square of the least prime number, has associated with it moral properties such as impermissibility, praiseworthiness, or harm? It makes no sense—a category mistake. Similarly for the logical state of affairs of a valid deductive argument guaranteeing the truth of the conclusion, if its premises are true.

Other types of states of affairs may or may not have moral properties associated with them. Importantly for us, however, physical states of affairs are types that may, or may not qua state of affairs-type, have moral properties associated with them. Take the physical state of affairs of Mont Blanc's having snow on its summit. I see no way that a moral property could be associated with this state of affairs. There is simply no feature here that is capable of taking a moral property: no "moral subject" is present in this state of affairs. Now contrast the state of affairs of a man being physically prevented from pursuing his own ends by another group of men. Certainly this state of affairs is under-described, but it is prima facie a physical state of affairs that *may* have associated with it a moral property. For this state of affairs contains entities, viz., *men*, which are the sort of entity that can have (necessarily do have?) associated with them moral properties. And depending upon how these entities are related to one another, they may well instance a moral property such as impermissibility, because the group may be enslaving, or otherwise mistreating the individual man in question. But the question now is, what does "depending on how these [moral] entities are related to one another" come to, given that we are dealing here with a physical state of affairs, and moral states of affairs seem to be different in kind from physical states of affairs? We are confronting, then, a manifestation of the notorious is/ought problem: one cannot get an "ought"—what things (morally) *should be* like—out of a description of what things *are* like.

Let's begin by noting that in several respects it appears that in order for a moral state of affairs to obtain, a physical state of affairs must obtain. For first, it seems highly doubtful that any moral states of affairs could obtain were it the case that no physical states of affairs obtained. Indeed, how could there be morality without a physical world? Speculations about the possibility of a wholly spiritual world utterly independent, both ontologically and causally, of a physical world seem totally untenable. *No physical world, no moral world.*[51]

Second, in most if not all cases, a specific moral state of affairs could not obtain unless a specific corresponding physical state of affairs obtained.

Take, for example, the moral state of affairs of its being morally wrong for Smith to burglarize Jones's house. How could this (moral) state of affairs obtain if no physical state of affairs obtained that instanced Jones's house? No house, no burglary; hence, no specific instancing of moral wrongness.

Third, as remarked in effect several paragraphs above, it seems that certain *sorts* of physical states of affairs must obtain if a moral state of affairs is to obtain. To use the same example as before, the physical state of affairs of snow being on the summit of Mont Blanc (at *t*) is incapable of instancing a moral property; but if Smith or Jones were to be on the snowy summit of Mont Blanc, the possibility (perhaps necessity) of moral properties comes into the picture: Smith could do something to Jones of moral import. But note that the same applies mutatis mutandis to Smith and Jones as it does to the snow: as we typically conceive of these things—certainly in scientific and legal terms, and seemingly in moral terms—Smith's and Jones's existence is predicated on their *physical* existence, just as the existence of the snow is predicated on its physical existence. (Consider: "Smith and Jones are here *literally*, but they have no physical presence." What are we to make of that statement?)

It seems, then, that the obtaining of physical states of affairs is a necessary condition for the obtaining of moral states of affairs. This is the case on broadly ontic grounds: moral states of affairs in general, for example, as a *type*, require that physical states of affairs obtain. More narrowly, this is also the case in order for the possibility of particular *instances* of moral states of affairs to obtain; that is, *this* instance of moral wrongness could not obtain unless *this* physical state of affairs, containing *these* particular physical entities, obtains.

Now the question: Are physical states of affairs *sufficient* for moral states of affairs to obtain? The answer would be a straightforward "yes" if moral properties were of the same ontic type as physical properties. Chapter 3 will be devoted to a discussion of moral properties, but something needs to be said here. Notice, first, that physical states of affairs obviously can, and I think *must*, instance more than merely physical properties. Take, for example, a physical state of affairs in which three apples are sitting on a table. This physical state of affairs instances the numerical (or mathematical) property of the cardinality of the set of apples on the table, *three*, and it also instances (three times over) the reflexive relational property of self-identity (each apple is identical with itself). But neither cardinality nor self-identity is a physical property.[52] Rather, in this case they *accompany* a physical state of affairs. So physical states of affairs instance more than just physical properties.

What, then, about (first-order) *moral* properties? As noted above, some physical states of affairs do not instance moral properties, but it certainly seems that some do. No moral properties are in evidence on the summit of Mont Blanc, but a man being stabbed to death on Mont Blanc's summit surely does. It is not, however, the physicality per se of the man's stabbing that makes this a moral state of affairs. Something different from bare physicality seems present in such states of affairs. Like the properties of the cardinality of the number of men present and their individual self-identities, the moral properties are additive—something over and above the merely physical. In fact, it appears that moral properties are irreducible to the physical properties, that they are *different in kind*.

Why think this? Well, one reason to think that moral properties can't just be, or can't be reducible to, physical properties is the apparent contrast in our epistemic access to them. Physical properties, at least of the most epistemically basic kind,[53] are commonly thought to be known (or justifiably believed) through the senses: visual, auditory, tactile, etc. It is highly doubtful that we "see" moral wrongness, permissibility, praiseworthiness, or what have you in precisely the same sense in which we see blue, or "feel" it in the way that we feel a rough surface. I will have much more to say about our epistemic access to moral properties in chapters 4 and 5, but for now, let us just say that it seems pretty clear that moral properties are not known empirically, at least not in any direct sense.

A second reason, connected with the former, is that it seems highly dubious that it is appropriate, conceptually speaking, to perform empirical scientific experiments to ascertain the moral rightness or wrongness of an act, policy, judgment, etc. Although further exploration of this point must await discussion in chapter 3, moral properties do not seem measurable in the same way that physical properties are measurable. Yes, we may establish a metric to discriminate between degrees of, say, moral wrongness or severity of a crime, but *what* is being measured does not appear to be the same sort of thing that is measured when we measure the speed of sound or the intensity of light. 'Moral wrongness' and similar terms simply aren't in the physicist's (or chemist's, or astronomer's) lexicon.[54] It appears, then, that moral properties, if there are any, are not the same sort of thing as physical properties. Ontically, they are different.

All this said, however, it seems clear that moral properties are related in some way to physical properties. One reason has already been stated: were there no physical world, it seems quite implausible that there could be a moral world. The physical world is a necessary condition of the moral world.

A second reason, admittedly indirect, stems from the plausibility of broadly naturalistic theories of mind—theories to the effect that minds are causally related to brains. That minded beings are capable of instancing (perhaps necessarily) moral properties *in virtue of* their mindedness, which is in some sense a product of their (physical) brain, surely suggests a connection between the physical and the moral. The plausibility of mind/body reductionism, that is, the thesis that mental properties are reducible to physical properties, however, is another matter. I do not think they are (chapter 3 will discuss this), but be this as it may, even if Cartesian (non-naturalistic) mind/ body dualism isn't dead, much of contemporary philosophy of mind is naturalistic in the broad (and somewhat misleading) sense that minds are considered causally connected with brains. One might even say that it is currently the orthodox view. I count myself among the orthodox on this matter, and take it to support a connection between the moral and the physical.[55]

A third reason is that an association of the physical and the moral is supported by our strong intuition that if two cases share all relevant physical properties, then ceteris paribus they share all relevant moral properties. The normative dictum, "Treat like cases alike" seems in part to reflect this intuition.

If the moral is neither reducible to nor unconnected with the physical, what relation, then, does it have? My answer is that moral properties *supervene* on physical properties. Physical properties constitute the *base set* of properties which are necessary and sufficient for the instantiation of moral properties which supervene upon them. When these ordered sets of physical properties give rise to states of affairs of certain types—states of affairs of a certain degree of complexity very hard to describe in the abstract—moral properties emerge in a way broadly analogous to the way that numerical and logical properties emerge when physical states of affairs obtain. Think of it this way: if a certain physical state of affairs *A* obtains, and what constitutes this state of affairs includes physical properties of a certain sort, ordered in a certain way, a state of affairs with mental properties emerges and therefore obtains, just as a set of numerical properties and a set of logical properties emerge, constituting numerical and logical states of affairs, respectively. *So, too, with moral properties.* In other words, if the physical state of affairs is right, a moral state of affairs will present itself: the obtaining of the former necessitates the obtaining of the latter.

I should add that I favor what is known as "strong supervenience" over "weak supervenience." Roughly put, a set of moral properties {M} *weakly* supervenes on a base set of physical properties {P} where, if individuals *A* and *B* within the *same* possible world differ in their moral properties, they differ also in their physical properties; while in *strong* supervenience, even if *A* and *B* are in *different* possible worlds, any difference in their moral properties entails a difference in their physical properties.[56] Strong supervenience seems preferable because it better captures the intuition that if full specification of the relevant (non-relational) physical properties of two individuals results in an isomorphic pairing of these properties, there would ceteris paribus be an isomorphic pairing of moral properties, if any, even if two individuals were in different possible worlds.[57] But I do not think that much turns on this for our purposes. If strong supervenience proves too strong, weak supervenience will suffice; for it preserves the core insight that moral properties are associated metaphysically with physical properties in a law-like way. Change one set of properties, and there is concomitant change in the other.

To the question, then, What is the relationship between physical states of affairs and moral states of affairs?, my answer is that moral states of affairs (strongly) supervene on physical states of affairs. Consequently, moral states of affairs obtain if and only if relevant physical states of affairs obtain. As we have noted several times, not all physical states of affairs have supervening moral states of affairs, but some do; and in the latter case a physical state of affairs is sufficient for the moral state of affairs to obtain—"sufficient" in the sense that when the physical state of affairs obtains, its corresponding moral state of affairs is necessitated.

Let's take stock of this complex discussion. The aim of this chapter has been to provide a foundation to understand what first-order moral truth comes to. In order to see this, I have argued for a realist conception of truth, one that not only preserves the T-schema, "the proposition that $p$ is true *iff* $p$," but also countenances a rather minimalist version of a correspondence conception of truth. The central point, then, is that propositions are true or false by virtue of the way the world is. I have explained the truth and falsity of first-order *moral* propositions in these same terms: they are true, or they are false, in accordance with the way the world is, morally speaking. Moral truths express moral facts, while moral falsehoods fail to do this. To understand the nature of facts in general and moral facts in particular, we developed an account of facts that drew heavily on the concept of a state of affairs, "something's being, doing, or having something." Further, we have seen that moral facts supervene on physical facts, because moral properties, hence moral states of affairs, supervene on physical properties and states of affairs. We can now see that first-order moral truth—the truth of propositions such as

> P7: It is morally wrong for anyone to walk into my office and shoot me to
> death as I sit here writing this book,

is firmly rooted in the world, not only in the sense that they are true or false because of the way the world is, as opposed to the way that we merely *believe* the world is, but also in the sense that the physical world *makes* moral truth and moral fact, even though moral truth and fact is not itself *physical* truth and fact.

We are now gaining some precision in understanding what makes some acts, policies, and so forth morally right, and others wrong. But we need to go still deeper if we are going to fully understand moral truth. To do so, we need to get a better handle on exactly what moral properties are. Chapter 3 is intended to do just that.

# NOTES

1. Some of what I say here has appeared in "Moral Facts and the Centrality of Intuitions," in *The New Intuitionism,* ed. Jill Graper Hernandez, (London: Continuum, 2011), 48-66.

2. Some would add a third category, "irrealealist," but I will take antirealism to cover any conceptual territory that denies a realist conception of truth. This will certainly do for our purposes.

3. I have discussed some of this in my "Introduction" to *Realism/Antirealism and Epistemology,* ed. Christopher B. Kulp (Lanham, MD: Rowman & Littlefield, 1997), 1–13, esp. 1–3.

4. John Stuart Mill, *An Examination of Sir William Hamilton's Philosophy and of the Principal Philosophical Questions Discussed in His Writings, Vol. 1* (Boston: William Spencer, 1866), chapter 11.

5. J. M. E. McTaggart, "The Unreality of Time," *Mind,* 17 (1908): 457 73.

6. After William P. Alston's terminology from the Greek word for truth, *aletheia.* More about Alston momentarily.

7. I pass over the truth characterization here of *p* in cases where the constant substituted for the variable *X* does not denote, for example, in cases where there are no such things as purportedly referred to. Such propositions are clearly not true, but whether they are false or meaningless, and precisely why we should regard them as such, need not concern us here. We will, however, be concerned with these matters in chapter 3.

8. William P. Alston, "Realism and the Tasks of Epistemology," *Realism/Antirealism and Epistemology,* ed. Christopher B. Kulp (Lanham, MD: Rowman & Littlefield, 1997), 57; my insertion. Actually, Alston does not think that the T-schema is a proper definition of truth: "First . . . it does not give us a contextual definition of 'true'. Second, it is not a statement at all, much less an unqualifiedly general statement as to the conditions under which a proposition is true. It is merely a scheme for statements," Ibid. Instead, he settles on the following version—a principle *about* the T-schema: "Any instance of [the T-schema] is necessarily true by virtue of the meaning of, *inter alia,* 'true'": Ibid., my insertion.

9. Ibid., 58. See pp. 58ff for elaboration. It is adequate here to understand 'analytically true' as "true by virtue of the meaning of terms." Cf. Richard Rorty on this conception of truth qualifying as realist in his "Realism, Antirealism, and Pragmatism: Comments on Alston, Chisholm, Davidson, Harman, and Searle," in *Realism/Antirealism and Epistemology,* ed. Christopher B. Kulp (Lanham, MD: Rowman & Littlefield, 1997), 159.

10. I will have more to say about the concept of "facts" in this and chapter 3.

11. Or more precisely, as James puts it, the true is "the name of whatever proves itself to be good in the way of belief, and good, too, for definite assignable reasons": William James, *Pragmatism and the Meaning of Truth* (Cambridge, MA: Harvard University Press, 1978), 42. I am indebted to William P. Alston for these and many other observations to follow regarding antirealist versions of truth.

12. See Charles S. Peirce, "How to Make Our Ideas Clear," *Collected Papers of Charles Sanders Peirce,* eds. Charles Hartshorne and Paul Weiss (Cambridge, MA: Harvard University Press, 1931–1935), paragraph 407. Actually, Peirce notoriously says a number of things, with doubtful compatibility, about what he means by truth, that is, that it we approach it asymptotically, which makes it sound rather realist.

13. See John Dewey, "Reconstruction in Philosophy," in *John Dewey: The Middle Works, 1899–1924,* Vol. 12, ed. Bridget A. Walsh (Carbondale and Edwardsville: Southern Illinois University Press, 1920), 77–201, esp. 156.

14. F. H. Bradley, *Essays on Truth and Reality* (Oxford: Clarendon Press, 1914), 1.

15. Ibid., 223.

16. Brand Blanchard, *The Nature of Thought, Vol. 2* (London: Allen & Unwin, 1939), 264.

17. I owe this point to Alston; see his "Realism and the Tasks of Epistemology," 62ff. Also see his *A Realist Conception of Truth* (Ithaca, NY: Cornell University Press, 1996), chapter 7.

18. I am indebted to Alston for this point: see his "Realism and the Tasks of Epistemology," 62f.

19. What follows is developed in much greater detail in John Searle, *The Construction of Social Reality* (New York: Free Press, 1995), 199–228. I discuss these same matters in "Moral Facts and the Centrality of Intuitions," 48–66 (esp. 50–51).

20. Searle, *The Construction of Social Reality*, 219. Italics mine.

21. Ibid.

22. Ibid.

23. Ibid., my insertion.

24. My wishing that there is a mailbox in front of my house may motivate me to build one (my wife would be astonished!), or to pay to have one installed; or my being happy that there is such a mailbox may mean that I am pleased that someone else installed it, or that I at some previous time saw to its construction. But none of this is to the point. The question is, is there a mailbox in front of my house? The proposition is true if the answer is yes, false if it is no. This is exactly how we naturally understand these things.

25. Searle, *The Construction of Social Reality*, 219.

26. Of course there are "conceptual truths"—truths that are a result of our concepts, but these truths are a matter of the way the world is with regard to our concepts

27. Much of the following has already appeared in my "Moral Facts and the Centrality of Intuitions," 53ff.

28. John Searle, *The Construction of Social Reality*, 220; quotation in my insertion from ibid, 206.

29. Ramon M. Lemos, *Metaphysical Investigations* (London and Toronto: Associated University Presses, 1988); and also his "Bearers of Value," *Philosophy and Phenomenological Research,* vol. LI, no. 4 (December 1991): 873–89. Lemos's work has a substantial bearing on much of what I have to say throughout §2.4.

30. Sentence-tokens such as this may not, however, be adequate to express fully a determinate proposition. It may, for example, be necessary to include a temporal, and perhaps a spatial indexical. But I will not pause over such details here. More about these matters in §2.6 below.

31. Lemos, "Bearers of Value," 873. I will refine this notion a bit momentarily, in a way that differs somewhat from Lemos.

32. See Susan Haack, *Philosophy of Logics* (Cambridge: Cambridge University Press, 1978), chapter 6, for an accessible and very useful discussion of the contrast between sentences, statements, and propositions as truth-bearers. For a thorough current discussion, some of it not sympathetic to my views, see Jeffery C. King, Scott Soames, and Jeff Speaks, *New Thinking About Propositions* (Oxford: Oxford University Press, 2014).

33. See Lemos, "Bearers of Value," 874–76, for elaboration.

34. Ibid., 876.

35. This is certainly not a canonical rendering of the implications of normative ethical relativism: there are a number of inequivalent ways it can be understood, which we will examine in chapter 5. This, however, will do for present purposes.

36. And similarly for the truth or the falsity of propositions like P3, although showing how this works is a bit more complicated, given that it deals with the relativity of moral norms, not specific moral judgments. I will not attempt to do this here.

37. I take my view here to be roughly compatible with Lemos: see his "Bearers of Value," 885–86.

38. This is of course to assume bi-valence. But even if bi-valence is rejected in favor of some other *n*-valent truth assessment, of truth at least *some* (if not most) first-order moral propositions clearly appear to be true and some false. For note that if there is at least one true proposition, its negation is false, and conversely.

39. Cf. '*All* oh my!' or '*Some* how is it?': neither appear to be propositional.

40. Subjunctive-conditionality will be an issue for us in chapter 3, §3.5.

41. It may be impossible to do so in practice. It would in any event be a specification of staggering complexity.

42. These are matters taken up in detail in chapter 3.

43. Karl Popper is perhaps best known in this regard for his systematic effort to discriminate between the scientific and the non-scientific, that is, between the physical and the metaphysi-

cal. See, for example, his *The Logic of Scientific Discovery* (New York: Harper & Row, 1965 [1959]).

44. See John Post, *Faces of Existence* (Ithaca, New York: Cornell University Press, 1986), for an informative discussion of the role that physics plays in determining the lexicon of physical entities.

45. Eliminative materialists like Paul Churchland project that only the ontic commitments of natural science will one day stand, and that all other spheres of inquiry will eventually be subsumed or eliminated as free-standing disciplines, leaving physics alone at the ontological table. See, for example, his "Some Reductive Strategies in Cognitive Neurobiology," *Mind*, Vol. 95 (1986). Cf. Post, *Faces of Existence*. Whether any and all current natural sciences are reducible to physics is a highly controversial issue, one of enormous complexity—in itself a whole subdiscipline of the philosophy of science—which I of course cannot deal with here.

46. We do not need what one might call a "deep understanding" of any of these terms in order to understand the proposition. I do not need a deep understanding of automobiles to know that it was an automobile that just ran over my foot.

47. It is, for example, highly dubious, and I think mistaken, to hold that an adequate conception of personhood can be given in strictly physical terms. But in this context, we can pass over such issues.

48. This is well represented in our ordinary moral thinking: you are not blameworthy or punishable for something that you have not yet done.

49. The following draws closely on my "Moral Facts and the Centrality of Intuitions," 55ff.

50. This is Lemos's wording.

51. What, for example, was the status of morality before the Big Bang? Assuming that this question even makes sense, the answer is, there wasn't any. This said, I admit that it is too much for me to dispute here radical conceptions of a non-physical universe.

52. Are these properties social constructs? In which case one might try to make the argument—a rather involved one—that they are after all physical properties; for all social constructs, as part of the physical world, are thought also to be physical. I think this is very doubtful. I will make the case against constructivism regarding properties—in particular, against constructed first-order moral properties—in chapter 3.

53. Some physical properties, for example, the atomic weight of a proton, may be knowable only (very) indirectly through the senses. Not so, for example, the color of a brick.

54. Is it, however, in the biologist's? Not properly, I think. We will discuss this in chapter 3.

55. See Russ Shafer-Landau, *Moral Realism: A Defence* (Oxford: Oxford University Press, 2003), 72ff, for a useful discussion of the relevance of a naturalist (physicalist) theory of mind to moral metaphysics. I largely concur with Shafer-Landau. Note that I do not mean to imply that only minded beings can instance moral properties. Any sentient being can (does), but non-persons (in the Kantian sense) can only instance a sub-set of the moral properties instanced by beings with minds. My discussion here has to do only with the moral properties instanced by persons

56. See David Enoch, *Taking Morality Seriously* (Oxford: Oxford University Press, 2011), 136ff, for the distinction between weak and strong supervenience. He too prefers strong supervenience over weak supervenience. I make the same point I am making here in "Moral Facts and the Centrality of Intuitions," 58.

57. See Jaegwon Kim, "Concepts of Supervenience," in *Supervenience and Mind: Selected Philosophical Essays*, eds. Jaegwon Kim and Ernest Sosa (Cambridge: Cambridge University Press, 1993), 53–78. This could be generalized to any type of base and supervening properties. Cf. David Brink, *Moral Realism and the Foundations of Ethics* (Cambridge: Cambridge University Press, 1989), 160–61.

# Chapter Three

# Moral Properties

## 3.1. A FEW PRELIMINARIES

We saw in chapter 2, §2.4–2.6, that when we know a first-order moral truth such as

> P7: It is morally wrong for anyone to walk into my office and shoot me to death as I sit here writing this book,

what is known is a proposition that expresses a first-order moral fact, in this case, the fact that it is morally wrong for anyone to walk into my office and shoot me to death as I sit here writing this book. We understand this fact to be a first-order moral state of affairs that obtains. Further, the obtaining of a first-order moral state of affairs requires the instancing of an ordered set of first-order moral properties. Our understanding of what all of this means, however, will be greatly enhanced if we can achieve a deeper explanation of facts, states of affairs, and properties than we currently possess.

In other terms, what we need is a deeper explanation, an analysis or explication, of *what* is known when we know a first-order moral truth. It is important to note that for us, this is fundamentally a metaphysical inquiry, not an epistemological inquiry. This is because of our commitment, as spelled out in chapter 2, §2.1 and §2.2, to a realist conception of truth: truth for a realist is not an epistemic concept, it is a *metaphysical* concept, viz., about the way the world is[1] independent of what we might think the world to be.

But there are different senses of "deeper analysis": an analogy may be helpful to see what I mean here by the term. Suppose we have a situation where an unfortunate Mr. X is found dead, and that the authorities have requested an explanation of the cause of death. Now imagine we are offered the following replies:

COD$_1$ (cause of death$_1$): Mr. X was shot to death.

COD$_2$: Mr. X's heart was destroyed by the violent force of a bullet, killing him.

COD$_3$: The destruction of Mr. X's heart caused a cessation of circulation of blood to the brain, resulting in death.

COD$_4$: The neurons in Mr. X's brain ceased to function due to hypoxia, resulting in death of the brain and subsequently of the entire neurological system.

COD$_5$: Physiological processes $A,B,C$ . . . *etc.* (to be filled out in terms appropriate to current physiology) ceased to function, resulting in cessation of all physiological processes throughout the entire biological system.

COD$_6$: (Molecules $m_1$ . . . $m_n$) constituting the chemical compounds ($d_1$ . . . $d_n$) involved in neuro-physiological processes ($p_1$ . . . $p_n$) under conditions $c$ caused molecules ($m_o$ . . . $m_p$) to act in ways ($j,k,l$).

COD$_n$: A description of physical events at the atomic level (?). At the subatomic level (?).

Note that any one of these replies may be said to constitute an "explanation of the cause of death" of Mr. X;[2] but note further that any one of them may be said to constitute an appropriate explanation of the cause of death only *relative to a set of criteria appropriate to the purposes at hand.*[3] Thus, surely the police or the courts would be interested in COD$_1$ and COD$_2$, and probably in COD$_3$ (which may seem banal because of its obviousness, given COD$_2$), but it is increasingly unlikely that they would be interested in COD$_4$ and so on (they would almost surely not be interested in COD$_6$). Why? Because in all likelihood these explanations would explain at a level not relevant to the primary purpose of the authorities' inquiry, which is to ascertain whether a law has been broken, whether a homicide has occurred, whether someone may be prosecuted, etc. The court is presumably not interested in physiological processes or molecular behavior per se, as would the physiologist or the chemist. But for that matter, neither would the latter two be satisfied with explanations at the level of COD$_1$–COD$_3$. Their purposes are different, requiring an explanation at a deeper causal level than the police or the courts.

Our cause of death case well illustrates, for our purposes, the notion of an "explanatory level." Roughly—this is a complicated issue that I shall not try to cast rigorously here[4]—as we descend from COD$_1$ through COD$_6$, our explanations deal with increasingly more basic physical entities and events— "basic" in the sense that the entities, processes, principles, and so forth, comprising a higher-level explanatory COD are in whole or in part explained by the entities and principles operating at the explanatory COD that immediately follows it. Thus, Mr. X's *being dead* (being caused to die) is explained by Mr. X's "being shot to death" (COD$_1$), which is in turn explained by the fact that Mr. X's "heart was destroyed by the violent force of a bullet" ($COD_2$), and so on with the succeeding explanatory CODs.

For the purposes of our inquiry, then, what we need is an explication of what is known when $S$ knows a first-order moral truth,[5] which provides an understanding of what constitutes such truths, that is at a more fundamental level than an explication in terms of propositional truth, or even in terms of facts and states of affairs. Schematically, what we have is something like this:

KMT$_1$ (knowing a moral truth): $S$ knows that (first-order moral proposition) $p$ is true.
KMT$_2$: $S$ knows that it is a moral fact that $p$.
KMT$_3$: $S$ knows that a moral state of affairs $p$ obtains.
KMT$_4$: $S$ knows that moral property $F_m$ applies to moral entity $E_m$.

KMT$_1$–KMT$_4$ are all aimed at explaining the nature of what is known when knowing a moral truth, each one providing a deeper, more fundamental explanation than the preceding one. In short, we need to get down to the level of moral properties, to the level of KMT$_4$, to see what really makes a moral proposition $p$ true or false.

But before exploring the relation of moral properties to moral truth and fact, we should keep firmly in mind that for us, given that a fact is a state of affairs that obtains, a proposition such as, 'There is snow on the summit of Mont Blanc' is true if and only if it expresses a state of affairs that obtains; and similarly, that a moral proposition such as

P1: Chattel slavery, such as was practiced in the southern states of the United States prior to the American Civil War, is morally wrong,

is true if and only if it expresses a moral state of affairs that obtains, namely, that such slavery is morally wrong.

Recall, too, that some states of affairs obtain, and others do not. Mont Blanc having snow on its summit obtains; President Obama's being twelve feet tall does not. Further, some states of affairs obtain temporally: the World Trade Towers being part of the New York City skyline is a state of affairs that obtained in the 1999, but not now. And it seems that some states of affairs obtain atemporally, or eternally. For example, it ever was and ever will be that $3 + 4 = 7$.

Let us also recall that a state of affairs $x$ may obtain in association with some other state of affairs $y$, but not with $z$. This may be the case within state of affairs-types, or across state of affairs-types. An example of the latter is, if the *physical* state of affairs $x$ of three apples sitting on a table obtains at time $t$, then the *numerical* state of affairs $y$ of the cardinality of the apples—in this case, three—also obtains at time *t*. But obviously *y* does *not* obtain when state of affairs *z,* of two apples sitting on a table at time *t* obtains.

There are of course many ways, far too numerous to mention here, in which states of affairs may be associated with one another; but one way that is important for us, as discussed in chapter 2, §2.6, is the relation of the physical to the first-order moral. On the view endorsed there, moral states of affairs *supervene* on physical states of affairs. This means that if there were no physical states of affairs—no physical objects of any sort; no physical universe—there would then be no moral states of affairs, that is, no instances of moral wrongness or praiseworthiness. And this of course means that were there no physical facts, there would be no moral facts. Physical facts and moral facts are intimately connected, the former serving as the ground or base of the latter.

So much we have said before. But at this point I should further note that what makes a state of affairs the ontic type that it is, is the type of properties to which the terms of its description refer. Thus, what makes a physical state of affairs-type a state of affairs of that type, is the type of properties, viz., *physical* properties, predicated of the subject as denoted by the terms of its description. The same applies mutatis mutandis for any other type of state of affairs, e.g., a mathematical state of affairs or a moral state of affairs. More-over, what makes a state of affairs-*token* a token of that type is the instantia-tion of those properties. Thus, a physical state of affairs-token is such be-cause of the (uniquely ordered) physical properties referred to by its descrip-tion—and similarly mutatis mutandis for any other state of affairs-token.

Now we are better positioned to get a handle on what it means to be "the way the world is, morally speaking." We may begin by saying that the meaning of 'the way the world is' in general, that is, in the abstract, is the uniquely ordered *n*-tuple of properties predicated of a set of entities which constitutes a unique description of that world. On the view developed below, if the properties of this description are instantiated, this constitutes a descrip-tion of the *actual* world; if uninstanti*ated* but instanti*able*, the description of a *possible* world. The description of the actual world is what we typically mean by 'the way the world is'. (Any deviation from this unique description consti-tutes a description of a different world—a different possible world.) A true proposition expresses (part of) this description of the world; a false proposi-tion does not: it fails to get this description right. [6]

We can understand the meaning of 'the way the world is' specifically with regard to morality to follow the same general pattern of explication. Thus, a true moral proposition correctly expresses a description of the way the world is with regard to (a set of) its moral properties; a false moral proposition fails to do this. To illustrate, again consider

P7: It is morally wrong for anyone to walk into my office and shoot me to death as I sit here writing this book.

Here the first-order moral property of moral wrongness is predicated of any act of an agent's walking into my office and shooting me to death as I sit here writing this book; and this is the way the world is, morally speaking. Actually, this point is more accurately expressed as a subjunctive conditional: *if* anyone *were* to walk into my office . . . *then* this act *would* manifest, or instantiate, the property of moral wrongness.[7] If this proposition were false, moral wrongness would *not* be instantiated if the antecedent of the conditional was fulfilled.

To take stock: the truth of the proposition *p* is a matter of *p*'s expressing the fact that *p*; and the fact that *p* is a matter of the obtaining of the state of affairs that *p*. Further, the fact that *p*, thus the obtaining of the state of affairs that *p*, is a matter of the way the (actual) world is. What makes a state of affairs the ontic type it is—physical, mathematical, or moral—is that the properties denoted by the state of affairs' description are of a given ontic type. We are here of course principally interested in moral truths, moral facts, and moral states of affairs, and the properties that make them such. Now to look at moral properties more closely.

## 3.2. ON PROPERTIES IN GENERAL

But before talking about moral properties in particular, I need to say something about the nature of properties in general. Owing to the great complexity of this issue, I will limit my comments to matters bearing directly on understanding first-order moral truth and knowledge.

What, then, are properties? I should first note that there are disputes over whether certain (putative) classes of properties should be admitted into our inventory of properties—for example, essential properties and internal properties—and disputes over whether different (putative) classes of properties have a different metaphysical (i.e., ontological) status—for example, external properties and relations. The appropriate limitations on the scope of our project—to understand moral properties—necessitates that I bypass these complex and specialized issues.[8] And in any event, for our purposes little hangs on such matters.

So to be clear at the outset: the sense of the term 'property' that I principally have in mind throughout this discussion is properties of particulars. And by the term 'particular', I mean an entity that is not a property, for example, material objects, events, persons, etc. We may call properties of particulars "first-order properties." On occasion, however, we will have reason to talk of properties of properties, that is, of "second-order properties," and also of relations, which I shall regard as yet another type of property, viz., relational properties. These simplifying stipulations understood, then, there are three main candidates for properties in the contemporary literature: properties as sets of particulars, properties as sets of tropes, and properties as universals. [9]

Understood as a *set of particulars*, a property $F$ is a construction of just those particulars that instantiate $F$. Thus, the property "green" is the set of green *things*—material objects, for example: the set of leaves, houses, bodies of water, and anything else that is green. This a nominalist conception of properties. Understood as a *set of tropes*, a property $F$ is the set of all of those *instances* or *cases* of *being F*. Thus, the property "green" is the set of all of those *instances* of being green—the "being green" of this house, the "being green" of this body of water, etc. Understood as a *universal*, $F$ is a characteristic or attribute that may be *instantiated* by a particular. Thus, the property "green" may be instantiated by a leaf, a house, a body of water, and so forth. This is a realist conception of properties. [10]

All accounts of properties known to me have significant challenges. Given a voluminous and often technical literature going back to Plato and Aristotle, which would take us far afield to pursue here, I will declare rather preemptively that I opt for an account of properties as universals. More about this below.

Let us suppose for now that properties are universals. In more detail, what, then, is a property? I shall understand properties to be features, or characteristics, or attributes—I mean these terms to be interchangeable—of the way the world is. Typically, these attributes are, in any of an indefinitely large range of systems of representation, predicated of or attributed to real or imaginary, possible or impossible particulars. Thus, in the proposition

> A1: The White House is white,

the property "whiteness" is predicated of a real particular, in this case a material object.

In the proposition

> A2: The unicorn is white,

the same property is predicated of an imaginary particular, a unicorn. According to this account, in the case of proposition A1, whiteness is instantiated: the White House (in Washington, DC) exists, and is white. In the case of proposition A2, however, whiteness is not instantiated; for we assume ex hypothesi that there are no unicorns. Some properties are *instantiable*—that is, they may take possible particulars as their actual instances—whiteness is an example—but others are not: round-squareness, for example. Thus, the proposition

A3: The rock is round-square (is a round-square; has the shape of a round-square),

predicates an *un*instantiable property of a material object. The property is uninstantiable because no (material) object could possibly possess the property of round-squareness.[11] One might retort that round-squareness is not really a property, that the term 'round-square' does not refer because it cannot apply in principle to any possible object. But given that locutions containing uninstantiable predicate terms are not only clearly intelligible, and candidates for truth or falsity (e.g., the proposition, 'Round-squareness is not equivalent to reddish-greenness' is true; the proposition, 'The candidate for president is the son who fathered his grandfather' is false); and also given that, *pace* W. V. Quine's and others' objections,[12] we can meaningfully quantify over properties (e.g., 'All properties such as round-squareness are spatial properties', and 'There exists the property of round-squareness and it is not a color property' are both well-formed locutions), I prefer to speak of their uninstantiability.

Some propositions predicate properties of abstract entities, that is, entities that do not have spatiotemporal location. For example

A4: The number 7 is prime,

predicates the property of "primeness" of the number 7 (on the plausible assumption that numbers are abstract entities). And as we saw in the previous paragraph, some propositions predicate properties of other properties. For example,

A5: Identity is symmetrical,

predicates the property of "symmetricality" of the property of "identity."

There is of course an indefinitely large number of properties of an indefinitely wide variety of types: physical, numerical, syntactic, moral, and so forth. Our concern being with moral properties, what I say in this and later sections of this chapter is aimed squarely at understanding them. But before looking more deeply at moral properties per se, it would be helpful to first say more about the *metaphysics* of properties in general.

## 3.3. THE METAPHYSICS OF PROPERTIES

In §3.2, I said that I take properties to be universals. Given that properties are universals, one way to view them is often called "conceptualism," or perhaps more aptly for our purposes, "constructivism," according to which although universals exist, they are mind-dependent. Some care is necessary here: a property may be mind-dependent in two broad senses.[13] In one sense of the term, the property of, say, "being a good logician" is mind-dependent in the sense that being a good logician requires possession of mind. In another sense of the term, however, the properties of, say, length or "rockhood" (being a rock) are mind-dependent in that we *construct* these properties. There are no natural kinds "rock" or "length"[14]: they are sociocultural or linguistic constructs. A rock is as much a construct as a baseball game. The second sense of the term is what is important here: the former sense is uncontroversial, a conceptual truth, but irrelevant for our purposes. The second sense of 'constructivism', however, is far from uncontroversial.

Antirealists, for example, hold some variation on the theme that reality is constructed, and because properties, whatever they are, are part of reality, they, too, are constructed.[15] Take an example we have already looked at in chapter 2, §2.1, John Stuart Mill's phenomenalism. According to this view, we construct the world out of sense-data. Say that you perceive a leaf, and attribute the property of greenness to it. As Mill has it, the green leaf is not a perception-independent material object, but a "permanent possibilit[y] of sensation,"[16]—that is, how things appear, or would appear, under a specified set of conditions. We construct the green leaf out of experience, out of sense-data: the greenness of the leaf, and the "leafiness" of the leaf, are not mind-independent existents, they are modes of being perceived. What "is" in the "material world" is not mind-independent in our second sense of the term. Quite the contrary, existence or ontological status is ultimately an epistemological matter.

Idealists are also in the antirealist camp. They see reality as ultimately a construct, because they think that the features of the world are features that mind brings to it. Mathematical and logical systems, for example, are on their view mental constructs, and likewise regarding the properties of those systems. Thus, we construct the "primness" of the number 7, and we construct argument forms and the validity and invalidity of those forms. On my view, the pragmatists are also antirealists regarding properties. Whether a material object has the property of whiteness or of redness, or of hardness or of softness, or of neither, ultimately comes down to whether we find it better, given a specified set of purposes, to call that object white or red, hard or soft, or neither. Indeed, the very existence of the concept of the property of color or of hardness is a matter of whether it serves our purposes.[17]

For all of these antirealists, then, what "is," is not mind-independent in the relevant sense of the term. Quite the contrary, existence is ultimately an epistemological matter, including the existence of properties.

Constructivism being one way of regarding universals, realism is another. On this view, we do not construct properties: properties are mind-independent in our second sense of the term. True, there are properties of things-that-we-construct, but the properties themselves are not constructs. Thus, we might construct a rectangular barn, but the barn's property of rectangularity is not a construct. The barn's property of rectangularity or lack thereof stands on its own.

There are, however, two major versions of this realist position: an *aristotelian* version, according to which properties are imminent in particulars, and therefore may be said to have spatiotemporal location;[18] and a *platonic* version, according to which universals are abstract objects which do not have spatiotemporal location. One might, after D. M. Armstrong,[19] call the former "imminent universals" (roughly, *universalia in rebus* in medieval terminology), and the latter, platonic account "transcendent universals" (*universalia ante rem*).[20] One reason to prefer the aristotelian account is that it obviates charges of "ontological queerness" of abstract entities by allowing spatiotemporal location of properties, namely, in the particular(s) in which the property is imminent. This appeals to those of an empiricist bent. But then there are some very strange, and I think deeply problematic characteristics of properties. As Alex Oliver observes, on this account "[(i)]one universal can be wholly present at different places at the same time and (ii) two universals can occupy the same place at the same time."[21] This is very curious indeed. For if something is wholly present at spatiotemporal point $y$, how could it *simultaneously* be wholly present at spatiotemporal point $z$? This seems a conceptual confusion. Further, how could two discreet things—in this case, two universals $U$ and $V$—occupy the *same* spatiotemporal point $y$? For it seems that the very notion of *individuation* precludes simultaneous occupation of $y$, otherwise $U = V$. In addition, one wonders what is to be made of the spatiotemporal location of a *property of a first-order property*, that is, the spatiotemporal location of a second-order property, for example, of the property of symmetricality of the property of identity—identity itself being a property? All this said, however, I readily admit that both versions of universals have their problems, many quite technical; and so to avoid complications not strictly relevant to our task, I shall declare, again rather preemptively, that I opt for the platonic account.[22]

In addition to the negative considerations of the previous paragraph, a major motivation for this choice—for properties as universals in general, and for the platonic account in particular—is epistemic. As I have emphasized in chapters 1 and 2, I want to reject moral skepticism in any of its general guises, and to support moral realism.[23] In chapters 4–6 to follow, I will defend a *non*-empiricist account of justified moral belief and knowledge, and therefore see no need to defend an account of properties that caters to empiricist sensibilities as provided for by an aristotelian account of universals, or for that matter by empiricist-friendly nominalist accounts of properties, according to which properties are sets of particulars. However, I still need to say a bit more about general concerns with platonic universals.

A salient reason to shun platonic universals is worries about their ontological status. Why think they exist? Now, there are several ways to come at
the general question, "Do entities of type *T* exist?" One way is to consider
whether we have cognitive access to such entities. A powerful reason for
answering in the negative is that we can come up with no plausible account
of how we do. Do material objects exist? Overwhelming evidence via the
senses indicates yes. Does God exist? Harder to say; for it is less clear what
cognitive access we might have to God. Do platonic universals exist? Perhaps harder still to say than in the God case, much less in the material object
case, but we might reply that if we endorse cognitive access to other kinds of
abstract entities—numbers and propositions, for example—then by analogy
we have good prima facie reason to endorse universals. Far from a definitive
answer, certainly, but I would emphasize that the moral realist should resist
allowing moral properties qua abstract entities to be singled out on epistemic
grounds for special skeptical treatment.[24]

A second way to come at the question "Do entities of type *T* exist?" is to
consider whether our best account of the world includes them. If it does, we
have reason to avow them; if not, not. Thus, many agree that our best account
of the world licenses material objects, but not ghosts. What about platonic
universals? Another question too big to deal with thoroughly here; but given
the concerns raised several paragraphs ago regarding an aristotelian account
of universals, and given the non-empiricist account of moral knowledge that
I shall advocate, which discounts the putative ontological advantages of
nominalism, the platonic account remains attractive.

A third way, one associated with the second way of coming at our question, is to ask whether positing entities of type *T* runs afoul of Occam's razor:
do not multiply entities beyond necessity. Assuming no loss of explanatory
power, choose the theory with the more economical ontology.[25] It is very
hard to do away with material objects, but what of platonic universals? Yet
another difficult question, but given the difficulties of dispensing with abstract entities tout court, and given the virtues of the non-empiricist moral
epistemology that I shall advocate—which does not incline toward a hard
line against abstract entities—I suggest that we see how far our platonic
account will take us.

On my view, then, all three modes of responding to the question "Do
entities of type *T* exists?" at least permit, even if they do not dictate, affirming platonic universals: (i) we appear to have cognitive access to them; (ii)
our best explanation of the world includes them; and (iii) Occam's razor does
not shave them from our ontological lexicon.

I have said little about properties as sets of tropes (i.e., the property *F* is
the set of all *instances* or *cases* of *being F*). I am unclear what is to be gained
by adopting trope theory over universals, and there is this to be lost: as Oliver
has observed, "it is usual to hold an aristotelian conception of tropes, accord-

ing to which tropes are present in their particular instances, and which does not allow for uninstantiated tropes."[26] However, as indicated earlier, I want to allow for both uninstanti*ated* properties (e.g., a twenty-foot-tall woman) and uninstanti*able* properties (e.g., round-squareness), so trope theory is unattractive.

In sum, our general account of properties is this: properties are platonic universals, understood as abstract entities which exist independently of their instantiations. When instantiated, they are instantiated by particulars (in the case of first-order properties), whether concrete or abstract—the whiteness of a house, the vividness of a color perception, the primeness of a number. We are now in a position to understand moral properties.

## 3.4. MORAL PROPERTIES

Recall our oft-discussed distinction between first- and second-order moral propositions (especially chapter 2, §2.3 and §2.5). First-order moral propositions are propositions about subject matters *within* morality, and second-order moral positions are *about* morality. Our concern has been with first-order moral properties, and they will remain our principal focus. So let's think about these properties more closely. Take first-order propositions such as:

> P7. It is morally wrong for anyone to walk into my office and shoot me to death as I sit here writing this book.
> P11: It is prima facie morally right to return a kindness with a kindness.
> P12: It is morally good to be a stalwart defender of your young children.

Whether true or false (all true, I am sure), these propositions are said to employ what are called in the current literature "thin" moral concepts, thin because there is an abstractness about them: they say comparatively little descriptively, and retain their meaning largely independent of their embeddedness in broader valuational contexts. We may say that moral rightness, wrongness, and goodness are relatively simple.[27] Such concepts are frequently contrasted with "thick" moral concepts, like those employed in the following propositions:

> P13: It is courageous to risk one's life to defend one's friend from serious physical harm.
> P14: It is important for the welfare of a child that her parents be compassionate toward her.

Here, "courageous" and "compassionate" are (adjectival forms of) thick moral concepts, which pick out thick moral properties. Descriptively, these concepts are less simple than moral wrongness et al., in that one needs an explanation of their embeddedness in a broader valuational context before the truth conditions of propositions containing them can be ascertained. This complexity leaves a good bit of room for disagreement. The concept of courage for Aristotle, for example, is a famously involved and subtle matter, being firmly embedded in his broader theory of the moral virtues (and which contrasts starkly with the concept of courage apparently endorsed by the leaders of al-Qaeda and ISIS).[28]

In the interest of simplicity, it will be convenient to focus on thin moral properties. In chapter 2, §2.6, we argued (i) that moral facts (strongly) supervene on physical properties; and (ii) that because mora facts and moral properties are related, moral properties are related to physical properties. More precisely, however, *how* are they related?

They are related thus: if a moral property $F_m$ is instantiated, then a physical property $F_p$, or more likely a larger set of physical properties which includes $F_p$, must also be instantiated. For example, suppose that Smith burns down Jones's house. We are talking here about a specific Smith, a specific Jones, a specific house, and a specific act of burning which occurs at time $t$ under a specific set of conditions $c$. Now assume that this is a *wrongful* burning: Smith shouldn't have done it—it was performed out of revenge, without Jones's permission, etc. (these factors would be among the conditions $c$). Clearly, then, this instantiation of moral wrongness could not have occurred without this instantiation of "houseness," that is, without the existence of this particular house. *No specific house, no specific instantiation of moral wrongness.* What this example points up is the general type of connection between physical properties and (first-order) moral properties: *instantiated moral properties supervene on instantiated physical properties, which serve as their base.*

Note that in the case just discussed, as is typical of such cases, it is likely that when one moral property is instantiated—wrongness, say—so will other thin moral properties, such as moral impermissibility or badness. (Perhaps thick moral properties such as spitefulness and vengefulness will be as well.) But this should occasion no surprise; for in general, when a property $Fx_1$ of type $T$ is instantiated, so will other properties $Fx_2$, $Fx_3$, and so forth, of the same type. For example, when the physical property of "tableness" (being a table) is instantiated, so, too, (in all likelihood) will the physical properties of "being a table leg" and "being a table top," and so forth. After all, just as one and the same physical event may be both an explosion and an event where a great quantity of heat is generated, so may one and the same act be an act of torture and an act of cruelty.[29] That is, virtually any event or situation admits of more than one description, each description of course involving the attribution of different properties. Further, when properties $Fx_1$, $Fx_2$, $Fx_3$ of one type are instantiated, it is also likely that properties $Fy_1$, $Fy_2$, and $Fy_3$ of a different type(s) will be instantiated. For example, the instantiation of a set of physical properties—this chair, this table, this house—also instantiates a set of numerical properties, for example, the cardinality of the number of these physical objects. And of course the same applies in principle regarding the instantiation of physical properties and the instantiation of moral properties.[30]

Now it is important to keep in mind that on the view propounded here, (first-order) moral properties are sui generis, irreducible to properties of a different ontic type. In a proposition such as

P1: Chattel slavery, such as was practiced in the southern states of the United States prior to the American Civil War, is morally wrong,

the *thin* moral property of "wrongness" is predicated of the policy of chattel slavery. Not all agree. Sociocultural moral relativists, for example, hold that whether or not an act is morally wrong, etc., is determined by, is a function of, the belief-set of the members of a specified social or cultural group. This means that moral properties are actually properties of sociocultural beliefs (not properties of beliefs *about* sociocultural beliefs; those aren't in the relevant respect "normative"). Other versions of moral relativism are essentially in the same boat. Some would tie morality to linguistic conventions or conceptual schemes, others to concepts constructed to suit our purposes. Moral wrongness and courageousness are for the former ultimately a function of which language is in play. What does 'morally wrong' mean? Look at how we use the term: *that* is what it means.[31] For the latter, moral concepts are just another set—albeit a particular *type* of set—of concepts that suit our purposes. But language and concepts are ultimately constructs, formed to suit the interests of mankind. Moral properties are simply properties of these constructs, and in this respect are constructs themselves. They are not sui generis. But all of this is also wrong if our moral realism is correct. For on our view, language may "get it right" or language may "get it wrong," as may our concepts, but the properties of language or the dictates of optional concepts do not make morality.

Moral nihilists would, for rather different reasons, also reject our interpretation of moral properties. They think that there aren't any moral properties of any sort. Take J. L. Mackie, for example:[32] he rejects moral properties because he thinks that they are metaphysically "queer," that if there were any such thing, that they must be unlike properties of other sorts for which we have clear epistemic access—physical properties, for example (color, heat, loudness, and the like). We in fact have no good reason to suppose that there really is any such type of thing as a moral property. What we are really doing is reifying our attitudes. We feel strongly about something, and mistake this strength of feeling, often shared by others, as signifying something objective, real, mind-independent.[33]

Reductive physicalists like Paul Churchland would have none of this sui generis moral property business either. On his view all genuine properties are physical properties, and "moral properties" are not physical properties. Moral discourse is just another form of superannuated "folk psychology" which will be eliminated by a thoroughgoing physicalist discourse.[34] And evolutionary ethics understands moral rightness and courageousness, wrongness and impermissibility, and so forth, in terms of the advantageousness or disadvantageousness of actions and dispositions for long-term reproductive success.[35] None of these views regard moral properties as sui generis.

Even many traditional moral thinkers reject moral properties as sui generis entities. For example, moral naturalists like John Stuart Mill and Henry Sidgwick, who have had an enormous influence on western ethics, think that moral properties are actually properties of natural individuals or systems. Take Mill: On his view an action is right insofar as it maximizes happiness for the greatest number in the indefinitely long run. And what is happiness? It is "pleasure and the absence of pain; [and] . . . 'unhappiness' [is] pain, and the privation of pleasure."[36] Pleasure, then, is a mental state, which in turn is the state of a physical organism. We are able to discern the nature of these physical states through experience—immediate first person psychological reports in the case of ourselves (Jones knows perfectly well if he is in pain), and through observation in the case of others (I may know that Jones is in pain: just observe his behavior). And this means that the properties we perceive are *physical* properties, not sui generis moral properties.[37]

There are many other views that deny that moral properties are sui generis, but these illustrations will suffice. In the next section, will have more to say in defense of the moral realist stance adopted here. For the moment, however, I simply note that there are prominent voices in opposition to us.

So our answer to the question, What are first-order moral properties?, is this: Moral properties, like other properties, are platonic universals, and therefore abstract entities. These universals may be instantiated or not: some are uninstantiated, but instantiable, others are uninstantiable. When instantiated, first-order moral properties are instantiated by particulars, for example, an act, a policy, a person.[38] Moral properties are a sui generis class of non-physical properties, which supervene on physical properties.

## 3.5. MORAL FACTS AND MORAL PROPERTIES

In a recent discussion of moral facts, Brian Leiter declares:

> I will use the terms 'moral properties' and 'moral facts' interchangeably. . . .
> So, for example, one might say that inflicting gratuitous pain on a sentient

creature has the property (or feature) of being morally wrong, or we might say that it is a (moral) fact that the infliction of such pain is morally wrong. [39]

Leiter is of course free to speak as he pleases, but this is confusion—at least it is if the analysis offered here is correct. Moral properties and moral facts are not interchangeable. They are certainly related, but they are distinct. To see this more perspicuously, consider our distinction between first- and second-order moral facts: thus,

P1: Chattel slavery, such as was practiced in the southern states of the United States prior to the American Civil War, is morally wrong,

if true, expresses a first-order moral fact; while

P15: There are non-relative, first-order moral truths,

if true, expresses a second-order moral fact. Let's grant the truth of both. P1 attributes the property of moral wrongness to the policy of chattel slavery; P15 attributes the property of non-relative truth to a class of entities, namely, first-order moral propositions, propositions like P1. Now I take it that Leiter has in mind first-order moral propositions when equating moral facts with moral properties, not second-order moral propositions like P15. If he wants to extend this identification of moral facts and properties to the latter, he is obviously in trouble, because P15 makes no reference to moral properties per se, but only to a *non*-moral property, viz., truth, *about* a class of first-order moral facts. Leiter's view cannot stand, then, as a general account moral facts and moral properties. Moreover, given his equating of moral facts with moral properties, one wants to know how he would talk about moral properties in the context of moral falsehoods, that is, in the context of *non*-facts? For certainly such forms of discourse are perfectly proper.

But the primary reason that it is a confusion to run moral facts and moral properties together is because moral facts are what they are owing to the *relationship* that obtains between moral properties and the entity or entities to which these proprieties are purported to apply. That is to say, the relationship between moral properties and the entities of which they are predicated determines what the moral facts are. This, I should emphasize, extends to facts and properties in general: facts are what they are because of the relationship of properties to that of which they are predicated. [40] Thus, sticking with first-order moral facts, what makes a moral fact a *fact* as opposed to a falsehood (a *non*-fact), is that the moral property(s) $F_m$ predicated of whatever $X$ is at issue *actually applies* to $X$. Conflating moral facts with moral properties, as does Leiter, obscures this relationship.

Let's look still more closely at moral facts and moral properties: In chapter 2, §2.4 and 2.5, I argued that facts are states of affairs that obtain. Thus, a proposition such as 'There is snow on the summit of Mont Blanc at *t*' expresses a fact if and only if the state of affairs of snow being on the summit of Mont Blanc at *t* obtains. Similarly, a moral proposition such as,

P1: Chattel slavery, such as was practiced in the southern states of the United States prior to the American Civil War, is morally wrong,

expresses a fact if and only if the moral state of affairs of chattel slavery's being wrong obtains. Analyzed in terms of our discussion of properties in this chapter, this means that the facticity of P1 requires that the platonic universal of moral wrongness be instantiated when an instance of chattel slavery—in this case, an *event*-entity—is realized or occurs. [41] Thus, the instantiation of a moral property, owing to that occurrence of instantiation, is what determines whether a moral state of affairs obtains. If the moral property is not instanced, then no moral state of affairs (of the kind in question) obtains.

We have here, then, the fundamentals of our "deep understanding" (§3.1) of what it is to be a first-order moral truth: the instantiation of moral properties is the *determinant* of moral truth and falsehood. *Moral properties are at the bottom of it all.*

This analysis, abstract though it is, accords well with the perspective of our ordinary, tutored moral thinking. To illustrate, go back to our example in the previous section of Smith's wrongful burning of Jones's house. We see that what makes it a fact that is a morally wrongful burning is the instantiation of the moral property of moral wrongfulness. And this instantiation is what makes it a moral state of affairs of wrongfulness *that obtains*. We therefore think that Smith bears some sort of censure: she has performed a wrongful act. If she did not burn down Jones's house—if, say, she only *considered* burning it, and therefore did not by her physical actions instantiate moral wrongness—then no censorship is appropriate. Only if Smith *did* burn down Jones's house would Smith be in the wrong, that is, would have committed a wrongful act, at least as we ordinarily think of these things. [42]

This last point brings out a need to be still more precise than we have been so far about moral truth and moral facts—an issue regarding the indexicality of propositions. Our inquiry into moral properties makes this possible. Propositions often incorporate indexicals, such as the time and location of the snow on Mont Blanc. And so the question: Is it true that it is wrong for Smith to burn down Jones's house (under the conditions *c* specified), *even if Smith has not committed the act?* The answer is yes, of course, it is "true," but not strictly so. For the proposition needs to be recast and analyzed as a subjunctive conditional: *If* Smith *were* to burn down Jones's house (under conditions *c*), *then* Smith *would have* committed a moral wrong. More generally, then, a first-order moral proposition of the sort we are considering here, is true or false *only if* the relevant moral property *were to be instantiated*.[43] If, however, the moral property is *uninstantiable*, that is, cannot be instantiated in principle, then the proposition is false due to presupposition failure: its truth presupposes the fulfillment of a condition that is not, and cannot, be met.[44] This type of analysis applies mutatis mutandis to propositions other than first-order moral propositions, but I shall not follow up on this here, a general theory of indexicality being quite beyond the scope of our project.

Let's take stock of where we are: I have argued in this chapter that first-order moral properties supervene on physical properties, and are not reducible to properties of any other type. Moral properties are in this sense sui generis. Further, since the relationship of moral properties to appropriate entities determines moral facts, which in turn determine (first-order) moral truths when these facts obtain, moral facts and moral truths are also sui generis in terms of the type of facts and properties that they are. Now a primary motive for making the case that moral properties (and moral truths and moral facts) are sui generis is to preserve the conviction, to be relinquished only if absolutely necessity, that in fact we know many things *in actuality* to be morally right or morally wrong, morally permissible or morally impermissible, and so forth. This is indeed a matter which motivates this entire study: *that the basic contours of our ordinary, tutored moral thinking are correct.* And our ordinary, tutored moral thinking, as elaborated in chapters 1 and 2, is that some things really are morally wrong (bad, impermissible, atrocious)—like the Lanza murders at the Sandy Hook shooting—and some things really are morally right (good, praiseworthy, commendable)—the Emancipation Proclamation of 1863 freeing the slaves seems an excellent candidate. On the account given here, there certainly *are* moral features of such acts, policies, agents, and so forth, but further, these moral features are *real* features of those acts, polices, and agents, not constructs of any sort.

To drive home the point, let's look again at the Sandy Hook Elementary School shootings. As discussed in chapter 1, §1.1, on December 14, 2012, Adam Peter Lanza shot to death twenty-seven people, including twenty school children, all of them six or seven years of age. The world was appalled. Our ordinary thinking is that killing these teachers and elementary school children was morally wrong, indeed, that it was horrendous, a moral outrage, utterly indefensible.[45] *If we abandon this attitude toward the killings, then we have abandoned the core of our ordinary, tutored moral thinking.* But we see no set of conditions, no desideratum, which mitigates against, much less exculpates the wrongness of this act.[46] We see no credible sociocultural perspective that could conceivably legitimize it: any society that thinks this sort of thing is even remotely permissible would be regarded as totally benighted. We would scoff at anyone who suggested that the wrongness of Lanza's deed is merely perspectival—that it is merely our particular social, or class, or historical perspective at work here. We have a similar, if not more dismissive attitude toward anyone who claims that the shootings were not really wrong because nothing is really wrong (or really right). In our ordinary thinking, such people strike us insincere, as adopting a pseudo-nihilistic pose *which would evaporate were it their own child cut down by Lanza's bullet*. And we do not think that our revulsion at Lanza's murderous act is only about our emotions: we think that we are revolted by the killings *because they are revolting*—that we have real and proper cause to be revolted; that anyone who isn't affected in this way has something wrong with them. In response to Mary Midgley's question, "What do we really think?" (see chapter 1, §1.1), I answer, *this is what we really think.*

This chapter and the previous one have been aimed at providing a rigorous explication of our ordinary moral thinking about first-order moral matters. And the Lanza killings, in all its atrocity and moral clarity, serves as a paradigm case to illustrate the foundations of this thinking. We believe that it is *true* that these killings were wrong, terribly wrong. In chapter 2, §2.1 and §2.2 we developed a realist conception of truth, according to which the proposition that *p* is true *iff* if *p*, and further argued that what makes *p* true is "the way the world is." In chapter 2, §2.3, we applied this perspective to first-order moral truths—truths such as 'The Lanza killings were wrong': this proposition is true if and only if the way the world is, morally speaking, such that the Lanza killings were wrong. In §2.4 and §2.5, we further explicated our realist notion of truth by developing a theory of facts, according to which a proposition is true if and only if it expresses a fact, which we further understand to be a state of affairs that obtains. Moral facts, and therefore moral states of affairs that obtain, were argued in §2.6 to supervene on physical facts.

In this chapter we sought to provide a still deeper conceptual underpinning of our ordinary moral thinking than our initial account of truth and moral facts afforded us. In §3.2 and §3.3, a broad conception of properties was developed, wherein we adopted the view that properties are platonic universals which are instantiated, *if* they are instantiated, by particulars in the case of first-order properties, or by other properties in the case of second-order properties or relations. We went on to develop a theory of first-order moral properties, according to which they supervene on physical properties. First-order moral facts, we argued in §3.5, are determined by the relationship between the first-order moral properties and the instantiating particular (or property, in the case of second-order properties) of which the property is predicated. A moral fact, being a first order moral state of affairs that obtains, obtains when the moral property is instantiated.

This is, admittedly, pretty heavy-duty metaphysical stuff. But some pretty heavy-duty justification is needed in the face of objections, emanating from many intellectual quarters, against our ordinary moral thinking. Just insisting, "I *know* that the Lanza killings were wrong!" only takes us so far. It is an excellent starting point, to be sure; and its very salience in the way we actually conduct our lives—and I suspect *must* conduct our lives—gives it great power. But having ready to hand a developed theory to back up our ordinary thinking not only provides a bulwark against our opponents—the views of some of whom, I despair to say, serve to undermine, if not by intent, then by effect—the very foundations of our moral life. We have here sought to clarify and justify those foundations.

But even if there is moral truth to be known, *how* do we know it? This question will occupy us for the remainder of this book. It is a very hard question. But any confidence in moral truth we might have would be greatly undermined if we cannot provide good answer. Let's now have a closer look at first-order moral knowledge.

## NOTES

1. It is important to remember that "the way the world is" is not a physical concept, but a *meta*physical concept, because we want to apply this concept to non-physical matters, such as mathematics, fictive discourse, morality, and so forth—in short, to non-physical realms of discourse in which speaking of "truth" is nevertheless appropriate.

2. Perhaps this is false, strictly speaking; for perhaps the concept of "biological death" is inapplicable at the level of $COD_6$, much less $COD_n$. Perhaps the concept of "cause of death" would not extend beyond $COD_5$. Or perhaps an explanatory bridge theory would be needed to connect explanations at levels $COD_1$–$COD_5$ to levels $COD_6$ and lower, if the notion of biological death is to be retained. These are very complicated matters, which I shall not go into here.

3. Note that a false explanation—that is, an explanation containing *relevant* falsehoods—is never, or at best only dubiously, appropriate in the sense of "truth-seeking appropriateness," no matter the purposes at hand. I discuss issues of explanatory satisfactoriness in "The Pre-Theoreticality of Moral Intuitions," *Synthese*, Vol. 191 (October 2014): 3759–778.

4. I am not aiming for a high degree of precision here. The number of discrete explanatory levels, and how they are related in this and other contexts, is a subtle and disputed matter. We need not be concerned with such issues. Other purposes—for example, erecting an explanatory hierarchy relevant to the natural sciences' explanation of the functioning of higher-order organisms—would certainly require close attention to the specifics of explanatory hierarchy. On explanatory levels and morality, see Fritz J. McDonald, "A Deflationary Metaphysics of Morality," *Acta Analytica*, 25 (2010), 285–98.

5. Even if the epistemic agent is unaware of, or utterly unable to perform, this explication. We will take up this issue again in chapter 4, §4.1.

6. Of course there may be both true and false propositions about a (merely) possible world. I shall not pause over this detail

7. There are deep problems with the truth-value of subjunctive conditionals. I will have a bit more to say about this issue in §3.5 below

8. For an excellent discussion of recent literature on the nature of properties, see Alex Oliver, "The Metaphysics of Properties," *Mind*, New Series, Vol. 105, No. 417 (January 1996), 1–80.

9. See Oliver, "The Metaphysics of Properties," for very useful discussion.

10. *If*, that is, universals are regarded as mind-independent. I take this up in §3.3 below.

11. One might say that round-squareness is the conjunctive property comprised of two incompossible simple properties, roundness and squareness. I take the truth of the uninstantiability of round-squareness to be knowable a priori. Just by understanding the proposition, 'No object could be a round-square', one sees, or may see, that it is true. These matters will come up again, in more detail, in chapter 5, §5.1.

12. Quine and others who have strong nominalist leanings are loathe to quantify over properties, and therefore reject second-order predicate logic, which does. The objection is on ontological grounds. See, for example, W. V. Quine's *Philosophy of Logic* (Cambridge, MA: Harvard University Press, 1970); and "On What There Is," reprinted in *From a Logical Point of View*, 2nd edition (Cambridge, MA: Harvard University Press, 1961). More about nominalism below.

13. We dealt with some similar issues regarding realism and truth in chapter 2, §2.2.

14. Not "length" in the sense of inches, meters, or miles. Everyone agrees that these *units of measurement* are human constructs. It is the very property of length itself, no matter how measured, that is at issue here.

15. We discussed a number of features of antirealism in chapter 2, §2.1 and 2.2 above. Also see my introduction to *Realism/Antirealism and Epistemology*, ed. Christopher B. Kulp (Lanham, MD: Rowman & Littlefield, 1997), 1–13.

16. John Stuart Mill, *An Examination of Sir William Hamilton's Philosophy and of the Principal Questions Discussed in His Writings*, Vol. 1 (Boston: William V. Spencer, 1866), chapter 11. I discuss these matters in my introduction to *Realism/Antirealism and Epistemology*.

17. See, for example, William James, *Pragmatism and the Meaning of Truth* (Cambridge: Harvard University Press, 1978), 42. Also see John Dewey, "Reconstruction in Philosophy," in *John Dewey: The Middle Works, 1899–1924* (1920), 12:77–201, 156. For Dewey, what is true, what we know, and what is, is a matter of what brings satisfactory resolution to a problem situation with which we are confronted. Richard Rorty, whom some term a "neo-pragmatist," is also in this camp. See his *Philosophy and the Mirror of Nature* (Princeton: Princeton University Press, 1979). Charles S. Peirce is admittedly harder to characterize: sometimes he sounds remarkably realist in his conception of truth. See, for example, his "How to Make Our Ideas Clear," *The Collected papers of Charles Sanders Peirce*, eds. Charles Hartshorne and Paul Weiss (Cambridge, MA: Harvard University Press, 1931–1935), 5: 388–410. In fact, there seems to be a kind of antirealist continuum among the pragmatists, with Peirce occupying the more realist pole, and Rorty the more antirealist pole. But in the end, they are all antirealists. For a very worthwhile discussion of pragmatism and realism, broadly concurring with the view I have just sketched, see Sally Haslanger, *Resisting Reality: Social Construction and Social Critique* (Oxford: Oxford University Press, 2012), chapter 2: "Ontology and Social Construction."

18. D. M. Armstrong, one of the leading current theorists on the subject, has suggested these two characterizations in *Nominalism and Realism: Universals and Scientific Realism*, Vol. 1 (Cambridge: Cambridge University Press, 1978). Armstrong favors the aristotelian account. See, for example, his "Four Disputes about Properties," *Synthese* (2005): 144, 309–20.

19. Armstrong, *Nominalism and Realism: Universals and Scientific Realism*, Vol 1.

20. See Oliver, "The Metaphysics of Properties," 25, n23.

21. Ibid., 25. See pp. 25ff for detailed discussion of these and other problems for the aristotelian interpretation of universals.

22. See Oliver, "The Metaphysics of Properties," §11, for very useful discussion of all of the matters mentioned above.

23. I develop the outlines of a version of moral realism in "Moral Facts and the Centrality of Intuitions," in *The New Intuitionism*, ed. Jill Graper Hernandez (London and New York: Continuum, 2011), 48–66.

24. I discuss these matters in "Moral Facts and the Centrality of Intuitions."

25. See Oliver, "The Metaphysics of Properties," for excellent discussion of various senses in which to construe Occam's razor.

26. Oliver, "The Metaphysics of Properties," 35.

27. The thick/thin distinction originated with Gilbert Ryle, but its current popularity is largely due to Bernard Williams, *Ethics and the Limits of Philosophy* (Cambridge, MA: Harvard University Press, 1985). Perhaps such thin properties are absolutely simple—for example, as G. E. Moore thought was the case with goodness: a simple, unanalyzable non-natural property. See his *Principia Ethica* (Cambridge: Cambridge University Press, 1903), chapter 1.

28. See Aristotle, *Nicomachean Ethics*, translated by W. D. Ross. *The Basic Works of Aristotle*, ed. Richard McKeon (New York: Random House, 1941), 935–1112, Bk. II. Aristotle's general view is often known as "virtue ethics"—a conception of ethics which has seen a major resurgence of interest in the last forty years, notably at the hands of Alasdair MacIntyre. See especially his *After Virtue* (Notre Dame, IN: University of Notre Dame Press, 1981). Aristotle would decry as barbarity the kind of violent tactics employed against unarmed civilians celebrated by al-Qaeda, ISIS, and other terrorist groups.

29. Torture ≠ cruelty, although any instance of torture is also very likely to be an instance of cruelty, and explosion ≠ heat-generating event, even if an explosion is very likely to be a heat-generating event.

30. As I noted in chapter 2, §2.6, no physical world, no moral world. I have no idea what a strictly non-physical (actual) world would be, and I have no idea what status morality could possibly have in such a world.

31. A view inspired by Ludwig Wittgenstein's *Philosophical Investigations*, 3rd edition, trans. G. E. M. Anscombe (New York: Macmillan, 1958).

32. J. L. Mackie, *Inventing Right and Wrong* (Viking Press, 1977). We briefly discussed Mackie in chapter 1, §1.4.

33. Mackie, "A Refutation of Morals," *Australasian Journal of Philosophy* 24, nos. 1 and 2, (1946): 77 90. I will have much more to say about moral nihilism and J. L. Mackie in chapters 4 and 6.

34. Paul Churchland, e.g., *Scientific Realism and the Plasticity of Mind* (Cambridge: Cambridge University Press, 1979). I should note that much discussion of eliminative physicalism has occurred in the context of the philosophy of mind—Churchland is a good example of this—and "moral properties" would on this account be eliminated in favor of properties of mind, which are in turn construed as physical properties. These properties are to be given canonical expression by an ideal physics. But see John F. Post, *The Faces of Existence* (Ithaca, NY: Cornell University Press, 1986) for good reason to think that even the physicalist must endorse mathematics, and therefore mathematical properties, given the seminal role that mathematics plays in contemporary physics. Thus, even physics appears to be committed to properties not accessible to the senses.

35. The spirit of this emanates, in scientific circles, from Charles Darwin, *The Descent of Man* (London: Penguin, 2004 [1871])—in particular, the chapter titled, "On the Development of the Intellectual and Moral Faculties of Civilized Times of Man." We will discuss the biological perspective on ethics in chapter 6.

36. John Stuart Mill, *Utilitarianism* (Indianapolis, IN: Hackett Publishing Co., 1979 [1861]), 7. Here I bypass the issue here of whether Mill was an act utilitarian or a rule utilitarian. Actually, I think that he had elements of both. Of course Sidgwick too was a utilitarian. See his influential *The Methods of Ethics*, 7th ed. (New York: Dover, 1966 [1907]).

37. A more complex matter than these remarks would suggest. For how are we to interpret the ontic status of physical properties for Mill? A propos of this, see my discussion of Mill in chapter 2, §2.1.

38. In the case of second-order moral properties, the instantiation would be by another property. Properties of this sort, however, are not our concern here.

39. Brian Leiter, "Moral Facts and Best Explanations," in *Moral Knowledge*, eds. Ellen Frankel Paul, Fred D. Miller, Jr., and Jeffrey Paul (Cambridge: Cambridge University Press, 2001), 79–101, 79n1; his insertions. Leiter, in any event, thinks that it is doubtful that there is any such thing as a moral fact.

40. I am not trying to give an exhaustive analysis here of the relationship between facts and properties. A more complex analysis would be required in the case of, for example, *general* facts, that is, facts expressed by propositions of the form, 'Any $X$ is $F$' or 'All $X$s are $F$', or of *hypothetical* facts, that is, facts expressed by propositions of the form, 'If $X$ is $F$, then $Y$ is F', or *subjunctive conditional* facts, that is, facts expressed by propositions of the form 'If $X$ were to do $A$, then $X$ would be $F$'. But see below for remarks bearing on a few of these matters.

41. Alternatively put, P1 is a fact when it is such that if there is an occurrence of a *token* of the event-*type* "chattel slavery," then there is a *token* of the moral property-*type* (the platonic universal) of "moral wrongness."

42. I pass over considerations of whether Smith deserves censure for "doing something less" than the actual act in question, for example, intending to burn down Jones's house, or fantasizing about burning down Jones's house, and so forth. We do not, however, ordinarily think that people deserve censure for merely contemplating an immoral act; for among other things, this imposes a degree of moral perfection that we think unattainable. There are also issues of an excessive psychological voluntarism presupposed in making demands of this kind. Controlling thoughts that just "pop into our heads," so to speak, may be exceedingly difficult, if not impossible. (One is reminded of the Kantian dictum, "Ought implies can.") All of this, however, presents complexities too extensive to enter into here.

43. One can easily see how this analysis applies mutatis mutandis to the symmetrical temporal indexical, where time *t* is in the past, that is, where *X was* wrong.

44. It is hard to think what an uninstantiable first-order moral property might be. Perhaps the property of "absolute goodness and absolute badness"?

45. What we might have to say about the killer himself, Adam Lanza, is perhaps a different (although certainly connected) matter, depending principally on what we take to be his mental state, his degree of moral agency, at the time of the shootings. But assuming he possessed even minimal moral agency when he performed the shootings, the shootings were wrong. (We do not consider a hurricane "wrong" for killing people in its path, nor do we consider the deaths "wrong"; there is a complete lack of moral agency here. Similar things apply mutatis mutandis to a rogue dog mauling a child to death. The deaths may in both cases be deeply unfortunate, but not wrong vis-à-vis the immediate or the proximate cause of death—the hurricane or the dog.) And note that what we have to say about the moral status of the Lanza killings provides an important part of the conceptual resources necessary to assess the moral status of Lanza the moral agent.

46. At least no *plausible* mitigating or exculpating conditions. Philosophers are very good at imagining circumstances that warrant qualifying judgment. But I am sure that Mr. Lanza was not given an ultimatum by Martians poised to destroy Earth, "Choose, sir, it's the Sandy Hook children or . . ."

*Chapter Four*

# First-Order Moral Knowledge

## 4.1. EXPLICATING 'S KNOWS THAT P'

We have spent several chapters wrestling with the nature of first-order moral truth. Our realist conception of truth has led us to a realist conception of moral facts, understood as states of affairs that obtain, and on to the development of a realist interpretation of moral properties, which in turn undergirds our realist understanding of moral facts and moral truth. All of this is well and good, and worth understanding on its own merits. But now it's time to apply what we have learned to understanding moral knowledge.

Chapter 1, §1.1, looked at a strikingly awful case of multiple homicide, the Sandy Hook Elementary School shootings, to underscore the conviction that our ordinary tutored moral thinking is correct: some acts are wrong simpliciter. We are convinced we *know* that shooting those children was wrong, and indeed, convinced that we know lots of other things to be wrong. The question now before us is, *What is it to know the truth or falsity of these things?*

In chapter 3, §3.1, we discussed various levels of explanation: some explanations are "deeper" than others. Thus, an explanation $E_2$ is deeper than another explanation $E_1$, if $E_2$ employs terms, concepts, laws, etc., which explain what is explained by $E_1$, but not conversely; and explanation $E_3$ is deeper than explanation $E_2$ if $E_3$ employs terms, concepts, laws, etc., which explain what is explained by $E_2$, but not conversely; and so on for any $E_{n+1}$ with regard to $E_n$. (Note that explanatory depth is transitive: $E_3$ is deeper than $E_1$.) What we are after here, then, is an explanation—actually, an *explication*, where we clarify the conceptual details—of what it is for $S$ to know that $p$. Our particular concern is of course to explicate what it is for $S$ to know a first-order moral proposition.

Now in providing this explication, it is important to see that in knowing that *p*, *S* herself may be quite unaware of the detailed conceptual underpinnings of this instance (or act) of knowing. A young child may know that someone is her mother, but may be able to say little if anything to defend her claim. We may even say that the dog Fido knows that Jones is its master, without being able to "defend" its belief: dogs aren't much in the business of providing an epistemic defense, adept though they may be at defending a bone.

The great pragmatist Charles Saunders Peirce drew a distinction between grades of clarity in understanding a word or concept. The first grade of clarity requires the ability to use a word. Our small child surely attains to this grade of clarity in understanding the word 'mommy' and to whom it applies: she can use it quite reliably. When she says, "That's my mommy," she's right. Fido, however, would founder here: dogs are, to put it charitably, weak language users, even though they may respond reliably to verbal commands (it is dubious, however, that they grasp the meaning of a command in terms of its semantics, as do we who speak the language). So Fido, on the Peircian scale, falls below the first grade of clarity, although I would insist that Fido still in some sense "knows" that Jones is its master. More about this latter.

Peirce's second grade of clarity requires the ability to provide a definition of a word or concept. Our young child may or may not be able to do this in the case of 'mommy'. Unless very young, however, I should think that under appropriate Socratic questioning she would be able to approach this level of understanding, if not actually attain it—to be able to say at least something that shows the ability to discriminate intellectually between being a mother and being a chair or a tree, or even an aunt, for example. Fido, of course, is long out of the game.

The third grade of clarity requires being able to provide the *pragmatic* meaning of the word or concept. As Peirce says, "If one can define all the conceivable experimental phenomena which affirmation or denial of a concept could imply, one will have a complete definition of the concept, and there is absolutely nothing more in it."[1] All of this is utterly beyond the capacities of the child, and for that matter, likely beyond the capacities of most adults in many circumstances—circumstances where we do not possess considerable expertise. But let's not be too worried that most of us do not usually understand much at this level of clarity; for it seems that Peirce is mistaken to think that the *meaning* of a term is its experiential implications. On the contrary, I would point out that although it is true that in many cases effects are rightly regarded as indicia of meaning, these effects should not themselves be identified with meaning per se. For one thing, terms or concepts referring to impossible objects—objects with which we can have no possible experience, such as a round-squares—can nevertheless be perfectly meaningful: one can formulate fully intelligible propositions that incorporate such terms, for example, 'A round-square is not a possible object', or 'A round-square is not equivalent to a spherical cube'. Another reason to doubt Peirce's view is that it interjects an excessive empiricism into our notion of meaning; for among other things, it unnecessarily complicates, if not rendering it impossible, a plausible account of the meaningfulness of mathematical and logical discourse. What experiential effects are entailed by the proposition '$(2.326 \div 6.3339) = .3672303$', yet no one doubts its meaningfulness?[2] And most importantly for us, Peirce's view does not square with the realist account of truth we developed in chapters 2 and 3, as well as the realist account of moral knowledge to be developed in this and subsequent chapters. For Peirce's view is in effect to (as William Alston would say) "epistemize" truth—to make the meaning, hence the truth conditions of a proposition, a matter of what we would agree upon, or what is useful for us, or what optimally organizes our experience, or some such thing—all of which are fundamentally epistemological notions. But this is ruled out by our realist conception of truth, which has served as the touchstone of our discussion of moral facts and moral properties. And of course it is this account of moral metaphysics which will ground the theory of moral knowledge to follow.[3]

I will come back to the issue of epistemizing truth and meaning later in this chapter. What I want to highlight here, and the reason that I have referred to Peirce in this context, is that clearly there are levels of understanding of any term or concept. And Peirce is quite right that the ability to use a term or concept (the first grade of clarity) is certainly not as advanced a level of understanding as the ability to define the term or concept (the second grade), which is in turn not as advanced as the ability to specify the experiential effects entailed but the term or concept (the third grade). That this is true is aptly illustrated by one's level of understanding of, say, macrophysics. It is one thing to use the term 'Einsteinian General Relativity' appropriately in day-to-day discourse (granted, rather elevated day-to-day discourse), but quite another to be able to define what general relativity is, and quite another still to be able to specify the possible experiential entailments of the theory, which few but bona fide physicists with relevant specialization can do.[4]

Nevertheless, I would insist that even if one does not have an understanding of a concept at a high—or perhaps for our purposes it is better to say, a *deep*—level, *it does not mean that we do not understand it at all*. Peirce in effect underscores this, and this will have major implications for the broadly commonsensist view of moral knowledge soon to be developed. Just as the young child may understand what 'This is my mommy' means and that this person is her mother, without being able to provide any kind of satisfying definition of the term or the conditions of its proper application, so may she also know what the proposition 'Hitting your brother Tommy is wrong' means and that it is *true* that she shouldn't hit Tommy. Granted, the child is not going to know it like an educated adult knows it, but she can know its truth nevertheless. Explicating the concepts involved here, however, is a different matter entirely.

So let's step back and ask the broad epistemological question, what is it for $S$ to know that $p$?[5] Well, we are clearly dealing with a certain kind of knowledge here, *propositional knowledge*—knowledge that such and such is the case. This kind of knowledge contrasts with other forms of knowing, such as knowing *how*—knowing how to ride a bike, for example. (A child may be able to go merrily on her way on the bicycle, but be able to say precious little by way of explanation of how she is able to do it.) Perhaps knowing *that* also contrasts with knowing *when*, knowing *where*, knowing *what*, knowing *why*, etc. In many cases, however, paraphrases may be appropriate, for example,

> '$S$ knows *when x* occurred' = '$S$ knows *that x* occurred at time *t*'
> '$S$ knows *what* occurred' = '$S$ knows *that x* occurred, and *that x* had characteristics *c*'
> '$S$ knows *where x* occurred' = '$S$ knows *that x* occurred at spatial location *l*'
> '$S$ knows *why x* occurred' = '$S$ knows *that x* occurred due to causal factors *y* and *z*'

Whether such paraphrases can be carried out in all cases is another matter: perhaps not, but I will not pause to consider the matter further. It seems clear that in many cases such paraphrases work.

But in other kinds of cases, such paraphrase clearly will not work. Knowing *how* (in the sense discussed above) is one example; another is *objectual knowledge*, that is, knowledge *of* an object which does not rise to the level of conceptual sophistication requisite to formulate a proposition. For example, one may have knowledge of an object to one's left, but not know anything in propositional terms about that object—what it is, its composition, its proportions, etc. Even under appropriate Socratic questioning, one may be unable to render a description of it.[6]

But we need not be too concerned about such reducibility matters, because much of what is standardly taken to be "moral knowledge" is clearly *knowledge that*. And further, as just illustrated, much discourse that is not cast in the "that $p$" idiom may be paraphrased as such. Recognizing, then, that although some first-order moral discourse may be resistant to the analysis to follow, we may nevertheless rest assured that a great deal of what we are after is captured in our net.

Given what has been said in chapters 2 and 3, we largely have ready to hand what is needed for an explication of '$S$ knows that $p$'. Let's begin by acknowledging the prima facie plausibility of the oft-cited necessary conditions of propositional knowledge. On this analysis, $S$ knows that $p$ only if:

(i) $S$ believes that $p$.

(ii) $p$ is true

(iii) $S$ is justified in believing that $p$.[7]

It was long thought, moreover, that conditions (i)–(iii) were not only neces-sary, but jointly sufficient for $S$ to know that $p$. But as is well-known to contemporary epistemologists, this is highly doubtful. A huge debate was ignited by the publication in 1963 of Edmund Gettier's paper, "Is Justified True Belief Knowledge?"[8] which argued that, even granting the necessity of conditions (i)–(iii), they are in fact not jointly sufficient. That is to say, even if $S$ satisfies all of (i)–(iii), it does not follow that $S$ knows that $p$. A famous example given by Roderick Chisholm,[9] which I paraphrase loosely here, well illustrates the point (and is more accessible, I think, than the two examples Gettier provided). Consider: $S$ is looking out over an undulating field and sees what he takes to be a sheep. The viewing conditions are good, as is $S$'s eyesight, and the object is within relatively easy viewing distance. On the basis of this observation, $S$ formulates the following proposition: 'There is a sheep in the field'. Now suppose, however, that what $S$ was looking at was not a sheep but in fact a life-size photograph of a sheep, pasted onto a cardboard cutout that had been propped up in the field by some trickster. And suppose further that just over the rise behind the sheep photograph, but out of $S$'s sight, is a real honest-to-goodness sheep. In this case, $S$ *believes* that there is a sheep in the field, and it is *true* that there is a sheep in the field. Moreover, $S$ as we normally understand these things, $S$ is *justified in believ-ing* that there is a sheep in the field, given that the evidence at $S$'s disposal good viewing conditions, good eyesight at reasonable distance—is actually quite strong: the kind of evidence we regularly appeal to while engaging in hazardous—indeed, potentially lethal—activities such as driving a car.[10] $S$ has therefore satisfied the three criteria of knowledge specified. Virtually everyone agrees, however, that $S$ nevertheless does not *know* that there is a sheep in the field.

Herculean efforts have followed to address the problem, which have often included specifying a fourth condition in addition to the original three, which will serve to rule out cases like the "sheep in the field" case—usually a condition to the effect that there cannot be relevant falsehood in $S$'s evidence base.[11] Whether philosophers have been successful in ruling out all such "Gettier cases" is disputed, but I believe it is plausible to hold that in large measure they have. Be that as it may, the analysis of knowledge is a rather specialized matter, the details of which we can in good conscience leave aside. Suffice it to say that, for our purposes, we can take an explication of '$S$ knows that $p$' to require that propositional knowledge demands satisfaction of the three conditions stated above, plus a fourth condition which rules out Gettier cases: $S$'s evidence must be free of relevant falsehood (as, for exam-ple, the sheep in the field case is not).

There are many other issues connected with the analysis of knowledge with which we must avoid getting bogged down. For example, one of the conditions of propositional knowing requires that $S$ believe that $p$. Another requires that $S$ be justified in believing that $p$. But what is belief—a mental state? A capacity quite independent of any (occurrent) mental state? And what exactly is it for $S$ to be epistemically justified in believing that $p$? How strong must the justification be? Does it require that $S$ be able to produce such justification? Etc., etc., etc. These are large and important questions, but we would be ill advised to pursue them here.[12]

The issue of truth, however, which is also required for propositional knowing, *is* of particular importance to us. This is because the nature of truth is of particular importance to making a case for realism in ethics, that is, in defending our ordinary tutored moral thinking. Chapters 2 and 3 have been devoted to this effort; and we may say that our explication of '$S$ knows that $p$' will take truth to be the sort of realist conception developed there. Thus, the truth of $p$ will be understood to consist in $p$'s preserving the T-schema, which we will recall is, "the proposition 'that $p$' is true *iff p*" (chapter 2, §2.2); and if $p$ is true, then $p$ will be understood to express the way the world is (in the relevant respect). Furthermore, the truth of $p$—the way the word is, as expressed by $p$—will be understood to be determined by the obtaining of a relevant fact; thus, if $p$ is true, then $p$ expresses a fact that obtains (chapter 2, § 2.4). And what determines that something is a fact is, as was developed at length in chapter 3, a matter of the way that properties are related to the entity of which the property(s) is predicated.

Here, then, is our explication of '$S$ knows that $p$'. $S$ has propositional knowledge that $p$ is the case if and only if:

(i) $S$ believes that $p$
(ii) $p$ is true
(iii) $S$ is justified in believing that $p$
(iv) $S$'s justification for believing that $p$ does not include relevant false-
        hood

Thus, if I *know* that there is a squirrel in the tree (at time $t$), an explication of my knowing this is that (i) I believe that there is a squirrel in the tree; (ii) it really is the case—because that's the way the world is—that there is a squirrel in the tree; (iii) I am justified in believing this in (iv) a way that does not rely on relevant falsehood. This explication is extendable mutatis mutandis to knowing first-order moral truths.

Now of course none of these explicatory details need be present to mind, or even dispositionally present in the sense that they could be brought to consciousness under appropriate Socratic questioning. After all, the young child may know perfectly well that there is a squirrel in the tree, yet get nowhere in the effort to provide, or even to follow, an explication of what she knows. Nevertheless, on our view this is what is going on under the epistemological surface. But let us see what this explication yields regarding some leading alternative conceptions of morality to the conception that we have been endorsing.[13]

## 4.2. MORAL NON-COGNITIVISM

Some would object that what we said in §4.1 is wrong, in whole or in part, as it applies to first-order moral claims. Moral non-cognitivists are prominent among them, the thrust of their claim being that there is no first-order moral knowledge, at least no knowledge of the sort I claim to have when I say that I know it is true that it is morally wrong for anyone to wlak into my office and shoot me to death as I sit here writing this book. And the fundamental reason is because they do not think that the truth condition has been satisfied here for propositional knowledge. Why? *Because they believe that there is no such thing as moral truth.*[14]

But we need to be careful here, because there are different versions of moral non-cognitivism, some more extreme in their denial of moral truth than others. In the end, however, we will see that they all come to the same conclusion: they deny that our ordinary tutored moral thinking is correct.

Let's start off with a strong version of moral non-cognitivism, one already discussed briefly in chapter 1, §1.4, A. J. Ayer's classic statement of emotivism given in *Language, Truth, and Logic*.[15] Ayer was one of the leading lights of logical positivism, a radical empiricist conception of philosophy appealing to those of a strong scientific and mathematical bent, which was substantially motivated by the logical atomism of Wittgenstein's *Tractatus Logico-Philosophicus* in the late 1920s.[16] In brief, Ayer held that Hume was correct: propositions are of two types, and two types only. Propositions are either *analytic*, in which case they are true or false in virtue of the meaning of their terms, or they are *synthetic*, according to which their truth or falsity is to be ascertained through empirical—which is to say observational—test. Thus, is '3 + 3 = 6' is an analytic proposition, which is true given the meaning of '3', the meaning of '+', the meaning of '=' and of '6', and the syntactic rules employed to connect them.[17] The truth of this and similar propositions is knowable a priori. Synthetic propositions, however, are not determinable as true or false simply by virtue of the meaning of terms. Their truth or falsity is ascertained by observational verification or falsification (later, replaced with "confirmation" or "disconfirmation"). Thus, 'There is snow on the summit of Mont Blanc' is ascertained as true or false in virtue of observational evidence.

For Ayer, then, as for the other logical positivists, all propositions are of either one of these two types. Now what about locutions like

P12: It is morally good to be a stalwart defender of your young children?

Ayer asks, is it true or false in virtue of the meanings of terms? *No*. Can we ascertain its truth or falsity based on observational evidence? *No*—what possible observational evidence could tell for or against its truth? Ayer says none. Where we are left, thinks Ayer, is with the recognition that P12, and other moral locutions like it, are in fact not propositional at all. We are fooled by their grammatical form into mistaking them for propositions. They are really just *expressions of emotion*, typically with the added feature of intending to evoke similar emotions in one's listener. They do not have cognitive import.

C. L. Stevenson, another prominent emotivist, came to much the same conclusion.[18] When we disagree with one another, the disagreement may be one of belief, or it may be one of (non-cognitive) attitude. In morals, it is the latter which is especially relevant. For the meaning of moral terms such as 'good', 'right', 'just', and so forth, is most fundamentally emotive. For example, Stevenson tells us that we may understand some representative moral terms thus:

(1) "This is wrong" means *I disapprove of this; do so as well.*
(2) "He ought to do this" means *I disapprove of his leaving this undone; do so as well.*
(3) "This is good" means *I approve of this; do so as well.*[19]

When we disagree over a moral issue, we may disagree over what the *non-moral* facts of the case may be—for example, the man was present; the man was not present; etc.—which of course is to have cognitive disagreement. But we may also have disagreement over whether the act was wrong, or just, etc., which is to have disagreement of moral attitudes—for example, I approve; you disapprove; etc.—but this disagreement is *non-cognitive* disagreement. At bottom, first-order moral locutions are about—are expressions *of*—non-cognitive attitudes.

What does this mean for our explication of '*S* knows that *p*' when, for example, '*p*' is instantiated by P12, etc.? Well, it means that our analysis is all wrong—or rather that it is inapplicable. It is inapplicable because we cannot have knowledge of P12, or of any other such locution, because there is *no moral fact or truth being asserted in the first place.* When I say that I *know* that it is morally good to be a stalwart defender of your young children, I am mistaken. For what is really going on here is that I am expressing a positive attitude about defending one's children, and trying to elicit similar sentiments among my listeners. Moral locutions like P12 are expressions of emotion, not expressions of moral fact. P12 may syntactically look like a proposition, but it isn't; it simply is not a truth bearer.

Expressivism is another important contemporary form of moral non-cognitivism, broadly similar to the emotivism in holding that first-order moral locutions fundamentally serve to express non-cognitive moral attitudes. But expressivists are also typically concerned about the semantic relation of moral locutions to psychic states. Take Allan Gibbard,[20] for example. His "norm-expressivist"[21] project seeks to construct a systematic semantics relating rationality and moral sentiments. We may, for example, feel guilt or resentment, but this is not to have reached a moral judgment per se; for we may experience such sentiments independent of judgment. Yet these sentiments exert a regulative influence on how we think we should live our lives. Are these sentiments, in any given case, defensible? Here moral judgment, and along with it rationality, enters the picture: "[t]o call something rational is to express one's acceptance of norms that permit it."[22] Gibbard goes on to work out a detailed analysis of how such moral discourse links up with the acceptance of norms which license acceptable use of moral terms. What is primary in moral discourse, however, is the expression of moral sentiments, *not* assertions of moral facts.

Prescriptivism is yet another influential version of moral non-cognitivism. At the hands of its most notable proponent, R. M. Hare,[23] first-order moral locutions are fundamentally imperatives—"Do *A*"; "Refrain from *B*"—but imperatives of a rather special sort, in that their prescriptivity enjoins universality: the imperative applies to all of those who are relevantly situated (hence Hare's "universal prescriptivism": there is an oft-noted Kantian element in Hare's form of prescriptivism[24]). But the prescriptive force of such locutions is not itself cognitive—not amenable to being classified as true or false. That is to say, first-order moral discourse is not in any primary sense moral fact-stating discourse.

There are other versions of moral non-cognitivism, some of which attempt to retain some features of a cognitivist ethics. In fact, in some cases it becomes difficult to classify them as cognitivist or non-cognitivist.[25] But in terms of bona fide non-cognitivisms, we have seen enough. A fundamental implication of all these theories is that the explication of '*S* knows that *p*', where '*p*' is replaced by some form of locution putatively predicating a first-order moral property of some particular entity—for example, a morally impermissible act, a morally wrong policy, a morally praiseworthy sentiment—is either that (i) our explication of '*S* knows that p' is inapplicable, because such locutions are not propositional, hence neither true nor false, and therefore incapable of being the object of propositional knowledge, as in the case of Ayer's view; or (ii) that *S* does not know anything specifically "moral," in a primary sense of the term. We may certainly know *non*-moral facts about the situation—we may know facts about human psychology, or facts about one's own attitudes and what one seeks to express—but one does *not* know that it is right (wrong, permissible, praiseworthy, etc.) to *x*, where '*x*' is filled in by any of the range of candidates typically thought appropriate for moral appraisal. Clearly, however, this is not how our ordinary, tutored moral thinking sees it.

Let's now have a look at views that are at least cognitivist—that is, views which hold that first-order moral locutions are cognitively meaningful, have truth values—but nevertheless hold that the analysis of '*S* knows that *p*' offered in §4.1 above is mistaken.

## 4.3. MORAL RELATIVISM

There is a variety of moral relativisms, construed as theories about the nature or status of morality, far too many to discuss here. I will look at several representative versions, all of which share commitment to what I will call the Relativist Evaluation Scheme (RES):[26]

> RES: *x* (act, policy, judgment, etc.) is morally *y* (right, wrong, permissible, etc.) relative to *z*.

Different forms of relativism are of course going to call for different instantiations of '*z*', the "relativiser": that's what makes them different forms of relativism. And all of them will of course differ in details regarding how to explicate '*S* knows that *p*' in moral contexts. We will see, however, that all of them are fundamentally at odds with the explication of '*S* knows that *p*' offered in §4.1 above.

Let's begin, then, with what is probably the best known version of moral relativism—doubtless the best known outside of philosophical circles—viz., *sociocultural moral relativism*, which we have already discussed briefly in chapter 1, §1.4, and chapter 3, §3.4.[27] The fundamental feature of this version of relativism is that societies or cultures create morality. The roots of this conception of morality are ancient, going back at least to the Greeks, and the general position has been elaborated by sundry thinkers over the age ages.[28] I will not pause to trace out its various iterations; I shall concentrate on its basic thrust, which is that moral values are sociocultural *constructs*. In a word, moral values are the creations of society. *How* they are created is not our concern here: historians and social scientists—sociologists, psychologists, anthropologists, economists, etc.—are largely responsible for providing that account, in general and in detail. Natural scientists, too—biologists, for example, and sociobiologists in particular (who straddle the natural/social scientific divide)—may have a lot to tell us. However, *what* these values are—not so much in terms of their evaluative content, but in terms of their ontic status—is the job of the philosopher to ascertain; and many philosophers have taken these values to be an expression of prevailing *moral beliefs*. That is to say, on this version of relativism, moral values are constituted by the moral beliefs of a society or culture. Therefore, this type of relativist would fill out the Relativist Evaluation Scheme thus:

RES$_{sc}$: $x$ (act, policy, judgment, etc.) is morally $y$ (right, wrong, permissible, etc.) relative to *prevailing societal-cultural moral beliefs*;

and in order to get the particularity of what those values are regarding a specific society or culture, one would have to go on to specify what those beliefs are.

The important thing to notice here is that moral values are identified with beliefs, that is, moral value is *constituted* by sociocultural moral belief. Thus, where there is no sociocultural belief $v$, there is no moral value $v$. And so, for example, the moral wrongness of, say, slavery is constituted by the prevailing moral belief of a society/culture that slavery is wrong. If the society or culture believes slavery is wrong, then slavery is wrong; if not, not. Note, too, that on this view, all moral value is fundamentally "local," so to speak— local in the sense that society $A$ determines society $A$'s morality, and *only* society $A$'s morality. Society $A$ does not determine society $B$'s moral values: $B$ does that.[29]

How, then, to explicate '$S$ knows that $p$' from the point of view of sociocultural moral relativism? Basically thus: if $S$ knows that $p$, then $S$ knows the proposition that $p$, which expresses a belief—a first-order *moral* belief— which prevails in the society or culture in question. In other words, what is known is a (set of) sociocultural belief(s).

Another version of relativism, thankfully little held and perhaps not often recognized as such, is *moral subjectivism*. If the sociocultural relativist thinks that moral truth and falsity is a function of the moral beliefs endorsed by a society or culture, the subjectivist goes one better by reducing moral truth and falsity to *the beliefs of the individual*. Thus, '$x$ is morally right (wrong, permissible, condemnable, etc.)' is to be understood as saying that some specific individual $S$ *believes* that $x$ is right (wrong, etc.). If I believe that slavery is right, then it's right—*for me*; if you believe that slavery is wrong, then it's wrong—*for you*. Thus, the moral subjectivist would fill out the RES thus:

RES$_{subj}$: $x$ (act, policy, judgment, etc.) is morally $y$ (right, wrong, permissible, etc.) relative to individual $S$'s *belief(s)*.

Note that on this view moral error is not possible; for morality is created by fiat. There is in fact no objectivity to morality: each of us creates morality for himself, and we are therefore each of us sovereigns over our own moral domain. (This makes morality look rather like mere taste. Is chrome yellow a pleasing color? Yes, if it is pleasing to you, no if it doesn't. And that is the end of it: *de gustibus non est disputandum*.) And so an act, policy, judgment, etc., *x*, is morally right, wrong, permissible, etc., if and only if *S believes* that *x* is morally right, wrong, permissible, etc. We might put this alternatively by saying that '*x* is morally wrong' *means* that *S believes* that *x* is wrong (and likewise the same for any moral predicate).

The fundamental similarity between radical moral subjectivism and sociocultural moral relativism is striking. For both, *first-order moral truth and falsehood is a matter of belief*—individual in the former case, collective in the latter. Both of these views, then, epistemize truth, in stark contrast to the realist conception of truth developed and defended in chapters 2 and 3, and which functioned as part of the explication of '*S* knows that *p*' in §4.1 above. For on our realist view, what makes *p* true, in moral contexts as in others, is the way the world is *independent of belief*. Someone's, *anyone's* believing that *p* has nothing whatever to do with *p* being true; *p*'s truth (or falsity) is "alethically independent" of *S*'s belief. Truth is one thing, belief is another. Moral truth is a matter of what the moral facts are; and of course it is theoretically possible, however unlikely, that everyone could believe that *p* even though *p* is false[30]—a possibility directly precluded in the case of radical moral subjectivism. For if *S* believes that *p*, then ipso facto *p* is true. The same applies mutatis mutandis to sociocultural moral relativism.

Notice that in addition to interpreting moral truth differently from realism, radical moral subjectivism implicitly rejects the constraint on *epistemic justification* emphasized in §4.1. There we pointed out that, according to the standard analysis of propositional knowledge which we accepted, it is possible for *S* to be justified in believing that *p* even though *p* is false. Not so for moral subjectivism. *S*'s belief in *p logically guarantees* moral proposition *p*'s truth, so *S* cannot believe that *p* without *p*'s being true. In other words, *S*'s believing that *p makes it the case* that *p*, from which it follows that *S* cannot believe a false moral proposition, and that therefore *S* cannot but be "justified" in believing any such proposition he believes. Alternatively put, for *S* to believe that *p* is for *S* to be justified in believing that *p*. This, however, is clearly to collapse what seems to us the exceedingly important distinction between truth and justification—a distinction central to our ordinary, tutored moral thinking. Most of us are convinced that *S* would be wrong simpliciter to believe that the Nazi's should have attempted to eradicate the Jews. But radical moral subjectivists cannot endorse this: if *S* believes that anti-Semitic genocide is morally right, then it is—for *S*. If *R* believes otherwise, then it is true—for *R*. Moral truth is determined by the believer. Note, too, that this collapses the conceptual distinction between finite and infinite beings, that is, between the omniscient and the non-omniscient. For every radical moral subjectivist is a god relative to his own moral sphere, rather like each of us is a god (of sorts) vis-à-vis our own gustatory tastes.

Notice also that sociocultural moral relativism, which is far more frequently endorsed than radical moral subjectivism, is at base in the same boat, the only difference being that, unlike moral subjectivism, this sort of relativism deals with a *collectivity* of moral beliefs: it is the preponderance of a society's moral beliefs that counts, not individual belief. But of course the collectivity analyzes into the sums of individuals; and just as radical moral subjectivism collapses justification and truth, so, too, does sociocultural moral relativism. If a society or culture *believes* that something is morally right or wrong, permissible or impermissible, then ipso facto it *is* morally right, wrong, or what have you.[31] And this is because, at base, moral truth and falsity is epistemized—a matter of belief, an epistemic concept. Also note that regarding the conceptual distinction between finite and infinite judges of moral truth, as with radical moral subjectivism, so, too, with sociocultural moral relativism: society/culture can't be wrong, morally speaking; it enjoys a godlike sovereignty over its own realm.[32] Assuming that a society genuinely believes that, say, slavery or systematic rape for political purposes (e.g., ISIS) is morally permissible, then it is. All of this of course deviates wildly from our ordinary moral thinking, as countless social reformers would insist.

We see, then, both sociocultural moral relativism and radical moral subjectivism conform at least superficially to the standard analysis of '*S* knows that *p*', viz.

(i) *S* believes that *p*
(ii) *p* is true
(iii) *S* is justified in believing that *p*
(iv) *S*'s justification for believing that *p* does not include relevant falsehood (i.e., our Gettier-blocking condition)

But the conformity is only superficial, because conditions (i) and (ii) collapse. For according to moral subjectivism, if *S* believes that *p*, then *necessarily p* is true. It also seems that condition (iii) would at best be otiose; for any lack of justification would have to issue from some other source than moral mis-valuation, given that *S* is himself the author of any such valuation. Sociocultural moral relativism is similarly situated. For if *S*, as a member of society *X*, believes that *p*, and if *p* is endorsed by (believed by the members of) *X*, then *S*'s moral belief that *p* is true. Put otherwise, as a member of the relevant valuation-determining set of believers, *S*'s belief that *p* makes *p* true.[33] Note that both of these forms of relativism contrast with moral noncognitivism, for both relativisms are cognitivist. They therefore entail that first-order moral locutions such as

> P7: It is morally wrong for anyone to walk into my office and (intentionally) shoot me to death as I sit here writing this book,

are genuinely, that is, in a primary sense, propositional. However, unlike the standard analysis of knowledge, which supposes that $S$ can be justified in believing that $p$ even if $p$ is false, these moral relativisms, both in their own way, deny this possibility. [34]

There are of course many other formulations of moral relativism. Take Gilbert Harman's influential version: [35] he, too, holds that there is no privileged set of moral norms which are "true" in an absolute, objective, non-relative sense of the term. Of course some acts, etc., are right and others wrong, some permissible and others impermissible, etc., but these terms apply properly only in the context of agreement between parties. Harman says of his "implicit agreement theory":

> My thesis is that morality arises when a group of people reach an implicit agreement or come to a tacit understanding about their relations with one another. . . . [M]oral judgments . . . make sense only in relation to and in reference to one or another agreement or understanding. [36]

And he further tells us:

> My moral relativism is a soberly logical thesis—a thesis about logical form, if you like. Just as the judgment that something is large makes sense only in relation to one or another comparison class, so to, I will argue, the judgment that it is wrong of someone to do something makes sense only in relation to an agreement or understanding. [37]

The details of Harman's theory need not concern us: for our purposes we have seen enough. Harman relativises moral predication, in principal and in specific cases, to agreement between agents. We may cast the thrust of his relativistic "implicit agreement theory" thus:

> RES$_{iat.}$: $x$ (act, policy, judgment, etc.) is morally $y$ (right, wrong, permissible, etc.) relative to a (set of) implicit agreement(s) between $S$ and $R$ (or some larger group of moral agents).

And so for Harman, the explication of '$S$ knows that $p$', where $p$ is a (Class A) first-order moral proposition predicating moral rightness or impermissibility inter alia of some act, etc., appears to be along the lines that $S$ has justified, true belief that the act is acceptable or not acceptable, in the particular respects connoted by the terms 'right' or 'impermissible' as *implicitly understood and accepted by the relevant parties in the case at issue.*

One more form of relativism, broad in scope and although applicable to the moral sphere, infrequently referred to directly as such, is what I will call "conceptual moral relativism." On this version of relativism, RES is filled out thus:

RES$_c$: $x$ (act, policy, judgment, etc.) is morally $y$ (right, wrong, permissible, etc.) relative to the set of moral concepts $\{c\}$.

So, act $x$ is wrong (right, etc.) if and only if sanctioned (positively or negatively) as such by the relevant concepts. For $S$ to know that $p$, then, is for $S$ to know that what is expressed by $p$ is sanctioned by these concepts. This of course allows, from the perspective of our ordinary moral thinking—that is, from a moral realist perspective—that what is sanctioned by the operative set of concepts is actually quite mistaken, because there is relevant error in the sanctioning concepts.[38]

So there is quite a variety of moral relativisms, a few representative examples of which have been canvassed here. They all explicate '$S$ knows that $p$', where $p$ is a moral proposition, more or less differently than does the moral realist, in some cases very differently indeed. Enough has been said to indicate that both the realist and the relativist cannot be correct. We will consider their respective degrees of defensibility later. We now need to consider a rather different perspective.

## 4.4. PRAGMATISM

Since the beginning of the twentieth century, American pragmatism has had a substantial influence on Anglo-American philosophy, especially, and not surprisingly, in the United States. While generally credited as having been founded by Charles Sanders Peirce, perhaps America's most original philosophical thinker, the beginning of the movement was largely driven by Peirce's friend, the highly respected Harvard psychologist and philosopher, William James. John Dewy, writing at roughly the same time, was also one of pragmatism's major developers, as was Clarence Irving Lewis during mid-century. There are significant pragmatist influences in the work of such leading contemporary philosophers as Willard Quine, Donald Davidson, and Hilary Putnam; and the late Richard Rorty has developed—notoriously, in many people's estimation, insightfully in other's—a "neo-pragmatist" (Rorty disliked the term) conception of philosophy which argues, in effect, that philosophers have very little proper role to serve.[39] Pragmatism's influence is largely centered on epistemology and metaphysics, notably less so in ethics. Nevertheless, given that this chapter is fundamentally a chapter on epistemology, albeit aimed at epistemic issues as they bear on morality, it is worth having a brief look at how pragmatism would view our question of how to explicate '$S$ knows that $p$' in first-order moral contexts.

The first thing we need to be clear on is that pragmatism comes in many forms—from Peirce's near-realism about truth, to Rorty's rejection of everything realist; from Dewey's celebration of contemporary science, to Rorty's view that science is at bottom, just another way we speak about human experience, as is literature, and not to be privileged in our quest for knowledge; from Lewis's insistence that some propositions are analytically true, [40] to Quine's famous rejection of the analytic/synthetic distinction. [41] I won't take time here to separate out the various pragmatist perspectives, which contrast widely in detail on exactly how we are to understand human knowledge. Rather, I shall speak in general terms. The nub of pragmatism is well-captured by Peirce's notion that pragmatism is most fundamentally to be understood as a theory of meaning, according to which, in Peirce's formulation of the "pragmatic maxim," "To ascertain the meaning of an intellectual conception one should consider what practical consequences might result from the truth of this conception—and the sum of these consequences constitute the entire meaning of the conception." [42] The meaning, then, of concepts and terms—of "intellectual conception[s]"—is to be cashed out epistemically, that is to say, in terms of what the actual and possible consequences are for human inquiry given application of those conceptions. In brief, and roughly put, the meaning of $X$ = the consequences of employing $X$. What does the concept of 'length' or 'mass' or 'rainbow' mean? The answer is, the set of discernible consequences that accrue for an indefinitely large number of inquirers, over an indefinitely long period of time, through the employment of these conceptions. Meaning is therefore fundamentally epistemic: it is tied to actual and possible consequences, and therefore to the interpretations supplied by actual and possible inquirers.

Like meaning, truth, too, is ultimately epistemological for the pragmatist, as we saw in chapter 2, §2.2—James holding that '$p$ is true' means "believing that $p$ is good . . . and good for definite assignable reasons" [43]; Pierce that '$p$ is true' means "that $p$ is fated to be agreed upon by all who investigate $p$" [44]; and Dewey that '$p$ is true' means that which successfully resolves a problem situation. [45] These and other pragmatist conceptions of truth fundamentally regard '$p$ is true' as *meaning* that $p$ is knowable, or epistemically defensible, or warranted, or justifiable, or some such thing as this. Epistemological conceptions of truth all. [46]

What we have with pragmatism, then, is an analysis of '$S$ knows that $p$' which, although complying broadly with the standard analysis of propositional knowledge, tends to collapse condition (ii), the truth condition, with condition (iii), the justification condition. Unlike the standard analysis, pragmatism appears to preclude the possibility that one can be fully justified—however the concept of "full epistemic justification" is to be developed in detail—in believing a falsehood; for to be fully justified in believing that $p$ entails $p$'s truth. Truth is to be understood in epistemic terms.

So where does all of this leave us regarding the explication of '$S$ knows that $p$' regarding first-order morality? Well, pragmatism is clearly cognitivist: first-order moral locutions have cognitive import in a primary sense, unlike non-cognitivist (emotivist and expressivist, for example) conceptions of such discourse. But in the end, pragmatism is yet another form of anti-realism; in fact, it appears to be, at bottom, another form of relativism in ethics. This is because, *pace* what Peirce at times seems to imply, pragmatism is committed to truth being relative to inquiry: what successfully completes inquiry *is true*. Indeed, Rorty has gone so far as to say that truth is what your contemporaries let you get away with,[47] an exceedingly weak notion of truth indeed. But all of this means that truth is relative to human judgment. This is not the banal observation that what we *believe* to be true is a matter of human judgment. Of course "what we believe to be true" is a matter of human judgment—at least "judgment" in the sense of what we take to be the case. How could it be otherwise? It is, rather, the far more controversial view that what *is* true just *is* a matter of human judgment, conditioned, of course, by human purposes. And so for pragmatism, the "relativiser" is human inquiry—or judgment, or human purposes, or whatever it is of this ilk that one's preferred version endorses. So with pragmatism, RES gets filled in along the following lines:

> RES$_p$: $x$ (act, policy, judgment, etc.) is morally $y$ (right, wrong, permissible, etc.) relative to the results of inquiry $i$.

That is, it is *true* that we should/should not perform act $x$ as determined by inquiry $i$: the results of inquiry *determines* moral (and other) truth.

I should note that rarely if ever does pragmatism lapse into a thoroughly implausible radical moral subjectivism. All of the great pragmatists have had far too much respect for the efficacy of collective human inquiry, and far too much respect for the efficacy of science in particular, to allow this to happen.[48] Nevertheless, on the view endorsed here, pragmatism is antirealist and relativist: there is no gap between truth and inquiry, as there is for realism. And like other forms of antirealism,[49] it is ultimately at odds with our ordinary, tutored moral thinking. 'It is true that slavery is morally wrong' means, for the pragmatist, something along the lines, as cast in Jamesian terms, of "It is better for us to believe, in light of our ends and purposes, that we should not endorse slavery"; or cast in more Peircian terms, something like, "The opinion fated to be believed by inquirers in the indefinitely long run is that we should not endorse slavery." I suggest that according to our ordinary moral thinking, however, it means something more along the lines that slavery is wrong, period, independent of our ends or purposes, which may themselves be morally bankrupt, and independent of whatever the opinions of inquirers in fact are, no matter how long investigated and by whom. Assuming finite intellects, inquirers could after all always be wrong.

Now to look at a view certainly more radically at odds with our normal moral thinking than pragmatism—second in its radicalness, perhaps, only to moral non-cognitivism.

## 4.5. MORAL NIHILISM

We have already briefly discussed moral nihilism in chapter 3, §3.4. It was pointed out there that moral nihilists hold that there are no first-order moral properties, hence no first-order moral truth. There are of course different versions of moral nihilism: we have already looked at an important contemporary version, J. L. Mackie's "error theory," in both chapter 1, §1.4 and chapter 3, §3.4, and it will be convenient to again take Mackie as an exemplar. How, then, would Mackie explicate '*S* knows that *p*', where '*p*' represents a first-order moral proposition?[50]

We first need to recall that Mackie agrees that first-order moral discourse is cognitively meaningful; so Mackie is no moral non-cognitivist. He is therefore at least in a position to embrace the standard analysis of propositional knowledge. Where he would balk regarding moral knowledge, however, is on the possibility of fulfilling the truth condition; for he thinks that first-order moral propositions such as the following are false:[51]

> P1: Chattel slavery, such as was practiced in the southern states of the United States prior to the American Civil War, is morally wrong.
> P7: It is morally wrong for anyone to walk into my office and (intentionally) shoot me to death as I sit here writing this book.

It likewise means that

> P8: It is always morally permissible for adults to have coercive sexual intercourse with young children,

is false (let that really sink in[52]), but by the same token it means that

> Not-P8: It is *false* that it is always morally permissible for adults to have coercive sexual intercourse with young children,

is false as well. And the reason he thinks propositions like this are false is because he thinks there are no first-order moral properties. Were there such properties, says he, they would be metaphysically "queer": unlike other types of properties—physical properties, for example—there just isn't any empirical evidence for them, and it is hard to imagine what kind of evidence *could* be adduced in support of them. We therefore have no reason to believe that there is any such category of properties. We might best put the issue by saying that such discourse suffers from systematic presupposition failure. All propositions like P1, P7, and P8 are false.[53] But if *p* is false, then we can't know that *p*.

To be clear, the moral nihilist is not necessarily saying that the standard analysis of propositional knowledge is wrong where propositional knowledge is possible. In fact, qua moral nihilist, one need have no commitment one way or the other regarding the adequacy of the standard analysis tout court. The standard analysis may apply in domains of human intellection other than morality, or then again it may not; that is a separate issue. Indeed, the moral nihilist may be agnostic on whether an analysis of knowledge in any domain is possible; for she may be among those who doubt that an analysis of knowledge, at least in terms of necessary and jointly sufficient conditions, can in principle be provided.

In any event, the explication of '*S* knows that *p*' in the context of first-order morality is, for Mackie, that there is no such knowledge—that *S* cannot know that *p*. And similarly for other moral nihilists. Nietzsche, for example: "*My chief proposition: there are no moral phenomena, there is only a moral interpretation of these phenomena. This interpretation itself is of extra-moral origin.*"[54] Indeed, Nietzsche tells us that the Greek sophists were right: "a 'morality-in-itself', a 'good-in-itself' do not exist . . . it is a swindle to talk of 'truth' in this field."[55] So for Nietzsche, clearly there cannot be any first-order moral knowledge of the type we have been discussing.

Now of course one doesn't have to be a nihilist to argue that skepticism is correct in the context of morality, or for that matter in the context of any or all domains of human belief on the grounds that, say, the standard analysis' justification condition cannot be fulfilled—because *S* cannot in principle obtain the degree of evidence requisite to genuinely *know* that *p*, even though *p* is true. Or perhaps there is something structurally unsound about any form of epistemic justification (there is no viable solution to the epistemic regress problem, for example[56]). But this is a different matter than what applies to moral nihilism per se. For the moral nihilist is saying that there are not any (objective) moral values; he is not saying that we cannot know moral values *if there were any*.

Need I say that this is not how we ordinarily think of such things? We typically think that, say, it is true that theft is prima facie wrong, or (however unlikely) that it is true that it is prima facie right. We typically do not think that it is false that theft is prima facie wrong, and also false that it is prima facie right. Our normal thinking is that the Law of Excluded Middle applies to such propositions: either the proposition or its negation must be true. Not for the moral nihilist, however.

## 4.6. MORAL REALISM

We have certainly not covered all of the conceptions of morality that philosophers have suggested as a way to understand, or to reject, the possibility of moral knowledge. But we have seen some of the important contemporary ones. Let's now look at a view that comports quite well with or our ordinary moral thinking about moral knowledge.

In chapters 2 and 3 we spent quite a bit of effort developing a conception of truth, moral facts, and moral properties to undergird and defend the propositionality and non-relativity of first-order moral discourse. We can now bring these considerations to bear regarding the explication of '*S* knows that *p*' for the *moral realist*. We may begin by stipulating that moral realism is well positioned to accept the standard analysis of knowledge; for after all, moral realism insists that first-order moral discourse is propositional, and therefore that first-order moral knowledge must be propositional. Further, moral realism is well positioned to accept the notion that *S* could be justified in believing that *p*, even if *p* is false, as is stipulated by the standard analysis. This is because moral realism, which is of course realist with regard to truth, recognizes that there is a gap between truth and justification; that owing to what we might call the "evidence transcendence" of truth, it is always possible in principle, however unlikely in fact, that *S* could be in possession of very strong evidence in favor of *p*'s truth, and yet be incorrect. Epistemic justification is not truth guaranteeing.

So we can allow that moral realism would explicate '*S* knows that *p*' as justified, true, (moral) belief, plus the Gettier-blocking condition. Fine as far as it goes, but let's look at this a bit more closely. We have seen in chapter 2, §2.2 that for a proposition of the form 'that *p*' to be true *means* that it must fulfill the T-schema, namely "the proposition that *p* is true *iff p*." So, the proposition 'It is morally wrong to torture children to death for fun and profit' is true, if and only if it is wrong to torture children to death for fun and profit. We have also seen in §2.2 that what makes *p* true is "the way the world is" in the relevant regard: in the child torture case, it is the way the world is with regard to morality. So for *S* to know that *p*, where *p* is a first-order moral proposition, is for *S* to know the truth of a moral proposition, which is to say, to know the way the world is in the relevant moral respect. In §2.4, we have further seen that true propositions express facts, and for true first-order moral propositions to express first-order moral facts, which we understand as states of affairs that obtain. So that when *S* knows the truth of the torturing children proposition, *S* knows a moral fact that obtains regarding the moral wrongness of torturing children.

Digging still deeper in our explication of '*S* knows that *p*', we understand, in light of our discussion in chapter 3, that what makes *p* the kind of proposition it is, is the kind of properties it predicates regarding the object of which these properties are predicated. So, moral propositions predicate moral properties of some (putatively appropriate) object, for example, a person, a policy, a psychological attitude, etc. The proposition is true if the properties actually apply to this object, that is, if, say, the property of moral wrongness actually applies to the act or policy—if it really is wrong to torture children to death for fun and profit.[57] Moreover, we have seen in §3.2 and 3.3 that properties of whatever sort, including first-order moral properties, are best regarded as platonic universals; and that when true, a first-order moral proposition asserts of an appropriate object that an instantiated property applies. Thus, if $S$ knows that it is wrong to torture children to death for fun and profit, then $S$ knows that the property of moral wrongness, when instantiated, apples to an instantiated type of action (in this case, an instantiation of torturing children to death for fun and profit).

I have of course not reviewed every detail developed in chapters 2 and 3 of the analysis of moral truth, moral facts, and moral properties, but enough has been said to indicate clearly how our theory explicates '$S$ knows that $p$' in moral contexts. We would do well to take a moment to contrast our results with the competing theories.

*Moral Non-Cognitivism*: There is no first-order moral knowledge, because there is no first-order moral truth—at least not of what we have been calling Class A first-order moral locutions. Neither, however, is there first-order falsehood, so $S$ cannot know either that $p$, or that not-$p$. First-order moral locutions (of the type in question) are not propositional. So "moral knowledge," if there is any, must have to do with second-order moral matters.[58] Second-order moral locutions *are* propositional, and we may have knowledge of them—locutions such as,

P6: There are no first-order moral truths, nor are there any first-order moral falsehoods.

So even though we may disapprove of—express a strong negative emotion about—Lanza's killing those twenty children at Sandy Hook Elementary School (chapter 1, §1.1), we cannot *know* that he shouldn't have done it.

*Moral Subjectivism*:[59] First-order moral locutions are propositional, and therefore truth-bearers: they are true or they are false. What makes any such proposition true or false is the conditions of assertion. Thus, if $S$ asserts (or believes) that $p$ is true, then it is true; if $S$ asserts (or believes) that $p$ is false, then $p$ is false. $S$ creates moral truth by fiat. So we may certainly have moral knowledge, but what this comes to is knowledge of what the asserter has declared, or the asserter's intent or belief regarding the proposition. (Presumably the person making the assertion is in a position of near absolute epistemic privilege on this matter.) So if $S$ says that Lanza shouldn't have shot those children, then Lanza shouldn't have. But if $S$ says that Lanza should have shot the children, *then Lanza should have shot the children*. And of course the same applies mutatis mutandis to any other moral agent $R$.

*Moral Relativism*: The moral relativist agrees with the radical subjectivist that first-order moral locutions are propositional, hence true or false, but locates the "moral truth-maker" elsewhere than in individual belief per se.

The sociocultural relativist locates morality in sociocultural norms, which are the moral beliefs of the collectivity of believers. Harman's implicit agreement relativism locates morality in agreement and understanding between agents; and conceptual moral relativism locates it in relevant moral concepts. All of these forms of relativism can agree that there is first-order moral knowledge, but see an explication of this knowledge in terms of knowledge of collective moral belief, knowledge of agreement (implicit or otherwise) between moral agents, or knowledge of the meaning and implications of moral concepts. So moral relativists of the sort we have discussed can agree that *S* knows that the Lanza killings were morally wrong *if and only if* (i) the collective belief is that the killings were wrong, or (ii) the implicit moral agreements in play imply that the killings were wrong, or (iii) the moral concepts employed (which are themselves not necessitated) indicate, directly or through entailment, that the killings were wrong. Clearly then, if these conditions are not fulfilled with regard to the respective version of relativism, then according to that version of relativism, the killings are not wrong. And clearly, we could not have moral *knowledge* to the contrary, no matter what we may think.

*Pragmatism*: First-order moral locutions are propositional, and given that skepticism is otiose, we may know *p* to be true or to be false. Such knowledge amounts to being in possession of what is good for us to believe (James), or what successfully concludes inquiry (Dewey), or some other variation on the theme that it optimally serves our purposes to believe that *p*. So yes, we could know that Lanza shouldn't have killed those children, if believing so is best for us, *given our purposes*.

*Moral Nihilism*: First-order moral propositions are propositional, but insofar as they purport to predicate a moral property of an act, policy, agent, etc. they are all false. This is because there are no first-order moral properties. First-order moral knowledge, then, is not possible.[60] And so we cannot *know* that Lanza shouldn't have killed the children. Killing them wasn't really "morally wrong," *because nothing is morally wrong*.

*Moral Realism*: There are first-order moral truths, because there are first-order moral facts and first order moral properties. Assuming a general skepticism to be incorrect, which moral realists perhaps invariably do, *S* can know these first-order moral truths. This means that, assuming that the Lanza killings were in fact morally wrong—a view hard to imagine any moral realist denying—*we can (and do) know the killings to be to be wrong*.

Moral Realism alone captures our natural response to Mary Midgley's simple but penetrating Moorean question, which we referred to in previous chapters: What do we *really* think about morality? The other responses seem deeply problematic—just how problematic will be a preoccupation of chapter 6. Our next step, however, is to probe still more deeply into the nature of first-order moral knowledge. Is it like other forms of knowledge? Is it sui generis? These and similar questions will be the topic of our next chapter.

## NOTES

1. Charles Sanders Peirce, "What Pragmatism Is," in *The Collected Papers of Charles S. Peirce*, eds. Charles Hartshorne and Paul Weiss (Cambridge, MA: Harvard University Press, 1931–1958), 5.411–5.415; his emphasis. For discussion of the three grades of clarity, see especially "How to Make Our Ideas Clear," in *The Collected Papers of Charles S. Peirce*, eds. Charles Hartshorne and Paul Weiss (Cambridge, MA: Harvard University Press, 1931–1958) 5.388–5.410.

2. At best, any effects would be indirect and highly attenuated. For a major pragmatist's efforts, broadly in the Peircean tradition, to show the pragmatic/empirical content of logical and mathematical discourse, see John Dewey, *Logic: The Theory of Inquiry*, in John *Dewey: The Later Works, 1925–1953*, Vol. 12, 1938, ed. Kathleen E. Poulos (Carbondale and Edwardsville: Southern Illinois University Press, 1986), 3–527.

3. Actually, Peirce is the most realist-leaning regarding truth of any of the classical pragmatists. This will come up again in §4.4 below.

4. And the Peircian view seems quite correct in that many contemporary scientists and philosophers of science agree that a necessary condition for a theory to qualify as scientific is that it be empirically testable in the sense that it entails observationally confirmable or disconfirmable predictions. Karl Popper, for example, has influentially argued this (in particular, for the observational falsifiability of scientific theories) in, among other places, *The Logic of Scientific Discovery* (London: Hutchinson, 1959); and *Conjectures and Refutations: The Growth of Scientific Knowledge* (London: Routledge, 1963).

5. This is well-traveled ground, and I do not propose to say anything new at the general level. I shall, however, endeavor to do better when it comes to explicating what it is to know a first-order moral proposition.

6. For an excellent discussion of objectual knowledge and belief, see Robert Audi, *Epistemology*, 3rd edition (New York: Routledge, 2011), chapter 1. I previously remarked upon objectual knowledge in chapter 1, §1.2.

7. These criteria are widely regarded as having its roots in Plato. See his *Theaetetus*, translated by Francis McDonald Cornford. *The Collected Dialogues of Plato*, eds. Edith Hamilton and Huntington Cairns (Princeton, NJ: Princeton University Press, 1961), 845–919: 201c–210b.

8. Edmund Gettier, "Is Justified True Belief Knowledge?" *Analysis* 23 (1963), 121–23. A precursor to the point of Gettier's famous paper, however, is to be found on Bertrand Russell, *Human Knowledge: Its Scope and Limits* (London: George Allen & Unwin, 1948).

9. Roderick Chisholm, *The Theory of Knowledge*, 1st–3rd editions (Englewood Cliffs, NJ: Prentice Hall, 1966/1977/1989).

10. Thus, on this analysis, it is stipulated—surely quite plausibly—that being justified in believing that $p$ does not entail that $p$. That is to say, one can be justified in believing a false proposition: justification is not truth-guaranteeing.

11. See, for example, James Cornman, Keith Lehrer, and George Pappas, *Philosophical Problems and Arguments* (Hackett, 1992), 43–44. For a broader perspective on the enormous literature that Gettier's paper has generated, see Robert K. Shope, *The Analysis of Knowing: A Decade of Research* (Princeton, NJ: Princeton University Press, 1983).

12. Epistemic justification will, however, be a matter of importance to us in chapter 5.

13. A note about the classification of the theories discussed below: there are various ways to group them, some theories to a greater or lesser extent crossing over into territory occupied by another. The taxonomy employed here, however, is pretty standard; and it would be wide of our purposes to spend time cross-referencing them. I do not think that the classification here, although certainly not exhaustive, will engender confusion, or materially detract from the rigor of discussion.

14. At least not with regard to what we have termed Class A first-order moral propositions.

15. A. J. Ayer, *Language, Truth, and Logic* (New York: Dover, 1952).

16. Ludwig Wittgenstein, *Tractatus Logico-Philosophicus*, translated by D. F. Pears and B. F. McGuinness (London: Routledge and Kegan Paul, 1961).

17. See Ayer, *Language, Truth, and Logic*, chapter 1. Ayer's analysis of analytic propositions differs from Kant's famous analysis, the latter's being that the concept of the subject contains the concept of the predicate. We will take up these matters in more detail in chapter 5, §5.1.

18. See his *Ethics and Language* (New Haven, CT: Yale University Press, 1944).

19. Ibid., 21; his italics. Actually, Stevenson regards these "definitions" as only "working model[s]" (p. 61), more refinement being necessary (see chapter IV). These renderings, however, are adequate to our purposes.

20. Allan Gibbard, *Wise Choices, Apt Feelings* (Cambridge, MA: Harvard University Press, 1990); and *Thinking How to Live* (Cambridge, MA: Harvard University Press, 2003). I here refer to his earlier, and perhaps better known, text.

21. Gibbard, *Wise Choices, Apt Feelings*, 8.

22. Ibid., 7. He refines this statement in ch. 2 and following.

23. See R. M. Hare, *The Language of Morals* (Oxford: Oxford University Press, 1952).

24. See Ibid., 16.

25. Simon Blackburn's "quasi-realism," for example, which emphasizes certain realist aspects of first-order moral locutions, without committing fully to realism regarding moral properties. See his *Spreading the Word* (Oxford: Oxford University Press, 1984).

26. For an excellent representation of the broad array of moral relativisms, see Paul K. Moser and Thomas Carson, *Moral Relativism: A Reader* (Oxford: Oxford University Press, 2000).

27. For the purposes of this and succeeding chapters, I will use 'society' and 'culture' interchangeably. For the sociologist or anthropologist, there is doubtless an important distinction—difficult as it may be to define rigorously—between society and culture. For us, however, little turns on it.

28. Thus, we see Plato inveighing against the sophists, who took the measure of man to be man himself. See, for example, his *Theaetetus*, translated by Francis McDonald Cornford in *The Collected Dialogues of Plato*, edited by Edith Hamilton and Huntington Cairns (Princeton, NJ: Princeton University Press, 1961), 845–919.

29. At least not in the direct respect intended. Of course society *A* may influence society *B*'s values, in which case *A*'s values may become *B*'s (i.e., *A* and *B* may share the same values); or society *A* could even impose its values on society *B*. These are complexities easily handled on this account, although I will not pause to trace them out here.

30. This will be an issue of major concern to us in chapter 5.

31. There are many problems with ascertaining "what a society/culture believes." We will look at some of these in chapter 6, §6.3.

32. Many sociocultural moral relativists will object to this characterization. More about this as well in chapter 6.

33. Whether condition (iii) is otiose from the perspective of sociocultural relativism, is a more difficult question than in the case of radical moral subjectivism. For example, internal (moral) valuational inconsistencies raise questions about whether, in the face of such inconsistencies, members of a society are actually justified in holding the moral beliefs that they do. We shall look at these matters in chapter 6, §6.3.

34. Again, keep in mind that we are here providing an explication of '*S* knows that *p*': an individual, even one who explicitly subscribes to radical subjectivism or sociocultural relativism may be unaware of, or even be unable to follow, these explicatory details.

35. See his "Moral Relativism Defended," *Philosophical Review* 84 (1975): 3–22; *The Nature of Morality: An Introduction to Ethics* (Oxford: Oxford University Press, 1977); and "Moral Relativism," in *Moral Relativism and Moral Objectivity*, Gilbert Harman and Judith Jarvis Thomson (Malden, MA: Blackwell, 1996), 3–64. The brief sketch given here most closely follows the formulation in "Moral Relativism Defended."

36. Harman, "Moral Relativism Defended," 3.

37. Ibid.

38. Note that this form of relativism may relinquish its relativist status depending on how one understands the grounding and status of moral concepts. We will consider this in §4.5

39. See, for example, Richard Rorty, *Philosophy and the Mirror of Nature* (Princeton, NJ: Princeton University Press, 1979); and *Consequences of Pragmatism: Essays 1972–1980* (Minneapolis: University of Minnesota Press, 1982).

40. See C. I. Lewis, *Mind and the World Order* (New York: Charles Scribner's Sons, 1929); and *An Analysis of Knowledge and Valuation* (La Salle: Open Court, 1946).

41. See W. V. Quine, "Two Dogmas of Empiricism," in *From A Logical Point of View*, 2nd edition (Cambridge, MA: Harvard University Press, 1961), 20–46. I do not mean to categorize Quine as a pragmatist, narrowly understood. An analytic philosopher, with pragmatist leanings, seems to me a more accurate description.

42. Charles Sanders Peirce, *Collected Papers of Charles Sanders Peirce*, edited by Charles Hartshorne and Paul Weiss (1931), Vol. 5: Para. 5.9 (1905).

43. James puts it thus: the true is "the name of whatever proves itself to be good in the way of belief, and good, too, for definite assignable reasons" (James, *Pragmatism and the Meaning of Truth*, [Cambridge, MA: Harvard University Press, 1978], 42).

44. Charles S. Peirce, "How to Make Our Ideas Clear," 5, 388–410. As noted in chapter 2, §2.2, Peirce says a number of things, with dubious compatibility, about what he means by truth. Sometimes he sounds quite realist on the subject, for example, "Every man is fully satisfied that there is such a thing as truth, or he would not ask any question. *That* truth consists in a conformity to something *independent of his thinking it to be so*, or of any man's opinion on that subject" (*Collected Papers*: 5.211; author's emphasis1; and "Truth [is] overwhelmingly forced upon the mind in experience as the effect of an independent reality" (*Collected Papers*: 5.564). These and similar quotations usefully collected in Susan Haack, ed., *Pragmatism Old and New* (New York: Prometheus Books, 2006), 677.

45. See John Dewey, *Reconstruction in Philosophy*, in *John Dewey: The Middle Works, 1899–1924*, Vol. 12 (1920), 77–201; 156.

46. I discuss this issue in "Moral Facts and the Centrality of Intuitions," in *The New Intuitionism*, ed. Jill Graper Hernandez (London and New York: Continuum, 2011). 48–66.

47. Richard Rorty, *Philosophy and the Mirror of Nature* (Princeton: Princeton University Press, 1979), 176. It appears, however, that Rorty backed off of this extreme view.

48. Rorty would be an exception regarding science, if indeed he qualifies as a great pragmatist. Dewey and Peirce are indubitably great pragmatists, and are exemplars of pragmatist admiration of science. On Dewey and science, and the implications of science for traditional epistemology, see my *The End of Epistemology* (Westport, CT: Greenwood Press, 1992), chapter 2.

49. See Sally Haslanger, *Resisting Reality: Social Construction and Social Critique* (Oxford: Oxford University Press, 2012), chapter 2, "Ontology and Social Construction" for illuminating discussion of the antirealism of pragmatism.

50. Regarding the following discussion, see J. L. Mackie, *Ethics: Inventing Right and Wrong* (New York: Viking Press, 1977); also see his "A Refutation of Morals," *Australasian Journal of Philosophy* 24, nos. 1 and 2 (1946), 77–90.

51. Note how this differs from the non-cognitivist. Non-cognitivism denies that moral locutions like P7 are *either* true *or* false, because they are not propositional in a primary, that is, *moral* sense.

52. In addition, it means that, 'It is morally permissible for an adult to have coercive sexual intercourse with *your* young child', is false. That doesn't look very good, does it?

53. It would appear, however, that propositions like, 'Kant's deontological theory of ethics entails similar treatment for persons under similar conditions'—which are arguably moral propositions of the first-order—may be true. For even if the entire theory is false, the theory may nevertheless entail this consequence. It is simply a matter of whether or not a set of propositions entails another (set of) proposition(s), even if all propositions concerned are false. Although the proposition just specified is of the first-order, it is not prescriptive in the sense that P1, P7, and P8 are, and it is doubtful that it purports to assert a first-order moral fact of the

same type asserted by propositions such as 'It is morally wrong to torture children for pleasure'.

54. Friedrich Nietzsche, *The Will to Power*, edited by Walter Kaufman, translated by Walter Kaufman and R. J. Hollingdale (New York: Vintage Books, 1968), sec. 258; italics in the original.

55. Ibid., sec. 428.

56. We will explore this issue in chapter 5, §5.3.

57. What does one say about, for example, 'Two divided by three equals four is morally right (praiseworthy, contemptible, etc.)'? I am inclined to say that it is simply false. Others might argue, however, that it is neither true nor false: the proposition 'two divided by three equals four' is not an appropriate candidate for predication of moral rightness. Sorting out this issue, however, would take as far afield.

58. And perhaps, too, propositions like 'Kant's deontology entails that lying is wrong', which is arguably best classified as a first-order moral proposition. But these issues need not concern us here.

59. In §4.3 I treated radical moral subjectivism as a species of relativism. It will be convenient here to treat it separately.

60. It is rather like "unicorn knowledge": there isn't any, at least in the primary sense, because there aren't any unicorns. Yes, we can know how people talk about unicorns in literature and fantasy, just as we can know how people talk about morality in philosophy and elsewhere. But there are no unicorns to know, just as there are no "morally wrong acts" to know.

## Chapter Five

# Our Epistemic Contact
# with Moral Truth

## 5.1. ANALYTIC AND SYNTHETIC MORAL PROPOSITIONS

In chapters 2 and 3, we concentrated on understanding the nature of first-order moral discourse, with special attention to developing the foundations of a version of moral realism, which, we argued in chapters 1 and 4, best captures our ordinary conception of moral judgments. On our view, some judgments are correct, others incorrect depending on whether they embrace propositions which are true or false simpliciter, not true or false only given

> RES: $x$ (act, policy, judgment, etc.) is morally $y$ (right, wrong, permissible, etc.) relative to $z$,

as moral relativists would have it. Nor are moral judgments disguised expressions of emotion, or assertions of non-cognitive prescriptions, or anything of the like. On the contrary, on our view we know, at least sometimes, the moral facts of the matter. In some cases we are so convinced of this that we are not only prepared to argue our case, but to fight and die for our beliefs. The profundity of these convictions for moral motivation and commitment deserves to be taken very seriously—and that includes moral theoreticians. In this book we have done this, and shall continue to do so.[1]

Our moral realism, then, commits us to the thesis that first-order moral discourse is truth-bearing discourse (chapter 2); and that if $S$ *knows* that $p$, where '$p$' expresses a first-order moral proposition, then $S$ knows a first-order moral truth (chapter 4). We have also seen that if a first-order moral proposition is true, then it appropriately expresses a first-order moral fact (chapter 2), which is a matter of the proposition properly expressing the relations of the relevant moral properties asserted by that proposition (chapter 3). We now want to inquire into *how* S knows these moral truths—how we come into epistemic contact with these truths. How do we know, for example, that it is true that chattel slavery is wrong, or that it is false that sex between adults and young children is permissible? We would best begin by having another look at the nature of first-order moral propositions.

As remarked in chapter 4, §4.2, propositions have traditionally been divided into two categories: *analytic* and *synthetic*. Analytic propositions, such as 'All bachelors are unmarried males', are usually thought to be necessarily true, if true, or necessarily false, if false (e.g., 'It is not the case that all bachelors are unmarried males' is necessarily false). Now there is a variety of analyses of analytic of propositions, and we can't go into all of them here. One historically important analysis, however, is Kant's, whose view is that in analytic propositions the concept of the subject "contains" the concept of the predicate.[2] Thus, the concept of bachelorhood contains the concept of being an unmarried male. Another important (more recent) analysis is offered by logical positivists like A. J. Ayer, who understands analytic propositions to be true or false in virtue of the meaning we assign to terms, along with the operative rules of syntax.[3] So take a proposition like '2 + 2 = 4':[4] it is true by virtue of the fact that we assign a meaning to the symbol '2', a meaning to the symbol '+', to '=' and to '4', and when these terms are concatenated in a certain licensed way, they yield a true proposition (while '2 + 4 = 2' would be false, and '2 + = 42' unintelligible because syntactically ill formed). Propositions such as 'All bachelors are unmarried males' receive a similar analysis. There is nothing "necessary" in the meanings we assign to terms or to the rules we that assign for their manipulation, but once set, it *is* necessarily true that '2 + 2 = 4' and that 'All bachelors are unmarried males'.

Propositions such as 'The house is painted green' are synthetic, and are true or false not by virtue of the meaning of the constituent terms (Ayer), or by whether the concept of the subject contains the concept of the predicate (Kant), but because . . . and here things become more complicated. Realists about material objects like houses will say that the truth of the proposition depends on whether the house really is painted green, that is, depends on the way the world is. Pragmatists are going to say something along the lines[5] that the proposition's truth or falsity depends on whether it is good for us, all things considered, given our ends and purposes, to believe that the proposition is true or that it is false. Idealists will say that the proposition's truth or falsity is a matter of how we conceive of the world: for example, F. H. Bradley's view is that truth is "that which satisfies the intellect"[6] and is "an ideal expression of the Universe, at once coherent and comprehensive."[7] Other schools of thought will answer in their own way.

But we can't go into all the ways that philosophers have interpreted the truth of synthetic propositions. And for that matter, some contemporary philosophers have denied the analytic/synthetic distinction—W. V. Quine, for example, has famously argued against analyticity.[8] All of this is a complex topic, so in the interest of manageability, let's take the easy way out and simply stipulate (we are in good company) that, *pace* Quine and his admirers, the analytic/synthetic distinction holds. And let's further stipulate—something implicitly defended at length in chapters 2 and 3—that propositions are true or false by virtue of whether or not they express *the way the world is*. This is, of course, to adopt a realist interpretation of syntheticity, which is fully in line with the realist interpretation of truth upon which our study is based.

Our next question is, how do we know these two types of propositions to be true or false?[9] Here again we have two traditional answers. Analytic propositions are known a priori, independent of appeal to experience; synthetic propositions are known a posteriori, through appeal to experience. But we need to be careful: to know that an analytic proposition is true is not to know it independent of all experience whatever. For in one sense, one can only have occurrent understanding of a proposition experientially. How could I know that 'All bachelors are unmarried males' is true unless I understood the meaning of the proposition, which in turn requires an understanding of its constituent terms and how they are concatenated—that is, understanding the proposition's syntax and semantics (albeit not at a theoretical level)? But this is to engage in a mental act, which is by definition experiential in the broad sense of the term 'experiential'.[10] Moreover, it is hard to imagine what a human mind would consist in (*pace* extreme eliminative materialists like Paul Churchland) without experience,[11] or in how a human mind could attain to any (or at least very much[12]) propositional understanding except against the background of a broad range of prior experiences. The point in being able to know an analytic proposition independent of experience is that one need not appeal to any *particular evidentiary experience* in order to know it. I don't need to make any observations; I don't need to do any polling to know that 'All bachelors are unmarried males' is true. Understanding the proposition is sufficient.

On the other hand, synthetic propositions such as 'The house is painted green' have traditionally been held to be knowable only a posteriori. How am I to know that the house is painted green? I need to make an observation.

But still more care is necessary here. A proposition may be analytically true, and therefore in principle knowable a priori, even though any given individual *S* may be quite incapable of grasping its truth because the proposition is, say, beyond *S*'s power to comprehend: it may be too complex, or its constituent terms too recondite for *S* to grasp. Many mathematical propositions (assuming their analyticity[13]), or propositions in formal logic are good examples. Not all of us, after all, are a Gauss or a Gottlob Frege! Moreover, *S* may know the truth of an analytic proposition a priori, or both a priori and a

posteriori. An example of the former is where the proposition is evident to *S*,
based on his comprehension of it; an example of the latter is where *S* first
comes to know that *p* on the basis of expert testimony—Gauss himself assured *S* that *p* is true (!); a reliable text book will usually suffice—and later
comes to comprehend *p*, and therefore know *p*'s truth a priori.

What, however, about propositions such as, 'No house can be green and
blue all over'? We seem to see its truth straightaway. Is it, then, analytic? Not
on the standard Kantian analysis; for the concept of a house does not contain
the concept of the predicate "green and blue all over." It isn't analytic on
Ayer's analysis either: we can understand the proposition's constituent terms
and their syntactic relations, but are still unable to determine its truth or
falsity. So the proposition seems to be synthetic. According to the analysis of
syntheticity we have adopted, the "way the world is" is such that it is not
possible for a house—or anything else, for that matter—to be green and blue
all over. But no observation is necessary to ascertain this: its truth is self-
evident. So there appear to be synthetic propositions knowable a priori. [14]

The point of this brief excursion into the analysis of propositions is to put
us in a better position to understand first-order moral propositions and our
epistemic access to them. So our next question is, What kind of proposition
are first-order moral positions?

Well, it appears that not all first-order moral propositions are the same
type. Consider this one:

P16: Murder (of a person) is morally wrong.

Is P16 true or false? Perhaps not so easy to say as it might first appear; for on
the one hand, it seems highly dubious that an act of murder is "morally
right," but on the other, we might say that under certain conditions an act of
murder is, all things considered, the right thing to do. But I doubt that we
would have the same reaction to this proposition:

P16*: Murder is pro tanto morally wrong.

The very concept of murder seems to imply that an instance of it is at least
pro tanto morally wrong. So P16* certainly looks like an analytic first-order
moral proposition, knowable a priori. And so with propositions such as:

P17: Rape (of a person) is pro tanto morally wrong.
P18: It is pro tanto morally right to treat loved ones with kindness.

How could raping someone be other than pro tanto wrong? And doesn't
loving someone entail the pro tanto propriety of treating them kindly? The
answers seem straightforward, self-evident assuming we understand the

proposition, given our use of the constituent terms and concepts.[15] We appear to know the truth of these propositions a priori.

Now contrast this proposition:

> P19: It is morally harmful to persons to tax their earnings at a rate exceeding 65%.

I see no case in favor of this being an analytic proposition, and in fact I personally have no real idea whether it is true or false. Ascertaining its truth seems to require, among other things, ascertaining whether taxing people at more than 65 percent in fact morally harms them, which seems at least in part an empirical question. After all, it scarcely appears a conceptual truth that taxing people at any given rate constitutes a harm—at least not a harm *all things considered*. One would have to ascertain the moral effects of such taxation on people *as embedded in a particular society*, and that almost surely requires observational evidence. On this interpretation, then, this is a synthetic moral proposition knowable only a posteriori.

Many philosophers would agree, for example, utilitarians like J. S. Mill. On his view, the truth of propositions of the form '*x* is morally wrong (right)' is determined by whether the action, policy, etc. that instantiates '*x*' maximizes utility for the greatest number of people in the indefinitely long run.[16] Utility, in turn, is to be understood in terms of whether the act, etc., conduces to that which has intrinsic value. Happiness alone possesses intrinsic value, and by happiness he means pleasure and the absence of pain. Pleasure, for Mill, is a psychological state, as is pain. And psychological states are physical states—brain states, if you will. So the property of happiness is a physical property, the obtaining of which is observationally ascertained in the case of second-person attributions, or introspectively in the case of first-person psychological reports. All of this is, however, knowable only a posteriori.[17]

But what do we say about propositions like this?

> P7: It is morally wrong for anyone to walk into my office and (intentionally) shoot me to death as I sit here writing this book;

or

> P8: It is always morally permissible for adults to have coercive sexual intercourse with young children.

Like P19, they certainly don't appear to be analytic. In P7, the concept of "walking into my office and shooting me to death as I sit here writing this book" does not seem to contain the concept of the predicate "moral wrongness." Neither does its truth or falsity turn on word usage alone. Similarly with P8, an obvious universal moral generalization. Yet what experience need I appeal to, what observation need I make, in order to see that P7 is true and that P8 is false? By the same token, what kind of cogent first-order moral argument can one offer against these judgments regarding P7 and P8? The answer to both of these rhetorical questions is, *none*. On the contrary, I suggest that in broadly the same way we see that the proposition, 'No house can be green and blue all over' is true, we see that it is true that it is wrong for someone, *anyone*, to come into my office and just shoot me, and that it is false that it is morally permissible for adults to have coercive sex with children at will. To genuinely comprehend these propositions is to grasp their truth or falsity. In other words, I claim to know them a priori.

Our position, then, is this: some first-order moral propositions are analytic, others synthetic. Analytic moral propositions are knowable a priori, while some synthetic moral propositions may be knowable only a posteriori, others a priori, depending on what type of synthetic proposition they are. On the moral realist view we are developing, all three types of proposition are candidates for moral knowledge. *Yet it is important to see that synthetic propositions are fundamental.*

A pivotal reason to regard synthetic propositions as fundamental is that were all true first-order moral propositions analytically true, there would be the inclination to see moral truth as a mere matter of conceptual relations or linguistic convention. The moral relativist may be happy with this, but we moral realists are certainly not. We want moral truth to be rooted in the world. After all, the wrongness of murder is not in our view a matter of how we think or speak: murder "really is" pro tanto wrong. And in fact there is a significant sense in which the importance of analytic propositions is parasitic on synthetic propositions. Consider, for example,

P16*: Murder is pro tanto morally wrong,

which is analytically true if any such proposition is analytically true. I dare say that P16* is morally important—in the moral foundations of criminal law, in the moral guidance of international political relations, in the very way we morally structure society. But it isn't the linguistic conventions or concept employment that gives P16* its punch; it is what underlies its analyticity that does this. For what is murder? It is standardly understood as something like the illicit killing of a person, the paradigmatic instantiation of which is the killing of a human being (who meets certain conditions of mental capability, etc.) under certain morally proscribed circumstances. The type of entity being killed is central here; for persons are entities that enjoy a unique moral status[18]—that instantiate a particular sort of, or set of, moral property(s)—and it is the moral violation of this entity's personhood, in terms of the termination of its existence, which bestows murder's pro tanto wrongness. But this isn't merely a conceptual or linguistic matter; it is a matter of moral fact. It is this rootedness in the moral world, clearly expressed by synthetic propositions, which bestows the "importance" upon those analytic propositions which we regard as morally important.[19]

Before saying more about our access to moral truth per se, however, we first need to deal with a more general epistemological issue important to our realist project. Our antiskeptical position demands it.

## 5.2. MORAL FALLIBILISM

I refer to the problem of the fallibility of the human mind, and its implications for knowledge. Long philosophic tradition, going back to the Greeks, has registered broad skeptical concerns owing to our liability to error. If, as is distressingly often the case, we can be very sure that we know something but turn out to be wrong, why think we ever have knowledge? Indeed, why think knowledge is even possible?

Let's put all of this a little more carefully. What I shall call the "Skeptical Argument from Fallibility" may be formulated in a variety of ways, but the following will be convenient:

*Skeptical Argument from Fallibility*

(1) S knows that p only if p is true.
(2) But belief per se does not guarantee truth, that is, S can believe that p even if p is false.
(3) However, if S does not possess certainty regarding the truth of p, then S's belief that p is not an instance of knowledge.
(4) S does not possess certainty that p is true.
(5) Therefore, it is not possible for S to know that p, that is, (propositional) knowledge is not possible.[20]

Premise (1) looks unexceptionable. As we saw in detail in chapter 4, §4.1, the concept of knowledge entails truth, so S could know that p, only if p is true. So far, so good. Premise (2) also looks good—*at least to us*. This is because on our realist conception of truth (chapter 2) and our realist analysis of knowledge (chapter 4), we insist that the truth, belief, and justification conditions of (propositional) knowledge not be collapsed. Thus, belief that p is one thing—a propositional attitude held by an epistemic agent; and p's being true is another, which is a matter of whether p comports with the way the world is. Certainly belief per se does not guarantee truth. That would require an additional property of belief, implicitly denied by the next two premises. So again, so far so good.

Premises (3) and (4), however, do not look so good—premise (3) being more problematic than premise (4). Let's look at (4) first, and ask, Is it true that we never possess certainty? This is an age old question, and the first thing we should do is get some clarity on what the term 'certainly' means. Philosophers have meant a variety of things by it, but principally three. '*S* is certain that *p*' may mean: (i) that *p* is indubitable for *S*; or (ii) that *p* is incorrigible for *S*; or (iii) that *S*'s belief that *p* is infallible.

The indubitability interpretation of 'certainty', construed as having to do with the subjective characteristics of *S*'s belief state or *S*'s capacity to be in such a state, in many cases gives the skeptical argument little traction. Of course *S* may find herself unable to doubt that *p*, but for reasons having little epistemic merit. Perhaps *S* is simply being epistemically irresponsible—hasn't thought about the matter with any care, or has allowed her prejudices to run unchecked. Or perhaps *S*, for well understood psychological reasons, cannot abide the thought that something is true—that her spouse, for example, is unfaithful to her, despite it being obvious to all the world that he is. *S*'s being "really, really sure" that *p* may say much about her predispositions, but little about the epistemic credibility of her belief. If that is all that indubitability means, why think certainty very important for knowledge?

We will come back to indubitability in a moment, but let's first look at the next candidate: incorrigibility. On this interpretation, '*S* is certain that *p*' is understood as meaning that *p* is irrevisable (irreplaceable, unimprovable) for *S*. For example, if *S* asserts "I am seeing a red patch"—that is, perceiving a red sense-datum, as much of the mid-twentieth century analytic tradition would put it—then that statement is incorrigible for *S* in that *S* will have no reason to revise it. Seeing a red patch is a "certitude" for *S*. This sense of 'certainty' surely seems to have more relevance to the Fallibility Argument than the indubitability interpretation just considered; but before thinking about this in more detail, let's look at the third possible interpretation of 'certainty', viz., infallibility.

On the infallibility interpretation, '*S* is certain that *p*' means that *S*'s belief that *p* cannot be false. Put otherwise, if *S* is certain that *p*, then *p* is true. This is the interpretation I prefer, owing to its unambiguousness, and because it seems to capture the main thrust of the other two interpretations. After all, the objective of the Fallibility Argument is to highlight the skeptical implications of human liability to error. The argument is to the effect that our fallibility undercuts our ground for holding that genuine knowledge is possible. So let's take infallibility as our canonical interpretation of certainty. Now the question, is premise (4) true? My answer is that, strictly speaking it is not, although it is very nearly true. Consider these two propositions:

Law of Identity: A=A
Law of Non-Contradiction: Not both A and not-A [or in symbols, $\sim(A \cdot \sim A)$]

Some may disagree, but I really cannot conceive of how I could be wrong about the truth of these two. Their truth seems to me a very condition of (propositional) intelligibility and understanding. If they are false, I do not know how to proceed; for nothing would *be* anything or *mean* anything. We would seem to jettison rationality. So I am prepared to claim that my belief in the truth of these two propositions is infallible; hence my judgment above that premise (4) is false.

But I can add little if anything to this exceedingly short list. Very nearly, but not quite in that category of certitude, is an indefinitely large set of propositions such as the following:

'$2 + 2 = 4$'
'If $p$ implies $q$, and if $p$, then it follows that $q$' (i.e., modus ponens)
'These are my hands before my eyes, as I sit here writing this book'.
'I am thinking about my wife'.

I suppose that I can at least imagine, *barely*, that I am mistaken about the first two; and perhaps just infinitesimally more likely would be the possibility that I am wrong about the latter two. But admittedly, whenever computation or inference occurs, or wherever classification plays a role (Is it really my wife I am thinking about, or someone else?—perhaps a dangerous example; or, is that sense-datum actually red, or more pink than red?), error is at least a theoretical possibility, however unlikely. And of course in many spheres of everyday life, to say nothing of scientific and (notably!) philosophic inquiry, the possibility of error is a constant companion. And so I think we are driven to admit that on the infallibility interpretation of certitude, premise (4) is, albeit not completely true, almost completely true: we virtually never have it.

Even on a more robust, and surely typically intended reading of certainty qua-indubitability, one lands in essentially the same place. The inability to doubt that $p$, even where the epistemic agent is well informed, attentive and exercising great care in judgment, nevertheless does not guarantee $p$'s truth, even if error is extraordinarily unlikely. Limitations of judgment always lurk. Ditto certainty qua-incorrigibility: one cannot absolutely rule out the propriety of revising judgment, for miscategorization, etc., is always a possibility. Certitude looks virtually unattainable. [21]

So premise (4) looks almost completely on target. But this in fact should not surprise us, given our commitment to a realist conception of truth. There is (virtually) always a "gap" between truth, and belief and justification, or as we have alternatively put it, truth is evidence transcendent.

What then about premise (3)? There is a long tradition going back to Plato, and prominently in evidence since Descartes, that equates knowledge with certitude. Thus, Plato in *The Republic* holds that the epitome of knowing is the direct acquaintance with the Forms (*noesis*), as opposed to mere belief (*pistis*), even if that belief is correct.[22] And Descartes in *The Medita-tions* seeks to answer his "methodological doubt" by appeal to clear and distinct perceptions, about which doubt (and error) is not possible.[23] This tradition has been carried through to the twentieth century in the work Ber-trand Russell, the logical positivists, and many others, who sought certitude in the immediate deliveries of the senses (i.e., in our perceptions of sense-data) and in introspection (the immediate experiences of our occurrent men-tal life). All of these efforts, however, have largely come to grief. The pos-sibility of error always works its way into defeating truth-guaranteeing jus-tification. So if premise (3) is accepted, then it indeed looks as though the argument goes through, the conclusion being: (5) Therefore, it is not possible for $S$ to know that $p$, that is, (propositional) knowledge is not possible.

Note that this skeptical conclusion has, at least in the eyes of many, special force in the context of morality. For they would argue that if we can't get certainty in domains like direct sensory reports or introspection, to say nothing of the elementary propositions of arithmetic or deductive logic, how could we possibly claim certitude in the domain of first-order morality? After all, moral claims are notoriously disputed—witness the interminable debates about abortion, affirmative action, capital punishment, etc.—so the only rea-sonable thing to conclude is that if the Argument from Fallibility applies to supposed paradigms of certitude like arithmetic and introspection, it applies a fortiori to morality. Indeed, moral disagreement has historically been a major impetus to embrace certain versions of moral relativism.

That last observation, however, is certainly not to the point, because the moral relativist is just as much caught up in this skeptic's net as anyone, whatever the impetus may be to relativism. For the relativist is claiming moral knowledge, *if* he is claiming knowledge (they typically do) that is relative to a set of norms, whatever their genesis (chapter 4, §4.3). But the skeptic is saying that you cannot have that kind of knowledge either. The Argument from Fallibility is general to all domains of knowledge.

There are other problems regarding what was said two paragraphs above about moral knowledge, which we will come back to in §5.3. It is clear, however, that if the Argument from Fallibility is correct, then we don't have moral knowledge, and our efforts to vindicate the fundamental correctness of our ordinary moral thinking—which is staunchly antiskeptical—are doomed. The argument's pivotal move seems to be premise (3): If $S$ does not possess certainty regarding the truth of $p$, then $S$'s belief that $p$ is not an instance of knowledge. *But why accept premise (3)? Why agree to play the "knowledge requires certainty" game in the first place?*

Many philosophers would insist we shouldn't. Wittgenstein would say that this is an ill-advised philosopher's game if ever there was one. Rather than listen to the skeptic prattle on about how we don't possess knowledge because it is possible that we are being deceived by an evil demon, or dreaming, or brains in a vat, or whatever it is that skeptics have cooked up to inject doubt, we should look to how we actually use the term 'knowledge' in ordinary discourse. And if we do, it will be as plain as day that knowing bears no such epistemic burden as the skeptic seeks to impose.[24]

G. E. Moore would have none of it either.[25] He thinks he knows an indefinitely large number of things, for example, that "external things" (e.g., physical objects) exit. He even thinks he can prove they exist: "here is one hand, and here is another, and therefore there exist at least two physical objects."[26] His proof, he tells us, meets the proper conditions of any such proof: the proof wouldn't be satisfactory,

> (1) unless the premiss which I adduced as proof of the conclusion was different from the conclusion I adduced it to prove; (2) unless the premiss which I adduced was something which I knew to be the case, and not merely something which I believed but which was by no means certain, or something which, though in fact true, I did not know to be so; and (3) unless the conclusion did really follow from the premiss.[27]

Moore says that he has fulfilled all three conditions of proof, but understands perfectly well that this will not satisfy many philosophers. For they will require that he provide a proof of the premiss—that we weren't being deceived by an evil demon, that he wasn't dreaming when he asserted them, etc.—and *that*, he says, he cannot do, and has no idea how to do. But this is what would be required to demonstrate certainty in the strong, infallibility sense at issue in premise (3) of the Skeptical Argument from Fallibility. As Moore sees it, however, "I can know things *which I cannot prove*."[28]

C. S. Peirce, too, would think little of the Argument from Fallibility. Insofar as the thrust of the argument is connected with the efficacy of radical doubt, that is, certainty qua-indubitability, Peirce would insist that the evil demon/brain in a vat/I might be dreaming type of doubts—the kind of doubt central to the Cartesian project—is spurious, ginned-up, mere "paper doubt."[29] Real doubt inclines one to action—action aimed at removing the psychological irritant of doubt[30]—but these merest of possibilities have no such effect. There are indeed many things about which we have no doubt, and many things about which we do. We are clear on the difference. In fact, we *know* many things, although it is surely true that we could, just possibly, be wrong in any given case.

There are important lessons here from these three great philosophers. We must admit, I think, that like most if not all philosophically interesting concepts, the concept of knowledge does not have a perfectly a precise meaning. The analysis of propositional knowledge presented in chapter 4 notwithstanding, no perfectly perspicuous, exhaustive, and *uncontroversial* analysis is available.[31] After all, even if we agree with the justified, true belief (plus Gettier-blocking condition) analysis, agreement on a full explication of knowledge would require agreement on the nature of its constituent concepts: truth, belief, and epistemic justification. We are far from being able to do that. But here, in the spirit of Wittgenstein, Moore, and Pierce, it is useful to consider how we actually use the term 'knowledge' in everyday discourse. And from this perspective, nothing could be clearer than that knowledge does not require infallibility. Here are several of an indefinitely large number of knowledge claims that I make with utter confidence:

1. I have a biological mother and father.
2. The planet Earth is nearly spherical.
3. George Washington was the first president of the United States.
4. If I say, clearheadedly and honestly, that am thinking about my wife, then I am thinking about my wife.

I *know* these propositions to be true. Anyone reading this would agree that they knew them to be true as well, *unless they were going philosophical*. At that point all bets are off—all sorts of possibilities are entertained, many completely divorced from life as we live it, and the door is open for doubt. But I maintain, along with Peirce, that these are mere *paper doubts*. They may serve an intellectual purpose in certain contexts: Peirce allows that a certain kind of "feigned hesitancy" is important in the conduct of scientific inquiry,[32] in that it can assist in the free and rigorous pursuit of truth. But none of us really doubts any of these assertions: that is my claim, in response to our oft-referred-to question of Mary Midgely, "What do we really think?"

Imagine you witnessed the following exchange at a certain Ms. White's oral defense of her doctoral dissertation on nuclear physics.

*Examiner*: "Ms. White, you know of course that based upon the elementary fact that atoms exist, it clearly follows that. . . ."
*Ms. White*: "Forgive me for interrupting, professor, but I don't *know* that atoms exist."
*Examiner*: "Whatever do you mean, Ms. White? Given the massive body of evidence supporting the existence of atoms, and the absence of so much as a shred of scientifically respectable evidence that they don't, you say that you don't know that atoms exist!?"
*Ms. White*: "No, I do not. After all, it is *possible* that they don't exist, so I can't really say that I *know* they exist."
*Examiner*: "That's what you mean? *That's all?*
*Ms. White*: "Yes, professor, that's what I mean."
*Examiner*: "But then you don't know anything, do you Ms. White? You don't even know that you are actually Ms. White, do you?"
*Ms. White*: "Well, I . . ."
*Examiner (to the other examiners)*: "It appears we have a philosopher here, not a physicist."

Would you, as one of her examiners, vote to pass this defense, especially if this kind of thing persisted throughout the examination?[33] Something is out of whack here: this just isn't the place where general skeptical concerns get any traction. Ditto in a court of law. Ditto in virtually all of practical life, where acting on our beliefs may have the most serious existential implications. It happens every time we drive a car.

Now I do not mean to dismiss out of hand general philosophical concerns. As Richard Feldman has astutely observed,

> Almost all arguments for skepticism make reference to seemingly ridiculous possibilities—we are deceived by an evil demon, life is just a dream, we are brains in vats. You might propose psychoanalysis, rather than philosophical reflection, for anyone who worries about these possibilities. However, advocates of *The Skeptical View* do not suffer from paranoid delusions. They think that these possibilities help us to see something about the nature of our evidence and provide the basis for strong reasons to think that *The Standard View* [*of Knowledge*, i.e., that we possess much knowledge of the external world, et al.] is mistaken.[34]

Taken in this spirit, the skeptic is certainly worth engaging. We stand to learn a lot by understanding and responding to his challenge. But do we really *believe* these possibilities? That is a different matter entirely. Of course I could be wrong that I have biological parents, that Washington was the first president of the United States, that these are my hands in front of my face. I haven't the slightest positive reason, however, to think that I am wrong. I am not in the least inclined to actively investigate the practical possibility that I am wrong, nor have I any evidence that I should be. As noted earlier, however, in the context of morality, the skeptical challenge from fallibility has admittedly enjoyed more sympathy than in most others. For moral disagreement is ubiquitous. That said, while I *could* be wrong that it's true simpliciter that no one should shoot me while writing this book (P7), or I *could* be wrong that it's false simpliciter that it is always morally permissible to have sex with children (P8), *do I really have cogent, positive reason to think so?* Well, if the non-cognitivists are right, then I would. Or if the moral nihilists are right, or if the . . . Yes, these folks *could* be right and I therefore wrong, but by the same token, the radical eliminative materialists (like Paul Churchland) could be right, and all of the garden variety material object talk (Earth, hands, chairs) and first-person psychological reports (thinking about my wife, my motives for performing this act) could strictly speaking be false, being remnants of an erroneous and obsolete folk psychology destined to be eliminated by a rigorous physics. Well, maybe. But in the meantime, I shall go on merrily speaking of Earth and hands and thoughts about my wife, and steadfastly avowing *knowledge* of the moral wrongness of shooting people writing books and of raping children.

Where all of this is pointing is this: Infallibility appears unattainable in anything like the amount requisite to ground virtually all of our knowledge claims. But we have found excellent reason to think infallibility too much to require. Our view, strictly in line with virtually all domains of human inquiry, including first-order morality, is that a *fallibilist* conception of knowledge is proper. Asserting the proposition 'I know that *p*' simply does not entail that it is not possible that I am wrong. *Of course* it is possible that I am wrong. And if I am wrong, then I didn't know that *p* after all. But knowing does not require that you know that you know—does not commit us to the once popular, but now widely discredited KK-thesis.[35] As fallibilists, we reject this as excessively demanding. The impossibility of error is *not* built into the concept of knowledge. It just isn't how the concept operates.

Summing up: Knowing that *p* does not require certitude in any sense of the term—not indubitability, not incorrigibility, not infallibility. On the contrary, *S* can know that *p* even if it is possible that *S* may be wrong, that is, even if *S*'s justification for believing that *p* does not guarantee that *p* is true. The possibility of error is a matter both of our conception of epistemic justification, and of our realist conception of truth: there is in principle always a gap between being justified in believing that *p*, and *p*'s being true, however minute this gap may be.[36] To eliminate this gap would be to turn truth into an epistemic concept, which as we have seen at length in chapter 2 is highly undesirable. We are, then, advocating a fallibilist conception of knowledge in general, and first-order moral knowledge in particular. That said, as with other domains of human inquiry, in some cases we have exceedingly strong reason to be confident in one's moral belief. The skeptic just does not present a persuasive case. Now to discuss more specifically some of the ways we come into epistemic contact with first-order moral truth.

## 5.3. MORAL INTUITIONS

We come into epistemic contact with moral truth at many points in human experience. To see how, it will be useful to consider another well-known problem in general epistemology. We have analyzed propositional knowledge as justified, true belief (plus the Gettier-blocking condition). What conditions, however, have to be satisfied in order for a belief to be properly justified? Two broad kinds of responses are relevant: domain-specific responses, which tell us how a belief in a specific epistemic domain, for example, mathematics, physics, biology, or morality are to be justified; and structural responses, which tell us what the proper structure of justification looks like. We are interested in both sorts of responses, but for the moment let's focus on the latter. Here is another skeptical argument of longstanding influence:

*The Infinite Regress Argument*[37]

(1) In order for *S* to know that *p*, *S* must have a good reason for believing it.

(2) Any chain of reasons must have one of the following structures:

  a. It is an infinite regress
  b. It is circular
  c. It begins with a belief for which there is no further reasons. However,

(3) *S* cannot have an infinitely long chain of reasons for any of his beliefs.

(4) Circular reasoning cannot produce knowledge.

(5) *S* cannot gain knowledge by structure 2c, because

  a. *S* would not know his starting beliefs to be true (from 1), and
  b. *S* cannot gain knowledge by deriving it from assumptions that *S* does not know to be true.

(6) Therefore, S cannot know that *p*.

This is of course an argument of general epistemological purport, not specific to moral knowledge. Answering it, however, will be helpful to get at our primary target

I do not intend to make a major issue of this argument (it has been exhaustively discussed in the literature)—certainly less of an issue than we did with the Skeptical Argument from Fallibility in the previous section. In fact, I think that we should accept its validity, and simply grant the truth of all of its premises except premises (1) and (5).[38] Premise (1) says that if *S* is to have a justified belief, requisite to possess knowledge, then *S* must have a good reason for believing it. But is this correct? The epistemic foundationalist says no; for foundationalism claims that there are basic, non-inferentially justified beliefs—beliefs that are self-evident, self-justifying, immediately justified: they have been characterized in many different (and I think inequivalent) ways—which stop the vicious regress of justification. Premise (1) denies this. For the view is that in order for *S* justifiably to hold that a putatively basic belief, $B_1$ is reliable (i.e., likely true), *S* would have to have a reason in the form of a second belief, $B_2$ that beliefs like $B_1$ are reliable. But then $B_1$ isn't basic after all. And so the dilemma: if $B_1$ is basic, then it isn't justified; or if $B_1$ is justified, then it is justified only relative to $B_2$, and therefore isn't basic after all.[39] (This is essentially the purport of premise [5].) The result: there are no basic justified beliefs, and so foundationalism does not rebut the Infinite Regress Argument. Assuming that alternatives

(2a) and (2b) aren't acceptable—and they are not—then we are left with the skeptical result that knowledge is not possible.

Many contemporary epistemologists, I among them, reject the Infinite Regress Argument, in particular the argument against basic beliefs, and therefore against epistemic foundationalism. To see this, let's distinguish between two broad forms of foundationalism, "strong" foundationalism, and "modest" foundationalism. Strong foundationalism holds that there are basic beliefs, and that these beliefs, if they are genuinely basic, are indefeasible, indubitable, immune to error. Cartesian foundationalism is a prominent example: Descartes sought certitude in "clear and distinct perceptions" of his own occurrent mental states. He could just read off, so to speak, the presentations of his own consciousness. No inference there, and no possibility of error; these are indubitable, basic beliefs. For the strong foundationalist, immediate justification is sufficient to ensure infallibility.

Modest foundationalism, however, eschews the indefeasibility of any belief, including basic beliefs. Error is always at least a theoretical possibility, and the justification of basic beliefs may well be augmented by their coherence with other beliefs, basic and non-basic. As the modest foundationalist sees it, the very nature of our experience is, at least in many cases, sufficient to justify belief $B_1$ without appeal to any second-order belief, $B_2$, justifying the reliability of $B_1$. In the normal case, if I have the visual experience of seeming to see my hand in front of me, and I believe that I am seeing my hand in front of me based on this visual experience, then I am ipso facto justified in believing that there my hand is in front of me. If I seem to have the occurrent mental event of thinking about my wife, then I am ipso facto justified in believing that I am thinking about my wife. Experience immediately justifies these beliefs. I may, or I may not, also have the second-order belief that my experience is in the relevant respect reliable, but such second-order beliefs are not necessary.[40] If these beliefs are corroborated by coherence with other carefully considered beliefs, so much the better. It of course remains a possibility, in some cases the barest of possibilities (such as those just mentioned), that I am wrong; but that doesn't mean I was not justified in my belief. What the modest foundationalist is committed to is that the broad architecture of knowledge and justified belief requires basic, non-inferentially justified beliefs—that inferential justification is not alone sufficient, even if in many cases highly augmentative.

The Infinite Regress Argument has force against strong foundationalism, but not against modest foundationalism. And our fallibilism, discussed in §5.2 above, is perfectly in line with modest foundationalism. So modest foundationalism it is for us. But our concern here is not the moral to be drawn for general epistemology, but the moral to be drawn for *moral* epistemology (pardon the pun). Specifically, if the regress of justification is to be stopped in the case of moral knowledge, there must be some form(s) of justified, basic first-order moral belief. But what is it?

Our answer: *moral intuition*. Moral intuitionism has had a long and somewhat checkered history, gaining particular prominence in the early twentieth century with the work of the British philosophers Henry Sidgwick,[41] a utilitarian, and W. D. Ross,[42] a neo-Kantian. But it soon came under heavy fire from a variety of quarters, notably moral non-cognitivists and moral relativists. Intuitionism is, however, enjoying a much deserved resurgence among contemporary moral epistemologists.[43] Robert Audi, one of today's leading intuitionists, has characterized intuitionism thus: "[Moral] intuitionism [is] broadly...the view that at least some basic moral truths are non-inferentially known, and in that very minimal sense known intuitively."[44] But what does it mean to know something intuitively?

Let's stick with propositional knowing, the form of knowing (and the type of truth) that has been our exclusive concern throughout this book. The type of intuition we are talking about, then, is that which takes a proposition as its object.[45] So the issue, then, is what is it for $S$ to know that $p$ intuitively?[46]

One way to come at this question is from the point of view of the psychologist or neuroscientist, that is, to attempt to explain the psychological and/or neurological processes that cause and characterize intuition. This is surely important, but is not our object here. We are concerned, rather, with the *epistemology* of intuition—its justificational character and potentialities, as these factors bear on moral knowledge. And the first matter to attend to is, what is a moral intuition, anyway? Here contemporary intuitionists are divided.[47] Some philosophers, such as Audi,[48] Walter Sinnott-Armstrong,[49] and Russ Shafer-Landau[50] interpret them doxastically: moral intuitions are a class of moral *belief*. Others, such as David Kaspar,[51] Clayton Littlejohn,[52] Michael Huemer, and Shelly Kagan interpret them non-doxastically. As Huemer puts it, "[a]n initial, *intellectual* appearance is an intuition."[53] And Kagan remarks: "In ethics . . . as elsewhere, we need to distinguish between intuitions and belief. . . . At best, intuition involves something like a disposition to believe."[54] Disputants cleave, then, into two camps, doxastic and non-doxastic.

Which interpretation is the correct? This is a complicated issue that I will not try to resolve here, but it is important to note that in ordinary discourse, we seem to use 'intuition' in both senses of the term. Consider these ordinary language locutions:

L1. 'My intuition is clear that, morally, we ought not do that to him'.
L2. 'I don't trust my intuitions about this issue'.

Both locutions seem unexceptionable,[55] the first more naturally interpreted doxastically, the second non-doxastically. If $S$ says that "my intuitions are clear," it would at least be surprising for *S* to go on say, "but I don't believe them." Not strictly nonsensical, but surprising nevertheless. For the natural interpretation is not that *S* is making a phenomenal report on, say, the vividness or distinctness of his intuitions, but rather on the strength of his conviction.

L2, however, seems more naturally interpreted non-doxastically, as a mere (intellectual) "appearance" or a "seeming-to-be," the kind of thing that Huemer and company are talking about. For what would it mean to assert,

> L3: 'I believe that *p*, but I don't trust that *p*'?

If one understands *believing* that *p* to entail *trusting* that *p*, then one is contradicting oneself.[56] It is of course possible to interpret L3 to be making a sort of second-order claim, along the lines of

> L3*: 'Although I believe that *p*, I am fallible, and thus I believe that, even though the belief that *p* is among my belief-set, *p* may in fact be false'.

But this explication of L3 reflects an atypical expression, one unlikely in ordinary, non-philosophical contexts—contexts in which the term 'intuition' often operates. The far more natural way to understand L2 is something like:

> L2*: 'Things (intellectually) *appear* to me to be thus and so, but I don't trust the way things (in the relevant respect) appear to me'.

This is a clear, non-doxastic way to interpret 'intuition', where an intuition is taken to be an (intellectual) appearance or a seeming-to-be.

By the same token, it strains ordinary usage to interpret L1 non-doxastically. If one's intuitions are clear that one ought (or ought not) to perform action *A*, it would be very odd to say that you do not believe, much less that you doubt, that you should perform *A*. There is of course a range of degree of conviction, from slightly more than suspension of belief to convictional certitude, but it would be strange indeed to construe L1 as falling outside this range, into the range of doubt. In other words, L1 connotes positive doxastic status.

Obviously, we may have intuitions about all kinds of things. We may have mathematical intuitions, intuitions about physical theories, intuitions about people's likely behavior, moral intuitions, etc. However, it is my sense, although I see no way to show this conclusively, that within the realm of first-order morality, the doxastic interpretation dominates. Consider again

> L1. 'My intuitions are clear that, morally, we ought not do that to him'.

Let us divide moral intuitions into first-order moral intuitions, for example, regarding the wrongness of a specific act, and second-order moral intuitions, for example, intuitions about whether moral non-cognitivism is the correct metaethical theory. If L1 is a typical first-order moral locution, and if I am correct that it would be odd to read L1 non-doxastically, this suggests the predominance of the doxastic reading in this domain.

Here are two further considerations. First, suppose I assert this:

> L4: 'I intuit that I ought to defend my wife against this unprovoked violent physical attack'.

L4 expresses an intuition of great practical urgency about a particular moral fact, viz., that it is morally obligatory for me, here and now, to defend my wife against this specific unprovoked violent physical attack. Surely L4 is most naturally read doxastically. This stems not only from (i) the degree of conviction that we think properly attends such assertions: if it merely "appears" to me, if it only "seems-to-be" that I should defend my wife here and now against this specific unprovoked violent physical attack, then I am open to (well-founded) criticism that I lack appropriate loyalty, that I am a coward, that I am morally insensible, etc.[57] But more fundamentally, it also stems from (ii) the fact that locutions like L4, which have to do with practice—often with overt physical action—involve a motivational component; and it is clear that *belief*, not mere "appearing" or "seeming to-be" is a more appropriate explanation, even if only partial, of this motivational component.[58] But if L4 is representative of much first-order moral discourse, discourse which the moral intuitionist wants to preserve at all costs given the grounding role he wants intuitions to play for justified moral belief and knowledge, this suggests the doxastic reading.

Here is a second and connected consideration:[59] moral intuitionists hold that intuitions provide an important source of grounding and support for *non*-intuitional moral belief and knowledge. (No contemporary moral intuitionist thinks that *all* justified moral belief and knowledge is intuitional.) Now let us ask, which are we warranted in thinking provides firmer grounding or support for the belief that *p*: a confirmatory *belief* that *q*, or a confirmatory (mere) "*seeming that*" *q*? Conversely, which are we justified in thinking is more likely to undermine or defeat a belief that *p*: a disconfirmatory *belief* that *q*, or a disconfirmatory (mere) "*seeming that*" *q*? In both cases it seems that the former would. For as we normally understand these things, believing carries with it responsibilities of epistemic commitment not shared by mere seemings. Failure to live up to these responsibilities, which include the responsibility to meet justificatory burdens such as consistency, relevance, coherence with other beliefs, and so on can be criticized. This is because of the connection, problematic though it may be, between belief, justification, and truth. If we believe that *p*, we take *p* to be true; if we take *p* to be justified for us, then we take it that there is something about *p*, or our relationship to *p*, that makes our belief that *p* true or likely to be true. Any such burdens, however, are much attenuated in the case of mere "seemings." It is indeed far less clear how an epistemic agent is to be criticized because something mere-ly "seems" to her to be thus-and-so, than if she *believes* that something is thus-and-so. But if moral intuitions are to play their foundational role in moral justification and knowledge, these burdens seem quite relevant.

I view none of these considerations favoring a doxastic reading of first-order moral intuitions as conclusive. But they do seem highly probative. Nevertheless, I will not press the issue further here; for much of what I shall have to say holds on either interpretation of moral intuitions. [60]

Audi has proposed the following criteria for intuitional beliefs: [61]

> *Non-Inferential:* The belief must not be evidentially based on a premise(s).
> *Firmly held:* One must be quite confident that the belief is true.
> *Comprehended:* What is believed must be understood thoroughly, that is, ade-quate to a clear grasp of what is believed.
> *Pre-theoretical:* The belief must not be evidentially dependent on a theory, or itself be a theoretical hypothesis.

Let's look briefly at each of these criteria, and to do so, consider my claim that I intuit that it is morally wrong for someone to shoot me as I'm writing my book (P7). [62] This is but one of an indefinitely large number of examples that I could provide. Certainly the "firmly held" and "comprehended" criteria are fulfilled. I am as sure as I can be that I believe P7 (!); and I am fully convinced that I know what the proposition means. I shall assume that in this case neither of these claims need defense. The other two criteria are, howev-er, another matter.

There has been a long-running debate among epistemologists regarding whether any justified belief qualifies as non-inferential. [63] We in fact encoun-tered this very issue earlier in this section in the Infinite Regress Argument. Our modest foundationalist answer was that yes, there are non-inferentially justified, basic beliefs. In some cases the nature of experience is such that the very experience itself justifies the belief, without need for a second-order belief that beliefs of the sort in question are reliable. Thus, my having the experience of seeing a red rock is typically sufficient, absent awareness of any abnormal viewing conditions, etc., in my being justified in believing that I am seeing a red rock. Note further that in this case I engage in no inference from the nature of my visual experience to the identity of the object I am perceiving, the red rock. I simply see it as a red rock, much as I see—much as I non-inferentially *recognize*—the person before me as my friend Peter. I am aware, as Robert Audi has usefully put it to me (in private correspon-dence), of no occurrent passage in thought from one set of propositions to another. I am simply reporting what I see; and on this basis I am justified in believing that this is a true claim about an external object. Although fallible, normally claims like this constitute knowledge. The non-inferential criterion, then, seems quite defensible.

Which brings me to the Audi's final criterion, *pre-theoreticality*: the intuitive belief must not be evidentially dependent on a theory, or itself be a theoretical hypothesis. Is this criterion defensible? This is a complicated business that I have dealt with in depth elsewhere, and so shall be (relatively) brief here.[64] Let's begin by getting a handle in what pre-theoreticality means. We may think of it in two ways:

> *Epistemic pre-theoreticality*: where $X$ is pre-theoretical if and only if $X$ is not epistemically dependent upon, or is not itself, a theoretical hypothesis;

and

> *Semantic pre-theoreticality*: where $X$ is pre-theoretical if and only if $X$ is not semantically dependent upon, or is not itself, a theoretical hypothesis.

As I am using the concept of "semantic dependence," $X$ is semantically dependent on $Y$ if and only if $X$ is intelligible, *meaningful*, only in the context of $Y$. To illustrate: the term (or concept of a) 'proton' has meaning only in the context of atomic theory—a theory (or set of theories) which provides at least in part the semantic conditions necessary for 'proton' to be intelligible. Without such a theory, 'proton' would be either meaningless, or if meaningful at all, mean something quite different than what contemporary physicists mean by it.[65] The same sort of thing applies to terms like 'irrational number', or 'exothermic reaction', or 'existential quantifier': none of these are meaningful, or would minimally have very different meanings, were they not contextualized in number theory, or chemical theory, or quantification theory. By the same token, $X$ would be semantically *in*dependent of $Y$ if $X$'s intelligibility did not require $Y$ (i.e., if $X$ is meaningful independent of the context of $Y$). Thus, 'human hand' is clearly semantically *in*dependent of atomic theory, chemical theory, number theory, and quantification theory.

Regarding moral intuitions, Audi's principal concerns have to do with epistemic pre-theoreticality, even if he doesn't specifically say so. To see this, note his reference to "evidential dependence" in his formulation of the pre-theoreticality criterion. If $X$ is *evidentially* dependent on $Y$, $X$'s dependence on $Y$ is clearly epistemic. What is it, then, for $X$ to be evidentially independent of $Y$? More specifically, what is it for a *moral intuition* to be evidentially independent of theory? Another complicated issue about which I shall be brief, nor shall I trace out all that Audi has had to say about it.[66] Clearly, however, a belief is not pre-theoretical if it is inferred from a theory—which in any case would be blocked regarding intuitions by the non-inferentiality condition.[67] Nevertheless, consider scientific observation of a vapor streak in a cloud chamber as evidence of the passage of an alpha particle (two protons and two neutrons bound together) due to radioactive decay. Surely the very notion of a vapor streak in a cloud chamber being able to provide observational *evidence* of the passage of an alpha particle due radioactive decay is thoroughly dependent epistemically on atomic theory for its status as evidence. The entire experimental set-up is thoroughly theory-dependent.[68]

Very well, then, we are talking about the epistemic pre-theoreticality of moral intuitions. And so our question is, are intuitions epistemically pre-theoretical? The answer to this in part depends what type of intuitions we are talking about. For we can have all kinds of intuitions, including intuitions about theories. For example, a physicist highly expert in General Relativity Theory may have an intuition that $p$ is true, where $p$ is a proposition that is (or may not be) a deductive consequence of the theory, or a proposition about the theory itself. Someone highly expert in, say, Kantian Deontological Ethical Theory may similarly have such intuitions. But in either of these cases, this is to have an intuition which is, in an important respect, *not* pre-theoretical, for absent the theory, there would be no intuition. So in this sense of "pre-theoreticality," the answer is no. This, however, isn't the pre-theoreticality that Audi is talking about. Rather, the issue is, are *all* moral intuitions, including first-order moral intuitions, theoretical? Audi thinks not, and I agree.

On my view, a lot depends on what one means by the term 'theory'. Some philosophers hold that all propositional belief is theoretical; and this is because they think that in order for anything to have cognitive significance, as propositions clearly do, it must be theory *de*pendent—moral intuitions, being propositional, included. The ground of this view is that nothing is meaningful in isolation. Thus, in order for $p$ to be meaningful, $p$ must be related to some other set of propositions $\{q,r,s\}$. And some of these "semantic holists" further believe that the term 'theory' is properly understood to refer to whatever confers meaning, in the sense that $p$ is meaningful only relative to the "theory" comprised of $\{q,r,s\}$. Consequently, whatever is propositional is theory dependent, hence not pre-theoretical—and this of course includes moral propositions.

The proper response to this view, I think, is to consider more carefully what we normally mean by the term 'theory'. And what we usually have in mind is typified by such examples as Euclidean Geometry, the Geological Theory of Plate Tectonics, the Big Bang Theory, John Stuart Mill's Utilitarianism, etc. These and similar paradigms are complex, structured sets of propositions, which their authors and defenders alike would agree must satis-

fy to some appreciable degree—the more the better—such general characteristics as:

1. Internal Consistency
2. Coherence with other (acknowledged) theories
3. Explanatory force
4. Testability
5. Simplicity
6. Truth entailment

In brief, characteristics such as these are widely considered to be desiderata
which apply across a broad spectrum of conceptual domains. Clearly, theories are supposed to *do* something; perhaps most fundamentally they are
intended to *explain*, hence the importance of a theory's *explanatory force*.
Indeed, if a theory explains little or nothing, it is worth little or nothing as a
theory. But in order for a theory to explain, it is important that it be internally
consistent; for an inconsistent set of propositions entails anything, which in
turn is to explain nothing. Further, that a theory *coheres* with other accepted
theories is highly desirable, in that this not only contributes to that theory's
cogence, but also contributes to a unified conceptual understanding of matters beyond the scope of the theory itself. And we of course want our theories
to be *true*, and for them to *entail other truths*, not falsehoods; otherwise, the
theory's explanatory force would be vitiated. There also need to be ways that
the theory can be *tested*, which will obviously vary across conceptual domains. A theory in the physical sciences, for example, will presumably be
tested in ways—observationally, primary among them—that a theory in
mathematics will not (or could not). Absent a way to test a theory, how are
we to ascertain its truth? *Simplicity*, too, is an important desideratum. Simplicity may of course be understood in different ways, but importantly among
them is the number of (types of) ontological commitments. Ceteris paribus,
the fewer ontological commitments a theory makes the better: do not multiply entities beyond necessity is the famously wise counsel of Occam's razor.
For economy of ontological commitment conduces to more satisfactory explanation—the raison d' etre of theories in the first place.

There are likely other general theoretical desiderata, and there has been
much discussion of what they may be, and which should be privileged. [69] And
of course there are less general desiderata specific to the theory *type* (i.e., the
particular conceptual domain) at issue. But I trust I have said enough to make
clear that it is to desiderata such as those just discussed that theories are
widely held to account. To the extent that a theory falls short of these desiderata, it is criticizable. [70] Thus, were one to say to a geologist, a mathematician, an historian, "Here is my theory," and what one presented had little
internal consistency, had no explanatory force, entailed no relevant truths,

failed to cohere with other theories in its respective domain—well, the response isn't hard to imagine. *Moral theorists would respond similarly.* Note,
too, that there is a difference between something's being a bad theory and its
not being a theory at all: not a perfectly sharp difference, perhaps, but a
difference nonetheless. A random set of propositions is no theory; a set of
propositions which explains nothing and which makes no pretense of explaining anything is no theory; a set of propositions with no obvious claim to
truth is no theory. A bad theory, in contrast, exhibits all or most of the
desiderata above, but in diminished degree—the less it does, the worse it is.
But on the flaccidly latitudinarian concept of theoryhood outlined several
pages earlier, once one has attained to propositionality, this distinction can't
be drawn. This is a very unhelpful, inadequate conception of theory indeed.

This generally understood sense of the term 'theory', which recognizes
the relevance of desiderata such as those I have discussed, is what I call the
"normal sense" of 'theory'. And this is the sense of theory I have in mind
when I claim that Audi is right, that many first-order moral intuitions are
epistemically pre-theoretical.[71] There are a number of reasons to think this.
One reason is that, assuming I am correct in thinking that I believe intuitively, for example, that it's wrong to shoot me while I am writing this book
(P7), careful introspection strongly suggests to me that this intuition is pre-
theoretical. As far as I can tell I understand it, I comprehend it, I did not infer
it, and I am justified in believing it *without appeal to any theory in my sense
of 'theory'.*

Another reason to believe this is that I knew many propositions like P7 to
be true or to be false immediately, non-inferentially, long before I ever heard
of Kant or utilitarianism or of "normative ethical theory"—long before, that
is to say, I possessed any moral theory to appeal to. After all, even small
children can be expected to know that it is wrong for someone to just walk in
and kill them, or their parents, or the family pet. And I would add that the
plausibility of such pre-theoretical moral beliefs is confirmed by my observations of beginning philosophy students, many of whom are quite theoretically
unsophisticated, but all of whom know straightaway that it is wrong to do all
sorts of things, including shooting people.

So it certainly seems that moral intuitions may be pre-theoretical. Of
course no one has intuitions ex nihilo. All such intuitions issue out of a set of
background beliefs and valuational commitments. But this doesn't entail that
they must be theoretical in any interesting sense of the term.[72] In short, then,
it seems that Audi is right regarding the pre-theoreticality criterion of moral
intuitions.

And fortunately so, because if intuitions were not pre-theoretical, they
could not serve an important role that intuitions are thought to serve. Ask
yourself this: How is one to assess the satisfactoriness of a first-order moral
theory, a normative ethical theory regarding the criteria of judgment of ac-

tions, for example? As discussed above, there are a number of desiderata to which any theory worthy of the name should be held to account: coherence, explanatory power, etc. That said, however, and thinking specifically of first-order moral theory such as that aimed at assessing human action, are there any particularly pressing epistemic considerations that need to be taken into account? The answer is, *there most certainly are: our moral intuitions.* As Sinnott-Armstrong, an important critic of moral intuitions, has observed, "Everyone relies on moral intuitions."[73] Indeed, we frequently rely on moral intuitions, perhaps especially in situations of uncertainty:

> "I just saw the neighbor boy break a window in the house down the street. Should I inform his parents?"
> "My boss repeatedly shows improper favoritism to my coworker. Should I tell my boss of my concerns? Should I tell Human Resources?"
> "I really don't feel like going to the party, but my friend Ann is expecting me. Do I need to go?"

Cases like this are ubiquitous, and we often respond to ourselves or to others with answers of the form, "Well, my intuitions are that I do such and such."[74] Sometimes these intuitions may rise to the level of near convictional certitude. I intuit the truth of

> P7: It is morally wrong for anyone to walk into my office and (intentionally) shoot me to death as I sit here writing this book;

and I intuit the falsehood of

> P20: Torturing my mother for my own personal pleasure is morally praise-worthy.

I am hard put indeed to even imagine what could lead me to reverse these judgments. These and similar intuitions are, if you will, "moral touchstones": if I am wrong about them, I can only conclude that I really know nothing about morality.[75]

Now some moral intuitions are about particular moral facts, and others are about general moral facts such as moral principles or generalizations. I intend P7 and P20 as examples of the former, and propositions like

> P18: All things equal, it is morally praiseworthy to treat one's friends with kindness,

and

> P21: It is always prima facie wrong to treat a person with cruelty.

as examples of the latter. Now while I am confident in the truth of all of these intuitions, I must say that if anything I am more confident regarding the particular moral intuitions than I am regarding the general moral intuitions. I invite the reader to reflect on this for himself. While I see no hard and fast rules on this, and exceptions abound, it seems that very often particular moral intuitions command greater confidence and motivational force than general intuitions—that the particular is epistemically pre-eminent. [76] In fact I suspect that our intuitive belief in propositions like P7 and P20 often precede our belief in general propositions like P18 and P21. For example, say I have (in a highly particularized situation) this intuition:

> P22: I ought to defend my wife against this unprovoked violent physical attack.

This is the kind of intuition that seems epistemically prior to having an intuition such as,

> P23: It is false that it is always morally impermissible to use physical force in defense against a violent attacker.

That is to say, it seems that in the case of propositions like P23, we are more likely to first have the intuition that it is permissible for *me* in *this* circumstance to defend *so and so* (e.g., my wife) against *this attack*, than we are to first intuit the generalization that it is false that it is always morally impermissible to use violence to defend against an unprovoked violent attack, and then later (but non-inferentially) have the particularized intuition. Belief in the particular moral fact often underlies belief in the general moral fact, if not occurrently, at least dispositionally. A kind of moral induction is at work here. Belief in the particular fact seems a necessary part of the "epistemic background" requisite to form beliefs regarding moral generalizations. Not necessarily, however: intuitive moral belief of moral particulars is certainly not *absolutely* epistemically prior to intuitions regarding moral generalizations or moral principles. There are many cases where belief in generalizations or in principles is a necessary part of the epistemic background requisite to form intuitions of particular moral truths. One might, for example, first intuit that "Everybody is created equal," and only later come to intuit that "Sue is created equal to me." Nevertheless, I suggest that the norm is that particular intuitions, in at least a large part of the domain of first-order moral intuition, are epistemically prior to moral generalizations both in being requisite for intuitive belief formation, and in strength of conviction. Note, incidentally, that even young children may have moral intuitions, but far more likely intuitions of the form, "It is wrong to do *X* to me," than of the form, "No one should have *X* done to them."

Whether or not I am correct that intuitions about particular moral facts typically take pride of place over intuitions about moral generalizations or principles, it is nevertheless clear that moral intuitions—non-inferential, comprehended, pre-theoretical, firmly held *beliefs*—are in many cases suitable candidates to stop the regress of epistemic justification requisite to ground moral knowledge. It is simply *evident* to me that it's wrong for someone to shoot me while writing this book (P7); and it is simply *evident* to me that it's false that torturing my mother for my own personal pleasure is morally praiseworthy (P20). *Really, isn't it the same for you?* I do not think it hyperbole to say that the likelihood of having to revise these claims approximates the likelihood of having to revise my claim that these are my hands typing on the keyboard before me.

In short, there is something central about moral intuitions like this in our evaluational lives—at times a kind of bedrock epistemic quality about them.[77] Moreover, these bedrock intuitions, such as my intuitions regarding shooting me (P7) and torturing my mother (P20), can and properly do serve a regulative role regarding the adequacy of normative ethical theory. Any normative theory entailing the falsehood of P7 or the truth of P20 would, on my view, almost certainly be incorrect, warranting either substantial revision or outright rejection. Or imagine a situation where a gunman runs into the room and demands to know where all the Jews (or Moslems, or Republicans, or . . .) are. May one legitimately "make a lying promise" to him that they have all left for a rally on the other side of town (or whatever)? *What is your intuition about that?* My intuition is crystal clear: yes, you most certainly may lie.[78] Many, however, interpret Kant as prohibiting it. According to Kant, the Categorical Imperative, *"Act only on that maxim whereby thou canst at the same time will that it should become a universal law,"*[79] entails that is *never* morally permissible to lie. For if one were to approve lying in one instance, even if highly advantageous, then one must be willing to approve lying in any instance—that is, be prepared to will that lying become a universal law, which leads straightaway to a contradiction (as do violations of all perfect duties), viz., that approving of lying renders the very act of truth-telling meaningless. So lying is never morally permissible.[80] My (exceedingly strong) intuition to the contrary, however, leads me to reject Kant's view. Minimally, adjustment to the theory is required.

The Kant case seems to me a clear one. Many cases, however, most certainly are not. Sometimes we may intuit that *p*, but embrace a normative moral theory that entails not-*p*, in which case it may be unclear which to accept, the theory or the intuition. Moral intuitions are not, after all, infallible: sometimes we revise them, sometimes we come to reject them outright. For that matter, we may well possess conflicting intuitions, in which case we know (or should) that something must be wrong somewhere. But the point is clear: moral institutions play a crucial role in normative theory construction and assessment. And I say the same, mutatis mutandis, for construction and assessment of metaethical theory. In some cases, if a theory runs against these intuitions, *so much the worse for the theory*. Ask yourself seriously if you do not, in the end, agree.

Moral intuitions, then, are of great importance. Practically, questions of the form, "What should I do?" are often answered by appeal to intuition. They are central to the phenomenology of our moral lives. They guide us, they give us confidence, they are often our first court of appeal to make sense of the welter of information, often conflicting, which confronts us when called to action. Theoretically, intuitions stop the infinite regress of (moral) epistemic justification. In many instances they provide immediate, non-inferentially justified moral belief, in some cases rising to the status of knowledge. Moreover, questions of the form, "What should my moral theory look like? Is this a good theory?" are likewise informed by appeal to intuition. Theories are erected upon, and judged by their appropriateness vis-à-vis moral intuitions. If our analysis is correct, intuitions provide a foundational source of contact with moral truth.

## 5.4. MORAL THEORY

I have argued that first-order moral intuitions may be pre-theoretical in the respect required to serve as regress-stopping justified moral belief, and therefore in some cases to serve as a foundational source of moral knowledge. But surely moral knowledge is not limited to intuitions: no contemporary intuitionist holds such an extreme view. Moral theory, too, has an important role to play in helping us achieve contact with moral truth. But what exactly is this role? Our reply is that most fundamentally, given the theory of truth developed in chapter 2, it is to help us grasp moral reality—to understand "the way the world is," morally speaking. At this point we need to recall the distinction between first- and second-order moral matters. The role of second-order moral theory—of metaethics—although in some respects similar to the role of first-order moral theory, is in other respects quite different. Second-order theory, the type of theory developed in this book, is supposed to enable us to understand the truth about the *nature* of morality, of what morality is like. First-order moral theory is to enable us to understand the truth of matters *within* morality. Note that of course one's second-order moral theory could be skeptical about there being any truths within morality, for example, on a nihilistic conception of morality. Our concern just now being first-order moral theory, and having in previous chapters rejected skeptical second-order theories, we can easily see that on our view the role of moral theory of any kind is to help us identify and understand which are and which are not true moral propositions—propositions which express moral facts. In short, the role of moral theory is to enable us to grasp first-order moral reality.[81]

The details of the criteria and/or desiderata of theory acceptability is a large and specialized topic beyond the scope of our remarks here. We have, however, briefly discussed several such desiderata in the previous section:

1. Internal Consistency
2. Coherence with other (acknowledge) theories
3. Explanatory force
4. Testability
5. Simplicity
6. Truth entailment

Minimally, moral theory—first- or second-order—should fulfill insofar as possible these desiderata. I will comment briefly on two of them.

*Truth entailment* is, for us at any rate, a very important theoretical desideratum. A first-order moral theory should entail first-order moral truths. This may be a straightforward matter, or it may be very complex, depending on the theory and the type of propositions inferred. If the theory entails moral falsehoods, or does not entail many, or many different kinds of moral truths, that is bad for the theory. All of this bears on the theory's *testability*.

Moral theories, according to the account of moral truth and moral properties that we have given, are not to be tested in the same way as theories in the sciences, whether natural or social. Although theories in physics or chemistry or sociology must sooner or later confront the tribunal of observation, this is not the case for moral theory, at least not in the sense of "observation" relevant to the empirical sciences. For on our account, scientific theories (primarily) have to do with physical properties, while first-order moral theories (primarily) have to do first-order moral properties which *supervene* on physical properties. Moral properties are sui generis, and ipso facto irreducible to physical properties; therefore, moral theories are fundamentally different from physical theories, as are the methods applicable to testing them. This isn't to say, of course, that moral theories may not include as subsidiary elements reference to both physical properties and the physical theories governing their ordering and interpretation. Moral judgment, after all, occurs in a physical world, and the nature and configuration of that physical world is often important to such judgment.

How, then, do we test moral theories? The degree to which they fulfill the remaining five desiderata is certainly relevant—and in this broad respect we may say that those five desiderata are in a sense subsumable under "testability." But more specific to testing first-order moral theory per se, we rightly ascertain how well the theory squares with other theories that we endorse, including moral theories, first- and second-order. On our view, it is of course very important to determine if the theory is compatible not only with our theory of moral intuitions, but with our specific intuitions as well. Thus, if theory $h_1$ squares with our (firmly held) moral intuitions better than does theory $h_2$, then ceteris paribus $h_1$ is to be preferred to $h_2$. The importance of this is not to be diminished, as do many critics of moral intuitions.[82] Again, moral intuitions appear to be an unavoidable and highly useful—albeit defeasible—tool for moral evaluation, including evaluation of moral theory. As noted in §5.3, my intuition that lying is sometimes morally permissible (even obligatory) leads me to reject a strict Kantian deontological theory.

Here is another example, although admittedly more controversial. On Mill's version of utilitarianism, it is prima facie wrong to lie about another person, on the ground that such lying will likely lead to more disutility than utility, that is, will likely not optimize the good, which is happiness cum-pleasure for the greatest number in the indefinitely long run. Imagine a case where Smith lies about Jones—knowingly avows something false and negative about Jones's character, say—although no harm comes to Jones or to anyone else: Jones never hears of it, those who have heard the lie, including Smith herself, quickly forget it owing to exigencies in their own lives, etc. It looks as if Mill's view would be "no harm, no foul": lying was not wrong in this case because no displeasure was generated.[83] My clear intuition is that Smith should not have lied about Jones, independent of any harm understood as non-maximization of pleasure. Lying was simply wrong here, being incompatible with the proper treatment of a moral agent independent of considerations of harm in any tangible, that is, disutilitarian sense of the term. And so the way that Mill comes at explaining the prima facie wrongness of lying is misguided. All of this is to say that, on my view, Mill's theory failed a test. Whether this means that the theory needs revision or outright rejection is a further matter, perhaps one of considerable complexity (as in fact I judge that it is).

Critics of intuitionism, as well as many critics of normative moral theory in general, despair of a "test" to discriminate between moral truth and falsity. They often contrast physical (e.g., scientific) theory with moral theory, arguing that observational test of the former provides a clear criterion for acceptance, while no analogously efficacious test is available for moral theory (or moral intuitions).[84] And it is true that, on our realist conception of morality, moral theory is not observationally confirmable in the same respect as is physical theory, because moral theory has to do with features of the world not similarly observable: one cannot see or taste a moral property in the same sense in which one sees redness or tastes saltiness. But it would be a mistake to conclude that physical theory is therefore to be elevated over moral theory in terms of testability. For problems with confirmation of physical theory are legion, both in practical and theoretical terms[85]; and it is remarkable how universal and enduring some moral judgments, largely grounded in moral theory, may be. Consider, for example, the virtually unanimous and enduring condemnation of slavery.

We may in fact look to interesting parallels with observation generally to better understand testing moral theory. Say that Smith reports seeing a small crack in the floor, and Jones reports seeing none. We have observational disagreement here. Now what? Do we conclude that there is no truth of the matter about there being a crack in the floor? Of course not. We ask both to have another look. Are they confident of their observations? Are there distorting lighting effects? Are the visual apparatuses of both observers working normally? Is either party able to confirm their visual observation with tactual evidence? Perhaps after all these checks Smith and Jones still disagree, and so we bring in others to have a look. Perhaps when all is said and done, we still have a 50/50 split on whether there is a crack in the floor. This may be a surprising result, and we may be inclined to think that there is something very odd about this putative crack, but we would not be at all inclined to draw any general skeptical conclusion about the efficacy of observation. Of course if inconclusive results were the rule rather than the exception, we may be inclined to skepticism, but not otherwise. And mutatis mutandis we may say the same about more theoretically oriented observational results. Yes, there may be divergent opinions, but principled consensus is often reached. Were this not the case, empirical science would be doomed.

We often reach consensus in moral judgment as well. The impermissibility of slavery appears a closed issue; there is unanimity condemning the behavior of Japanese troops during the Nanking Massacre (a.k.a., the Rape of Nanking); the basic goodness of honesty and kindness and courage, and of many similar character virtues has long enjoyed wide assent. Any normative theory which runs against these judgments is in serious trouble—and deservedly so. Just as consensus among well-positioned observers is strong evidence in favor of, or against, a physical theory, so consensus among well-positioned judges of moral situations or principles is strong evidence in favor of, or against, a moral theory. Not a truth-guaranteeing consensus, of course: no evidential consideration can be on the realist view that we have developed. But in some cases consensus properly warrants great confidence in judgment.

Just as we have a good idea of what it is to be "well positioned" in the context of observational judgment, so we have a good idea of what it is to be well positioned regarding moral judgment. To be informed of the relevant situational facts, to grasp the valuational context, to be able to draw appropriate inferences, to be as free as practicably possible of bias—these and other epistemically advantageous factors conduce to soundness of judgment in moral matters. It is simply disingenuous to claim that in morality all opinions are equal, that no one is better positioned than anyone else. No one believes that, *not in matters that count*. We dismiss the vicious, we discount the callow and the dissembler and the bigot—and we know perfectly well what it is to be all of these things, and why such opinions are undeserving.

To be clear, our purpose here is not to specify which normative moral theory we should adopt. We can, however, rule out some theories, or at least partially rule them out, and rule in, or at least partially rule in, others. For any first-order moral theory makes second-order moral, that is, *metaethical* commitments, and if those commitments are incompatible with the metaethical views we have developed, then we are to that extent warranted in holding that theory unacceptable. For example, a hedonic version of utilitarianism such as Mill's, which defines the central moral property of goodness in terms of pleasure, which is in turn presumably to be cashed out in terms of physical brain states, will not secure our approval. Our theory of moral properties being incompatible with this, we cannot endorse Millian utilitarianism. We have not therefore ruled out utilitarianism per se, however, because utilitarianism is not necessarily committed to a physicalist conception of moral properties. G. E. Moore, for example, held that the Good is a "simple, unanalyzable, non-natural property," yet endorsed a version of utilitarianism (perhaps 'consequentialism' is a more apt term). [86]

For different reasons, we can rule out, or at least demand modification of, a strict Kantian normative ethical theory, assuming (i) that the Categorical Imperative really does prohibit all instances of lying; and (ii) that one shares my strong intuition, discussed in §5.3 above, that in some instances lying is permissible. The ground of rejection here is not metaethical, as in the Mill case, but epistemic. It is, in other words, a first-order moral objection to Kant's first-order moral theory: the theory entails a first-order moral falsehood. [87]

First-order moral theory, then, should help us grasp first-order moral truth. This will require that the theory have the right kind of second-order moral commitments, for example, that there *are* first-order moral truths. In addition, it should state and entail true moral propositions, and should fulfill insofar as possible the other theory desiderata discussed above. Moral theory should help in structuring and interpreting our moral lives. Consider these two questions:

> Q1: Is it permissible to waterboard Jones for the sheer pleasure of it?
> Q2: Should waterboarding suspected terrorists be absolutely prohibited under any and all circumstances, no matter the exigency of the situation?

Many will think Q1 a ridiculous question. Of course the answer is no: their *intuition* could not be clearer. Few, however, will think Q2 a ridiculous question; if they do, I suggest that they lack imagination. There may be those who have a confident answer to Q2 based strictly on intuition, but many, I among them, do not. This, I submit, is the kind of case where moral theory comes into play. It provides the organizing and interpretive structure requisite to engage complex moral situations—situations where competing moral considerations are present.[88]

Yet, the relationship between moral intuition and moral theory is fluid. There are times when intuition takes priority, and times when theory takes priority. Knowing which to favor, in any given case, requires judgment, a kind of moral wisdom, if you will. Experience and knowledge of associated non-moral matters all contribute to sound moral judgment. Relevant, too, is consideration of the implications of what flows from the intuition, and what from the theory, as is consideration of the respective strengths of conviction. But in fact, there is often an interplay between intuition and theory, ideally each informing the other so as to bring us ever closer to moral truth. When falsehood is thought to be encountered, it may be a matter of some subtlety what to do: Keep the theory, but revise it? Jettison the theory? Reject the intuition as more likely false than the theory? It is difficult to answer these questions in the abstract. But in the final analysis, we are best advised to rest judgment on *reflective equilibrium*:[89] all things considered, which view best stands inspection? Which best comports with our deeply held intuitional commitments? Which best squares with our theoretical commitments? With our broad life experience? Which best accommodates all relevant data, theoretical and non-theoretical, moral and non-moral? In the end, these are the considerations that bear most heavily on where we should plant our flag.

What, really, is our alternative to assessing moral judgment other than in these terms? An absolutely definitive litmus test in moral matters seems rarely if ever obtainable. So, too, in politics, in aesthetics, in literary criticism—indeed, in nearly any realm of inquiry, including the natural sciences.[90] There are virtually always considerations in favor of $X$ that may at least in principle be overridden by considerations against $X$, and conversely. Rank ordering priorities, balancing desiderata, ascertaining levels of confidence, etc., can be devilishly difficult. Such are the demands of serious thought. But I think the most epistemically responsible position is clear: believe what best provides reflective equilibrium.[91]

To take stock of where we have been in this chapter: in §5.1 we argued that some first-order moral propositions are analytic, others synthetic. The truth of analytic moral propositions is in principle knowable a priori, while the truth of some synthetic moral propositions is self-evident, knowable a priori—in particular, moral intuitions—and others only a posteriori. All three types of proposition play a role in our quest for moral truth. Synthetic moral propositions, however, are fundamental to our realism. They are the ones that most clearly enable us to come into contact with realist moral truth, *with moral facts*, and the ones that undergird the importance of important analytic moral propositions.

In §5.2, we made the case for the viability of a fallibilist moral epistemology. Skeptics are wrong to demand freedom from all possible error as a necessary condition of knowledge. Certitude in any sense of the term—indubitability, incorrigibility, infallibility (the latter our preferred interpretation)—is to ask too much. Knowledge, as we understand the concept, of course requires truth, but it does not require the impossibility of being wrong. We in fact know many things, but virtually none with absolute certitude. In particular, we know many first-order moral truths—our justification for holding such beliefs in some cases warranting an extremely high degree of conviction. Nevertheless, the possibility of error is an ever-present theoretical possibility. But nowise should this lead to a general moral skepticism.

In §5.3, we made the case that moral intuitions can answer skeptical worries about a vicious infinite regress of justification in the context of moral belief and knowledge. Moral intuitions, especially on our preferred doxastic interpretation, can and often do provide a firm grounding for moral knowledge: they are in many cases justified basic beliefs, often rising to the level of knowledge. Although not immune to error, intuitions provide a source of unmediated contact with moral truth, and consequently are able to serve many roles, including a pivotal one regarding the construction and assessment of moral theory, both first- and second-order. The moral epistemology advocated here is a fallibilist moral intuitionism.

In §5.4, we emphasized the role and importance of moral theory. Moral intuition can do a lot of work for us, but moral theory is needed, too, especially in situations of moral complexity where competing moral considerations are present. In countless ways, moral theory can help order and structure our moral lives. It can provide the possibility for a deeper and more complete apprehension of moral reality. It can also serve as a check on moral intuition, which we must remember is not infallible. Moral theory and moral intuition properly play complimentary roles. It is hard to see how theory can arise other than on the back of intuition, but it would be profoundly limiting if we relied only on intuition. I suggest that ceteris paribus the person best informed by sound moral theory is the one most likely to have sound moral intuitions. In the end, however, we should seek reflective equilibrium in moral matters: this is our best avenue to moral truth, fallible though we are.

We need, however, to get a still firmer fix on what it is to possess moral knowledge, and to see in still finer detail, in more specific terms, where the skeptic has gone wrong. This shall fulfill the promissory note issued in chapter 1, §1.5.

## NOTES

1. Consider the case where $S$ is convinced that she did a grievous wrong, and out of overwhelming feelings of guilt, takes her own life. Consider a second case in which $R$ is

convinced that she *did nothing wrong whatever*, but out of overwhelming feelings of guilt, takes her own life. We may (or we may not) find *S*'s behavior rational. What, however, are we to say of *R*'s behavior? In epistemic, not psychological, terms, are the two cases parallel? Hardly. Belief and the epistemic constraints which attach to it, matter a great deal.

2. Immanuel Kant, *The Critique of Pure Reason*, translated by Norman Kemp Smith (New York: St. Martin's Press, 1965 [1787]), 48ff.

3. A. J., Ayer, *Language, Truth and Logic* (New York: Dover, 1952), ch. IV

4. Which Kant would not consider analytic, but rather synthetic. More about this below.

5. Different pragmatists will provide importantly different detail. Thus, Dewey is going to say something different than Peirce, who in turn says something (quite) different from Rorty. For Dewey, *p* is true if and only if asserting *p* brings to fruitful conclusion an inquiry that was instigated by a felt problem situation; for Peirce, *p* is true if and only if *p* is the proposition to be assented to by the collectivity of inquirers in the indefinitely long run; for Rorty, *p* is true if his contemporaries let him get away with asserting it (or some other such implausible criterion). See John Dewey, *Reconstruction in Philosophy*, in *John Dewey: The Middle Works, 1899–1924*, Vol. 12 (1920), edited by Bridget Walsh (Carbondale and Edwardsville: Southern Illinois University Press, 1982), 77–201, 156; Charles S. Peirce, "How to Make Our Ideas Clear," *Collected Papers of Charles Sanders Peirce*, eds. Charles Hartshorne and Paul Weiss (Cambridge, MA: Harvard University Press, 1931–1935), paragraph 407.

6. F. H. Bradley, *Essays on Truth and Reality* (Oxford: Clarendon Press, 1914), 1.

7. Ibid., 223. And Brand Blanchard takes the truth of such propositions to mean that it coheres with an "all-comprehensive and fully articulated" whole. See his *The Nature of Thought*, Vol. 2 (London: Allen & Unwin, 1939), 264.

8. Willard V. O. Quine, "Two Dogmas of Empiricism," in *From A Logical Point of View*, 2nd edition (Cambridge, MA: Harvard University Press, 1961), 20–46.

9. A similar question is how do we achieve justified belief with regard to each of these two types of propositions? The answer about to be provided with regard to knowledge will track closely with a proper answer with regard to justified belief.

10. Propositional understanding (i.e., occurrent propositional understanding) is, as John Searle famously argues, an "intentional," that is, "mentally directed" act, which is, as I am using the term, experiential. See his "Minds, Brains, and Programs," in *The Behavioral and Brian Sciences*, Vol. 3, Issue 3 (Cambridge: Cambridge University Press, 1980), 417–24; and also his *Intentionality: An Essay in the Philosophy of Mind* (Cambridge: Cambridge University Press, 1983).

11. These people think that "folk-psychology," that is, mental talk as we commonly employ it in everyday and even most philosophical discourse, will someday be eliminated, and that the discourse of contemporary physics will become the coin of the realm. See, for example, Paul Churchland, *Scientific Realism and the Plasticity of Mind* (Cambridge: Cambridge University Press, 1979).

12. Innate knowledge would be a counterexample, if there is any. But if there is any, it cannot be very much—certainly not adequate to account for the vast scope of knowledge with which we are acquainted.

13. Kant, for example, did not consider arithmetical propositions analytic. See *The Critique of Pure Reason*, B14–18. More about this below.

14. Not everyone agrees. The great pragmatist C. I. Lewis, for example, famously argued against the synthetic a priori in *An Analysis of Knowledge and Valuation* (La Salle, IL: Open Court, 1946), chapter VI, §13 and 14.

15. I mean to be as neutral as possible here regarding how one construes analyticity.

16. See John Stuart Mill, *Utilitarianism* (Indianapolis: Hackett Publishing Co., 1979 [1861]): ch. 2. In the discussion to follow, I leave it open whether Mill is an act or rule-utilitarian.

17. The great virtue ethicist Aristotle is similarly situated. The truth of instantiations of propositions of the form '*x* is courageous (temperate, loyal, etc.)' is to be determined according to whether or not the individual manifests moral virtue. Moral virtue, in turn, is to be understood in terms of action as appropriate to man as a rational animal. Courage, as with other moral virtues, is to be interpreted in terms of habits of character which lie between the extremes

of excess (e.g., recklessness) and deficiency (e.g., cowardice), as would be determined by a rational individual, and relativized to that individual's capacities and circumstances (what is appropriate for an expert may be ill-advised for a novice). Thus, 'Smith behaved courageously when he fought Jones', is true or false depending on whether Smith's act of fighting Jones was virtuous as regards courage—that is, insofar as Smith's act of fighting was an appropriate expression, given all of the relevant situational variables, of ideal character. For our purposes, however, the important thing to note is that, as with Mill's utilitarianism, the truth or falsity of this proposition is an empirical matter. For whether Smith behaved courageously is a matter of whether she behaved virtuously, and that is ultimately a matter of whether Smith's act was appropriate to Smith's flourishing qua-rational animal. Was Smith's act in line with what is good for man, *given her capacities as a natural being?* Knowing moral truths for Aristotle, then, is a matter of knowing empirical truths; and gaining knowledge of these truths ultimately depends on making observations. See Aristotle, *Nicomachean Ethics*, translated by W. D. Ross, edited by Richard McKeon, *The Basic Works of Aristotle* (New York: Random House, 1941), 935–1112, Books I–V.

18. We do not, after all, typically speak of a bear hunter "murdering" a bear, and certainly not of a logger "murdering" a tree.

19. Of course what is important in one context may be unimportant or utterly irrelevant in another. The point here is that our version of moral realism is not content to allow first-order moral truth to lie exclusively in the domain of the conceptual or the linguistic. Note, however, that on our view it makes perfectly good sense to say that *X is purpose-independently important*. Note further how the analysis just given applies to other moral concepts such as rape. 'Rape of human beings is pro tanto morally wrong' appears to be an analytically true proposition, but its truth clearly "hooks in with the world"—and is only implausibly a "mere matter of words"—in the sense captured by the paraphrase, 'Coercive sexual intercourse with human beings is pro tanto morally wrong', which, although also true, certainly does not appear to be analytically true.

20. Some philosophers prefer to separate skeptical concerns about fallibility from skeptical concerns about certitude, and so would see two arguments here. I, however, see these concerns as thoroughly entwined, and do not think that relevant confusion will result in presenting the skeptical challenge to knowledge in this way. The reader is free to restructure the argument in the way implied if he sees fit. If my argument below is correct, however, we will end up in the same place.

21. I except the two propositions put forth earlier: the laws of identity and non-contradiction. I simply cannot doubt either one, and can conceive no case for revising them. (One can easily see, however, how these propositions can be given alternative expression.)

22. Plato, *The Republic*, translated by Francis MacDonald Cornford (Oxford: Oxford University Press, 1945), Book VI, 507c–511e.

23. See Rene Descartes, *Meditations on First Philosophy*, translated by Donald A. Cress (Indianapolis: Hackett Publishing, Co., 1993 [1941]), Med. 2. More about Descartes in §5.3.

24. See Ludwig Wittgenstein, *On Certainty*, edited by G. E. M. Anscombe and G. H. von Wright (New York: Harper & Row: 1969); and *Philosophical Investigations*, 3rd edition, translated by G. E. M. Anscombe (New York: Macmillan, 1958).

25. A theme first broached by us in ch. §1.1. I here repeat for the reader's convenience much of what was said there.

26. This is a paraphrase from Moore's "Proof of an External World," in *Philosophical Papers* (New York: Collier Books, 1959), 126.

27. Ibid., 144.

28. Ibid., 148, my italics.

29. Charles S. Peirce, "Some Consequences of Four Incapacities," *The Collected Papers of Charles S. Peirce*, Vol. 5, edited by Charles S. Hartshorne and Paul Weiss (Cambridge, MA: Harvard University Press, 1913–1935), 264–317, esp. 264–268; and "How to Make Our Idea Clear," *The Collected Papers of Charles S. Peirce*, Vol. 5, edited by Charles S. Hartshorne and Paul Weiss (Cambridge, MA: Harvard University Press, 1913–1935), 388–410.

30. Peirce, "The Fixation of Belief," *Collected Papers*, Vol. 5, 358–387, esp. §III.

31. Wittgenstein, for example, would be quite unhappy with what we have said. Forget this business about necessary and jointly sufficient conditions. You want to know what 'knowledge' means? Look to ordinary language use. And there's a lot of variability there.

32. See Peirce, "How to Make Our Ideas Clear," §II.

33. Of course everything would be different if Ms. White were to adumbrate cogently a theory that overthrows the atomic theory of matter. In that case, we may have another Einstein on our hands.

34. Richard Feldman, *Epistemology* (Upper Saddle River, NJ: Prentice Hall, 2003), 114; his italics, my insertion.

35. For a study showing the implications of the KK-thesis, see Jaakko Hintikka's classic, *Knowledge and Belief: An Introduction to the Logic of the Two Notions* (Ithaca, NY: Cornell University Press, 1962).

36. Excepting the examples provided earlier in this section, the Law of Identity and the Law of Non-Contradiction.

37. This formulation of the augment is Michael Huemer's, "Three Skeptical Arguments," in *Skepticism and the Veil of Perception* (Lanham, MD: Rowman & Littlefield, 2001), 9–15. I have made minor modifications to better comply with our text.

38. Each of these other premises have been challenged in the literature, to greater or lesser— I think for the most part lesser—effect. Premise (1) is the one that has traditionally received the most attention.

39. This argument against basic beliefs was famously put forward by Lawrence BonJour, *The Structure of Empirical Knowledge* (Cambridge, MA: Harvard University Press, 1985).

40. Surely young Johnny is justified in believing that that is his mother, even if Johnny is perfectly incapable of formulating a second-order belief about the reliability of his senses. We could say roughly the same thing, mutatis mutandis, about our dog Fido's recognitional capacities.

41. See Henry Sidgwick, *Methods of Ethics* (London: Macmillan, 1907; reissued by Dover Publications, 1966).

42. W. D. Ross, *The Right and the Good* (Oxford: Oxford University Press, 1930).

43. See, for example, the fine set of essays recently published in Jill Graper Hernandez, ed., *The New Intuitionism* (New York & London: Continuum, 2011). Other recent developments and defenses of moral intuitionism are to be found in Michael Huemer, *Ethical Intuitionism* (New York: Palgrave Macmillan, 2005); and David Kaspar, *Intuitionism* (London & New York: Bloomsbury, 2012).

44. Robert Audi, *The Good in the Right* (Princeton, NJ: Princeton University Press, 2004), 5, my insertions. This book is the best discussion of moral intuitionism known to me. It also develops Audi's own highly insightful version of intuitionism. My views on moral intuitionism are deeply indebted to, and largely compatible with, Audi's.

45. See Robert Audi, "Intuition and Its Place in Ethics," *Journal of the American Philosophical Association*, vol. 1, issue 1 (2015): 57–77, for excellent discussion of other forms of intuition, for example, objectual intuitions, "a direct apprehension of either a concept, such as that of obligation, or of a property or relation, such as the property of being justified or the relation of entailment" (p. 60). Propositional intuition will do the required work for us here.

46. I have discussed many of the matters in this section in previous publications: "Moral Facts and the Centrality of Intuitions" in *The New Intuitionism*, ed. Jill Graper Hernandez, (London: Continuum, 2011): 48–66; "The Pre-Theoreticality of Moral Intuitions," *Synthese*, Vol. 191 (October 2014): 3759–778; and "Disagreement and the Defensibility of Moral Intuitionism," *International Philosophical Quarterly*, Vol. 56, Issue 224 (December 2016): 487–502.

47. The discussion that follows is based in part on that of my "Disagreement and the Defensibility of Moral Intuitionism."

48. Audi, *The Good in the Right.*

49. Sinnott-Armstrong, "Moral Perception and Heuristics," *The Modern Schoolman*, 86 (2009): 327–47: "As I will use the term, *moral intuitions* are roughly strong, stable, immediate moral beliefs" (327, his emphasis).

50. Shafer-Landau, *Moral Realism: A Defence* (Oxford: Oxford University Press, 2003).

51. David Kaspar, *Intuitionism* (London: Bloomsbury Press, 2012).

52. Clayton Littlejohn, "Ethical Intuitionism and Moral Skepticism," in *The New Intuitionism*, ed. Jill Graper Hernandez (New York and London: Continuum, 2011), 106–27.

53. Michael Huemer, *Ethical Intuitionism*, 102, his emphasis.

54. Shelly Kagan, "Thinking About Cases," in *Moral Knowledge*, eds. Ellen Frankel Paul, Fred Miller, and Jeffrey Paul (Cambridge: Cambridge University Press, 2001), 44–63, 45n1.

55. In common usage, the singular (as in L1) and the plural (as in L2) forms of 'intuition' are used nearly interchangeably. I use the plural form in L2 because it seems a more natural expression. But this is of no real concern here: if you prefer to use the singular for the sake of consistency, please do so.

56. As John Searle points out in *The Construction of Social Reality* (New York: Free Press, 1995), 199ff., we assess statements as true when we consider them trustworthy. So to believe that *p* is to consider *p* trustworthy. We noted this in chapter 2, §2.2; and I discuss it in "Moral Facts and the Centrality of Intuitions."

57. This is tricky: I am not open to punishment, of course, as we normally see these things, but my character would be open to criticism were these attitudes known. People would hardly think me admirable.

58. I don't intend to get involved here in the complex debate between motivational internalists and motivational externalists. But note that the internalist—Kant, for example—would hardly find a mere "seeming-without-believing" motivationally sufficient.

59. This paragraph comes almost directly from "Disagreement and the Defensibility of Moral Intuitionism," 489.

60. See Robert Audi, "Intuitions, Intuitions, and Moral Judgment," *The New Intuitionism*, ed. Jill Graper Hernandez (New York and London: Continuum: 2011), 171–98, for useful discussion of the different interpretations of moral intuitions. Also see his "Intuition and Its Place in Ethics," *Journal of the American Philosophical Association*, Vol. 1, Issue 1 (2015): 57–77.

61. Robert Audi, *The Good in the Right*, 33–35; this is not direct quotation.

62. To forestall objections to some of the example intuitions I will use in this chapter: intuitions may be simple or complex, which is likely in part a function of the sophistication of the intuitor and her familiarity with the subject matter at hand. Someone highly familiar with a subject matter will likely have more complex intuitions than someone who is not. Additionally, a person may have an intuitive belief that *p*, and also believe that *p* inferentially (although perhaps not at the same instant). For the most part I have chosen relatively simple exemplar intuitions. The reader is free to substitute others of a similar nature more to her liking.

63. A huge literature attends this, which I cannot begin to deal with here. Among many useful discussions of this issue are: Roderick Chisholm, *The Theory of Knowledge*, 1st–3rd editions (Englewood Cliffs, NJ: Prentice Hall, 1966/1977/1989); Paul Moser, *Empirical Justification* (Dordrecht, Holland: D. Reidel Publishing Company, 1985); Lawrence BonJour, *The Structure of Empirical Knowledge;* and Robert Audi, *Epistemology*, 3rd ed. (New York: Routledge, 2011)

64. See my "The Pre-Theoreticality of Moral Intuitions."

65. Strictly, matters are more complicated than this. For 'proton' may be meaningful relative to any of a variety of particular atomic theories, although it may not, or then again it may, have the *same* meaning relative to theory $h_1$, as it does to theory $h_2$. We may safely ignore such complications here.

66. See Audi, *The Good in the Right*, 35ff, for useful discussion

67. One might suspect that pre-theoreticality follows from non-inferentiality, since if *S* believes that *p* and theory *H* is part of *S*'s evidence for believing that *p*, then *S* inferred that *p* in whole or in part from *H*. But then why think that pre-theoreticality is distinct from non-inferentiality? This, however, seems to me mistaken. *S* could believe that there is a hand in front of his face, which is grounded in his perceptual experience, even though *S* performed no inference. Similarly, *S* could believe that it is prima facie wrong to kill his dog, which is grounded in his belief-set regarding, say, the moral parameters of treating higher mammals.

68. In this case semantic dependence on theory is also evident, for example, in the very meaningfulness of the term 'alpha particle' et al. I suspect that where there is epistemic

dependence on theory, there is very often semantic dependence on theory as well. I will not pause to sort this out.

69. For example, *consilience*, that is, how much a theory explains, is likely another general desideratum, and distinguishable from explanatory force; for how *well* a theory explains, and how *much* the theory explains are not equivalent. Perhaps one desideratum can be maximized only at the expense of another, for example, simplicity at the expense of consilience, and vice versa. The proper weighting of theory desiderata is a complex business, in part dependent on what one wants the theory to do. See, for example, Paul Thagard, "The Best Explanation: Criteria for Theory Choice," *Journal of Philosophy* 75, No. 2 (1978): 76–92. Also see Brian Leiter, "Moral Facts and Best Explanations," in *Moral Knowledge*, edited by Ellen Frankel Paul, Fred D. Millar, and Jeffrey Paul (Cambridge: Cambridge University Press, 2001), 79–101.

70. A desideratum is not equivalent to a necessary condition: it is a criterion of judgment that must, or at any rate should, be fulfilled insofar as possible. Thus, theory *H* could be lacking in internal consistency or explanatory power and still qualify as a theory. However, to the extent that it lacks these qualities, this counts as a deficiency. Specifying exactly what conditions must be fulfilled for something to qualify as a theory, especially across all possible conceptual domains, is very difficult at best. I cannot attempt that here.

71. It seems, in fact, that many moral intuitions are *semantically* pre-theoretical as well— that semantic pre-theoreticality can be fulfilled not only in principle, but in practice. For consider the implications for propositional intelligibility if one takes this "ubiquity of theory-dependence" thesis seriously. If proposition *p* is intelligible only relative to some theory $h_1$ (in what I have called the "normal sense" of theory), but $h_1$ is only intelligible relative to some (other) theory $h_2$, and $h_2$ only relative to some (other) theory $h_3$ . . . , we would have a vicious regress on our hands which threatens the very possibility of propositional intelligibility. But it is obvious that propositional intelligibility *is* possible, so any such conception of radical theory dependence cannot be correct. (Huemer, *Ethical Intuitionism*: 103, makes a similar point in this context: "moral intuitions are not in general caused by antecedent moral beliefs, since *moral intuitions often either conflict with our antecedently held moral theories, or are simply unexplained by them*"; my italics.) The semantic pre-theoreticality of moral intuitions is in principle fulfillable.

72. I discuss all of these matters in much greater detail in "Moral Facts and the Centrality of Intuitions"; and in "Moral Disagreement and the Defensibility of Moral Intuitionism."

73. Walter Sinnott-Armstrong, "Reflections on Reflection in Robert Audi's Moral Intuitionism," in *Rationality and the Good: Critical Essays on the Ethics and Epistemology of Robert Audi*, edited by Mark Timmons, John Greco, and Alfred R. Mele (Oxford: Oxford University Press, 2007), 19. Shelly Kagan, "Thinking About Cases," in *Moral Knowledge*, edited by Ellen Frankel, Paul Miller, Jeffrey Paul (Cambridge: Cambridge University Press, 2001), 44–63, also a critic of moral intuitions, agrees. Sinnott-Armstrong arrives at a skeptical conclusion regarding ethics; Kagan has skeptical leanings as well.

74. Note that such intuitions may be either of the doxastic or the non-doxastic type. Again, my emphasis here is on the doxastic interpretation.

75. This assumes realism in ethics. That is, *if* moral realism is true, *then* I am completely at a loss if P7 is false and P20 true. I would know nothing at the level of first-order morality.

76. I have argued in "Moral Facts and the Centrality of Intuitions," for the epistemic preeminence of intuitions about particular moral facts, for example, in the context of norm testing and theory construction.

77. But not always: as with other forms of belief, *S* my hold certain intuitions with greater confidence than others.

78. Actually, my intuition is stronger: one has a *pro tanto obligation* to lie to the gunman.

79. Immanuel Kant, *Fundamental Principles of the Metaphysics of Morals*, translated by T. K. Abbott (New York: Prometheus Books, 1987), 49, italics in the original.

80. See ibid., 50–1.

81. Remember that this is an explication (as per chapter 4, §4.1) of what first-order moral theory is supposed to do. One can know perfectly well that killing innocent people is prima facie wrong without knowing any of the fancy metaethical theory underlying it.

82. Shelly Kagan, for example. See his "Thinking About Cases."

83. I am under no illusion that this constitutes a full analysis of Mill's resources to deal with this case. For one thing, we would have to stipulate whether we are interpreting Mill as an act or a rule-utilitarian, and what we say on one interpretation may well be different than on the other interpretation. I bypass these issues here, but nonetheless take the example to be adequate to our purposes of demonstrating the role of intuitions in theory assessment.

84. The logical positivists, like A. J. Ayer, are perfect examples of this.

85. The long-running dispute over the theoretical adequacy of the (now largely discredited) Deductive-Nomological Model of scientific explanation is but one salient illustration.

86. G. E. Moore, *Principia Ethica* (Cambridge: Cambridge University Press, 1903).

87. It is concerns like this about Kant's view which recommend a deontological theory like W. D. Ross's, where one obligation, such as to refrain from lying, may be overridden by another obligation, such as to preserve innocent human life (i.e., duty to non-injury). See Ross, *The Right and the Good* (Oxford: Oxford University Press, 1930).

88. Of course what may at one time require moral theory to answer, may not at another. I am sure that all of us have the strong, virtually indefeasible intuition that Smith, who is black, is utterly underserving of slavery. Some of us may not have had this intuition two hundred years ago, even if we would have agreed on theoretical grounds that Smith should not be enslaved.

89. John Rawls, in his landmark *A Theory of Justice* (Cambridge, MA: Harvard University Press, 1971), brought the importance of reflective equilibrium to the fore in the philosophical community, and it has been widely regarded ever since.

90. Thus, it was that Karl Popper's litmus test of falsifiability in the sciences came to grief. A theory can always be saved, if one is willing to make enough adjustments elsewhere. Some spheres of mathematics and formal logic, however, may exceptions.

91. This, of course, is far indeed from the full story. But I do take it to be a central component in any adequate conception of epistemic responsibility.

# Chapter Six

# Knowing Moral Reality

## 6.1. FIRST-ORDER AND SECOND-ORDER MORAL KNOWLEDGE

We began in chapter 1, §1.1, with an account of the revolting murder of twenty-six people, including twenty innocent children ages six to seven years—the notorious Sandy Hook Elementary School killings perpetrated by Adam Peter Lanza. I claimed to *know* that these killings were seriously morally wrong,[1] and that virtually everyone else familiar with the case knows it, too. I also argued that there is something very powerful at the root of our ordinary, tutored moral thinking.[2] Although moral judgment is certainly fallible (chapter 5, §5.2), our broad moral perspective is fundamentally correct. It is now time to put more theoretical muscle behind these claims.

We have already laid the foundations necessary to get a firm grasp on what it is to know moral truth. We now look to those foundations to develop a broader and deeper understanding of moral knowledge, and to see what is wrong with what our opponents have had to say. In order to best do this, we first need to recall our oft-mentioned distinction between first- and second-order moral claims—the former having to do with matters "within morality," the latter with matters "about morality." Chapter 2 developed a theory of truth intended to apply inter alia to both first- and second-order moral propositions, as well as a theory of first-order moral facts. Chapter 3 went on to develop a theory of first-order moral properties, intended to deepen our understanding of first-order moral truth and facts. Together, chapters 2 and 3 were aimed at developing the metaphysical underpinnings of moral knowledge, while chapters 4 and 5 were aimed at understanding the general features of such knowledge, as well as some specific ways that we come into contact with moral truth. The present chapter furthers the effort of the previous two.

Thus far, the emphasis has been on first-order moral knowledge. This shall remain our focus, principally because on our view, understanding first-order morality is the gateway to a proper understanding of second-order morality—that is, of *metaethics*—which is, after all, one of the two central topics of this entire study. We have done little to argue in favor of any particular moral policies or normative ethical theories. We have done little, for example, to provide an argument in deontological terms, or in utilitarian terms, or in terms of virtue ethics or what have you, that it's wrong to shoot me will I'm sitting here writing this book (P7), or that it's not the case (!) that it's always permissible to have sex with children (P8). The strategy employed here is to appeal to many uncontroversial exemplars of first-order moral truth or falsity to enable us to go on to make broader metaethical or epistemological points. We now need to consider more carefully the distinction between first- and second-order moral knowledge.

From our realist perspective, we can possess a good bit of the former but little of the latter, and conversely. The first is nothing new to us. An unsophisticated adult, even a child, can know many things to be right or wrong, but know nothing about metaethics. To require that they possess knowledge of such theoretical matters would be to set the bar far too high. Many of our opponents, however, will balk at this. Non-cognitivists and moral nihilists (moral error theorists like J. L. Mackie; some would include non-cognitivists in this category as well) are going to say that we are very much in the dark without metatheory, that we systematically misunderstand what we are saying when making first-order moral pronouncements. Even moral relativists might balk: they may press the need for metatheory to straighten us out—to move us off the mistaken idea that 'It is wrong to do that to him' means that it is "really" wrong to do that to him in some objective, much less absolute sense of the term. So no, it is hardly uncontroversial to hold that we know a lot about ethics without appeal to metaethics.

Our commitment to the second point—that we can know a lot about metaethics but little about first-order ethics—may be a bit more difficult to see, but is clear on a moment's reflection. Let's distinguish between '$S$ knows that $p$', and '$S$ knows the theoretical foundations of $p$'. So take these two propositions:

> SK: $S$ knows that the proposition 'Coercive sexual intercourse with young children is prima facie wrong' is true.
> SKF: $S$ knows the metaethical foundations upon which the truth or falsity of the proposition 'Coercive sexual intercourse with young children is prima facie wrong' rests.

I see no reason to doubt that *S* could fulfill SKF—could know the metaethical foundations on which the truth or falsity of the proposition 'Coercive sexual intercourse with young children is prima facie wrong' rests—without knowing whether it is true that coercive sexual intercourse with children is prima facie wrong. That is to say, it is clear that *S* could fulfill SKF, but not SK. For all that is required for *S* to fulfill SKF, is for *S* to know the metaethical foundations upon which the truth or falsity of *any* first-order moral proposition of the sort under discussion (viz., Class A propositions like P7) rests, and to know that 'Coercive sexual intercourse with young children is prima facie wrong' is a first-order moral proposition. *S* need not know whether this particular proposition is true or is false; *S* would just need to know that this is such a proposition, which would of course presumably require that *S* understood the proposition. To require that fulfilling SKF demands fulfilling SK is roughly parallel to the previous case: to require too much.

Obviously, then, first-order and second-order moral knowledge are not necessarily connected, at least not in any thoroughgoing sense. But in any event, linking them too closely would result in mistakenly thinking that there is far more "moral ignorance" than seems plausible, especially given our fundamentally antiskeptical stance. Not only would the theoretically unsophisticated be condemned to moral know-nothinghood, but metaethicists would be severely limited in the range of first-order moral propositions with which they could properly deal   apparently, limited to those the truth value of which they know. That would be a severe restriction upon theorizing: *unacceptable.*

I also want to make room for the possibility, even if unlikely, that one may be sophisticated on the level of theory—about metaethics—and still hold many, even unusually many false first-order moral views. Broadly and roughly put, theoretical sophistication does guarantee practical sophistication.[3]

And yet first-order and second-order morality *are* connected, and in myriad ways. In fact, we think the connection is profound. While the thrust of much of this book has been to understand second-order morality, we have, as noted above, continually appealed to the first-order for guidance in our theorizing. We now need to explore this connection more closely.

## 6.2. THE EPISTEMIC PRIMACY OF THE FIRST-ORDER MORAL

Whence come our moral views? A large and multifaceted question, one to which the psychologist, the sociologist, the historian, and the philosopher all have important things to tell us. It is, alas, a question the magnitude of which prohibits our being able to entertain it exhaustively here. Nevertheless, there are a few things to be said to help orient the remarks to follow.

Alasdair MacIntyre has recently and to much acclaim emphasized the situatedness of our moral lives—of our moral beliefs and other valuational attitudes.[4] We learn our morals from specific people, in a specific place(s), during a specific historical epoch, etc. We are all members of a moral community, broadly understood, which forms us as moral beings. My beliefs, and *your* beliefs, regarding the legitimacy of democratic rule; the rights of women; obligations to nation, family, friends, and so on are what they are because of the situatedness of our moral experience. I am not here going to assess MacIntyre's broadly Aristotelian account of morality, a version of "virtue ethics" which he develops with great depth and insight, and with which he provides a powerful critique of the "liberal moral tradition"—the tradition of Kant and Mill and all the others who see morality as a system of rules or principles applicable to all, divorced from their rootedness in the specificity of concrete community.[5] But I do want to note that MacIntyre implicitly raises a point apropos of our study: the role of moral education.

Let's ask our question again, whence come our moral beliefs? One way to answer is look to our moral education. Where does that start? Without trying to put too fine a point on it, it starts with our parents' telling us, "No, Johnny, don't do that," and moves on to "Johnny, you shouldn't do that because it's not nice," and then on to "Johnny, how would you like it if someone did that to you?" and continues on to . . . perhaps a close reading, in the German original, of Kant's *Foundations of the Metaphysics of Morals.* Very well, it probably won't go that far, but the point is clear: we do not start with sophisticated, high-flown normative ethical theory.[6] And we absolutely do not start with abstruse metaethics—prescriptivism, emotivism, Moore's *Principia Ethica,* or anything remotely like that. We could not: the young intellect is simply incapable of comprehending it. We need to start "down low"—with simple, specific cases lacking in nuance and ambiguity—and build up from there. As we become more mature, more intellectually and practically able, we can think in more abstract, general terms. Some of us, alas, never get very far in this regard.[7]

Although but roughly sketched, and open to refinement and subject to qualification, nothing said here really seems controversial. The point is obvious: the trajectory of our moral education moves, for the most part and in most respects, from the simple and concrete toward the abstract and general. What makes this point other than a banality is the theoretical work it can do for us.

To wit, in chapter 5, §5.2, we emphasized the point that in philosophical inquiry, as in other spheres, we "start where we are." We do not, for example, begin with radical Cartesian doubt. Yes, we can feign radical doubt if we wish—and I do not rule out a priori the efficacy of doing so, as long as we are fully self-aware of what we are doing—but this isn't where we really start. We in fact start with puzzlement of some sort—in Deweyan terms, with a "problem situation"[8]—and go on from there to resolve it. This puzzlement has specificity; it is not puzzlement "in general." There is a situation confronting us, with a significant (although variable) degree of definiteness, which we feel the need to address. This is a mark of inquiry, as opposed to mere daydreaming or musing (not that the latter two cannot play a role in inquiry).

We can of course begin in puzzlement over myriad things, from the brutely practical where the press of imminent existential threat looms, to cogitations over the most subtle and recondite of matters. Moral inquiry manifests the full range of practical exigency—from extreme to all-but absent—yet unlike some areas of inquiry, in morality the more practical end of the continuum is frequently in evidence. This often presents itself as a matter of what to do about *this* issue, in *these* circumstances, *here and now*—not a theoretical matter in the sense of being at far remove from tangible effects. In this sphere of moral experience, I think it plain that the first-order predominates, not the second-order. We might put the point in other terms by noting that propositions like

> P22: I ought to defend my wife against this unprovoked violent physical attack,

have a kind of priority, not just practically, but epistemically and in a sense even metaethically, over propositions like

> P6: There are no first-order moral truths, nor are there any first-order moral falsehoods.

The practical priority is obvious: I ought, and I recognize that I ought, to defend my wife under these circumstances, no matter my metaethical sensibilities. Even the moral nihilist is going to come up with sort of justifying "ought"—perhaps a prudential ought, given that it would, say, make him feel better about himself, or better serve the (non-moral) interests of society, etc., were he to defend his wife than if he didn't.[9]

But it is the epistemic and metaethical priority which is our primary interest here. And in moral matters generally, for the most part the specific takes priority. *Epistemically*, because I am far more convinced that I know the truth of propositions such as that I ought to defend my wife against this violent attack (P22) and that I shouldn't be shot will writing my book (P7), than that I know the truth or the falsehood of propositions such as like

> P5: Moral judgments are true or false only relative to a specific society or culture.

I say this even though I have spent many pages in this very book arguing that P5 is false. The fact is I am about as sure of P22 and P7 as I can be, probably just as sure as you are that it is morally wrong for anyone to walk into *your* office and shoot *you* to death as you sit there writing *your* book. The epistemic priority of the first-order morality assets itself here. It is not, of course, an absolute priority. As we saw in chapter 5, §5.4, theory can trump intuitions, and the force of moral generalizations can lead to retraction of individual judgments. But the fact remains that there is often a kind of bedrock quality about particular moral judgment. Appreciating this is essential for a proper understanding of how moral knowing works.

*Metaethically*, the first-order asserts a kind of priority as well, in that it forms the foundation upon which a proper conception of the nature of morality is built. We begin with our ordinary, everyday moral discourse, and then—if we are curious or otherwise motivated—we examine the nature of that discourse, what underlies it, what gives it authority. Some have concuded that we are unable to make sense of that discourse on its own terms, that we are deceived as to its true nature: our "judgments" are really expressions of emotion, or reifications of moral sentiments, or commands issued to others and perhaps to ourselves. But wherever one comes down on metatheory, no one—or no one who is *thoughtful*—lightly dismisses commonsense morality. Hence, the often Herculean efforts to show that even though there may be no objective moral truth, morality's regulative purport can nevertheless be saved. Our view, stated and elaborated from chapter 1 onward, is that if a metaethical theory cannot accommodate the truth of the wrongness of certain things—such as walking in and shooting someone to death for the fun of it (P7)—*then so much the worse for the metatheory*.[10] For from a practical point of view, what is morality if it is incapable of speaking to the proper limits of *actual human conduct*? Or can speak to it only in the most anemic of ways? Morality at its core, after all, has to do with *praxis*. To conceive of morality otherwise is rather like formulating a conception of science, a metascientific theory, which renders the practice of science otiose. Very attractive.

But we overstate things a bit here; for our considered view, also with us since chapter 1, is that if our ordinary conception of morality truly cannot be defended—if our opponents really do get the better of us—then we may have no choice, on pain of irrationality, other than to relinquish our position. Let's now see how some of our opponent's fare.

## 6.3. MORAL SKEPTICISMS: NON-COGNITIVISM,
## NIHILISM, RELATIVISM, EVOLUTIONARY ETHICS

In chapter 1, §1.4, I offered the following admittedly non-standard interpretation of moral skepticism:

> Moral skepticism = *df*. Any conception of morality that systematically denies either (i) non-relative truth or falsity to first-order moral discourse on the grounds that there are no non-relative first-order moral facts; and/or (ii) that such moral truth and falsity is often known to us.

Some, perhaps many philosophers would reject this definition on the grounds that it is too broad, even question-begging. They prefer to reserve the term 'moral skepticism' for views that reject morality wholesale—moral nihilists and advocates of the stronger varieties of moral non-cognitivism, for example.[11] Many would certainly balk, for example, at saying sociocultural moral relativists are skeptics, because, so these folks say, moral relativists believe in morality, and believe that we can know "moral truths," it's just that they understand these things in different terms than do we in what I have been calling our "ordinary, tutored moral thinking." We will come back to relativism shortly, but let's begin with an examination of what most would agree is a version of—or perhaps better, a *category* of—moral skepticism.[12]

*Moral Non-Cognitivism:* Two paradigms of non-cognitivism—ones that we have already examined—are A. J. Ayer's[13] and C. L. Stevenson's[14] versions of emotivism. Although differing in detail, they agree that first-order moral locutions, which appear to morally assess actions, etc., are in fact not propositional; they express emotion. So take a locution such as,

> P24: Adam Lanza should not have shot those twenty children to death at the Sandy Hook Elementary School.

This does not express a moral truth or moral fact. In its primary sense it expresses a negative moral emotion when sincerely uttered or otherwise asserted. There may be legitimate implicit assertions of fact in such expressions—that it was Adam Lanza who shot the children to death; that the scene of the killings was Sandy Hook Elementary School—but what appears to be its main propositional gravamen, *the moral wrongness of Lanza's act*, is an illusion. Ayer thinks that we are fooled by grammar—the locution syntactically resembles an analytic or a synthetic proposition, the only kinds that there are, but in fact it is neither. Stevenson denies that moral avowals are descriptive, and that we are failing to recognize the centrality of emotion in such discourse ("This is wrong" means *I disapprove of this; do so as well*[15]): moral agreement/disagreement is non-cognitive.

Given our earlier remarks, I won't belabor exposition of Ayer's and Stevenson's views. But nothing could be clearer than that they are almost diametrically opposed to the realist theory propounded here. For we think that Lanza was *really and truly wrong*—that it is an objective moral *fact* that he was wrong—in shooting those children. Consider now what would follow if the emotivists are correct.

First, it is doubtful that *S* could coherently assert

P24: Adam Lanza should not have shot those twenty children to death at the Sandy Hook Elementary School,

unless *S*, at the time of the assertion, possessed a negative attitude toward the shootings. (Here, as always, I assume sincerity of assertion.) This means that *S* could not coherently say, "Look, I know that Lanza shouldn't have shot those kids, but frankly, I really don't care one way or the other." Of course we would be appalled by *S*'s remark, we may not comprehend what value-system could lead to this attitude, we may even question the psychological possibility of *S*'s feeling this way, but our normal thinking is that *it is at least coherent for* S *to say this*. But take a less provocative example: suppose *S* were to say, "I know that Smith should not have lied to Jones, but it's a quite trivial matter and I simply have no feeling about it one way or the other." Or what about, "I know that Smith should not have lied about Jones, but I don't like Jones, and I'm glad Smith lied about him"? Even if perhaps a bit out of the ordinary, all of this seems perfectly intelligible—the conditions of assertion perfectly coherent. Our point is that a propositional analysis of P24, such as we have offered, far better explains the coherence of the assertion conditions than either Ayer's or Stevenson's emotivism.

Take other forms of first-order moral discourse, which not infrequently assert subjunctive conditionals. Suppose *S* asserts, "*If* Smith *were to* lie to Jones, *then* Smith *would have* committed an immoral act." Surely this is intelligible. It looks perfectly propositional, whatever may be the complications involved in explicating the truth conditions of subjunctive conditionals involving moral facts.[16] Ayer's view falls flat: How are we to make any sense of it at all in terms of the expression of emotion? Remember, Ayer is not claiming that locutions like P24 are first-person psychological reports; such locutions would have truth-value. P24 is supposed to be an *expression* of emotion. Stevenson's version of emotivism does little better. But it seems strained, to put it mildly, to hold that *S* is actually expressing an emotion that S *would have* if Smith *were* to lie to Jones. For one thing, how does one express an emotion that is not yet realized? For another, if taken as a projection of what will be the case regarding *S*'s emotions, then this looks like a *proposition* regarding *S*'s probable future emotions. On our view, it is much more plausible to take this locution to be what it appears to be—a straightforward subjunctive conditional *proposition*.

Second, locutions like P24 would of course have no (moral) truth value, no (moral) cognitive import. Ayer spends a lot of time arguing that we are being fooled by grammar, and Stevenson that we miss the fundamental emotive import of moral locutions. But on our view, these explications of first-order morality are highly dubious. One reason is that it fails to account for the way moral discourse functions. For example, we engage in moral argumentation, and we hold that argumentation to essentially the same standards to which we hold other forms of argumentation—scientific argumentation, for example. Good moral argument has to be coherent, relevant, inferentially rigorous. Failure in any of these regards counts against it, just as it does in science or in other non-moral affairs. We level no such restrictions on expressions of emotion.[17]

Another reason for doubting emotivism is that on our normal perspective regarding the relation of emotion to fact in moral contexts, we are prepared to insist that, *no matter how I feel about the matter*, it either is or it is not the case that something is right or wrong, permissible or impermissible, etc.: Lanza was either wrong to have killed those children, or he wasn't, *period.* But one way or the other, feelings just don't have anything to do with it, even if feelings may be indicators, even reliable indicators in the case of some morally perceptive individuals, of the instantiation of (first-order) moral properties like wrongness and rightness. What we normally want is for our emotional stance to line up with the truth; but emotion doesn't *determine* truth. Put otherwise, truth, not emotion, has priority in the moral realm. And it hardly seems to beg the question to say that this is a conceptual fact about morality. We may even be tempted to suggest that any theory that misses this fundamental moral tenet is talking about a different subject—but that does, alas, look rather question-begging.

Which leads to a third consequence of emotivism: our normal moral assessments of human experience would be radically misplaced, because "there is no there, there," cognitively speaking. If taken seriously, the implications of this are profound: neither moral denunciation nor moral approval would have cognitive significance. Emotive significance qua expression thereof, yes, but the moral "ought" of rationality disappears. 'Don't discriminate on the basis of race or sex'; 'Refrain from sexual activity with small children'; 'The Nazis should not have killed millions of Jews in the concentration camps' become mere instantiations of the grammatical form, 'I don't like *X*, and I want you to share a similar emotional (i.e., non-propositional) attitude'. *How impressive.* I take it that the distinction between the degree of "wrongness" of a teenager's back-talking his parents and the Nazi's systematic murder of millions of Jews is to be cashed out in terms of the strength of one's negative emotion. That just can't be right. Again, Mary Midgley's question is apt: What do we *really* think about this? My answer is that no one could think this to be correct who is not in the grip of a theory.

One might respond to our arguments with a big, "so what?" You realists are simply privileging commonsense morality, and that is exactly what is being challenged. The emotivists' claim to fame is that they have been able to see through commonsense morality's conceptions: if it was easy, it would have been done eons ago, but it isn't. And the emotivist may go on to point out that broadly speaking, there is nothing new in this. Science does it all the time. Look at a bar of molybdenum-alloy steel. What distinguishes it from, say, a bar of nickel-alloy steel? The machinist will probably have something useful to tell us, but his remarks will only take us so far. For on his account, there is nothing to rule out a certain type of nickel-alloy steel having precisely the same machining qualities as a certain type of molybdenum steel. We have to go to the metallurgist for a real answer, and what she has to say is deeply grounded in the chemistry of steel compounds. And chemistry is deeply grounded in physics. And physics takes us all the way "down" to quantum physics, and all the "up" to General Relativity. Absolutely nobody thinks that quantum physics or General Relativity Theory is "commonsense," in anything like the usual sense of the term. But our best understanding of the physical world takes us in these two theoretical directions. The emotivists are simply doing the same thing with morality.

To which we say, fair enough—as far as it goes. But we realists do not for an instant think that "moral reality" is simple or commonsensical *at the metaethical level*. Anyone who has worked through chapters 2 and 3 of this book will surely agree with that. Our claim, rather, is that we are able to construct a plausible second-order conception of the nature of morality which supports the "simple" first-order conceptions of commonsense morality. The emotivist, on the other hand, constructs a second-order conception of morality which vitiates the cognitive thrust of ordinary moral discourse. The reader will have to decide which account is more compelling, ours or theirs.

There are of course many other versions of non-cognitivism. We have already (in chapter 4, §4.2) looked at two, the expressivism of Allan Gibbard, and R. M. Hare's prescriptivism. Expressivism being more like emotivism, let's take that first. Expressivists agree with emotivists that first-order moral locutions fundamentally serve to express non-cognitive moral attitudes. But unlike emotivists—certainly one's like Ayer—expressivists are concerned with the semantic relation of moral locutions to psychic states. Gibbard pursues this in his "norm-expressivism":[18] he seeks to construct a systematic semantics relating rationality and moral sentiments. Perhaps we feel, for example, guilt or resentment, but that doesn't mean that we have come to a moral judgment: we may simply be experiencing an emotion. Such sentiments, however, exert a regulative influence on our lives, and sometimes it is important to consider whether they are defensible. Here rational judgment enters the picture: "[t]o call something rational is to express one's acceptance of norms that permit it."[19] Gibbard's project is to work out a detailed analysis of how such moral discourse links up with the acceptance of norms which license acceptable use of moral terms. What is central for us here is that on Gibbard's view, what is primary in moral discourse is the expression of moral sentiments, *not* assertion of moral facts.

Well, this is better than emotivism, but on our view still misses the central point of first-order moral discourse. For expressivism is nevertheless a version of non-cognitivism; it denies the moral fact-stating role of locutions like these two:

> P1: Chattel slavery, such as was practiced in the southern states of the United States prior to the American Civil War, is morally wrong.
> P2: It is prima facie morally praiseworthy to return kindness with kindness.

Whatever our psychological states vis-à-vis these propositions—that is, however they may or may not link up with norms we accept which license use of terms like 'wrong' and 'praiseworthy'—none of this is to the point regarding what we believe to be the primary function of moral discourse. For as we see it, expression of emotion, although often accompanying assertion of moral propositions like P1 and P2, is strictly speaking *additive*—a possible, but not necessary, feature of the assertorial event.

Prescriptivists see first-order moral locutions as fundamentally imperatives. R. M. Hare,[20] the theory's most noted proponent, takes these imperatives to enjoin universality—hence his "universal prescriptivism"—so, 'Don't do *X*' is not a merely self-regarding command; it is intended to apply to all who are relevantly situated. However, the prescriptive force of locutions like P1 and P2 is not cognitive—not amenable to being classified as truth-bearers. And so first-order moral discourse of the sort in question (viz., Class A propositions) is not in any primary sense fact-stating.

Like expressivism, prescriptivism looks like a more plausible theory than the emotivism of Ayer and Stevenson: much first-order moral discourse is indeed intended to have prescriptive force, and is indeed intended to entail universal implications. So when I assert,

> P7: It is morally wrong for anyone to walk into my office and shoot me to death as I sit here writing this book,

I mean to imply (i) Don't shoot me, and (ii) *Nobody* should shoot me; and I regard both (i) and (ii) as having prescriptive force against any would-be assassin. Note, however, that both (i) and (ii) may be regarded as entailments of the *cognitive meaning* of P7; for if it is wrong to shoot me, then (ceteris paribus) you should not shoot me—that's just what "being wrong" means in this propositional context—and if it is wrong for anybody to shoot me, then *nobody* should shoot me, which is universal in scope. All of this, however, is straightforwardly cognitive. And so the gravamen of our claim against Hare is that his theory, as compelling as it is in some respects, nevertheless misses the central point of first-order moral discourse, namely, its cognitive import. We therefore classify it, along with the other versions of non-cognitivism, as "skeptical" vis-à-vis our ordinary conception of morality.

*Moral Nihilism*: Another form of moral skepticism; they deny that there is any such thing as morality—at least "morality" in the sense that we typically think of it, certainly in the sense in which there is moral truth and falsity. Nietzsche, for example, famously tells us that when it comes to ethics, "it is a swindle to talk of 'truth' in this field."[21] Given our previous discussion (chapter 1, §1.4 and chapter 4, §4.5), it will be convenient to stick with J. L. Mackie[22] as our exemplar nihilist; for all versions fundamentally assert the same thesis: *there is no such thing as morality because there are no such things as "real" moral properties.* Were there any such properties, says Mackie, they would be metaphysically "queer," unlike properties of other sorts to which we have clear epistemic access—physical properties, for example. We can see and feel, and we can employ observational instrumentation to detect features of the physical world. But there is nothing epistemically analogous when it comes to detecting "moral properties."

Mackie's argument is of the following form: we move from epistemological premises to a metaphysical conclusion. And we can agree that there is prima facie merit in arguments of this type. After all, the root of belief is, as Dewey and Peirce and the other great pragmatists have emphasized, *experience*. Why believe that *p*? Because the belief that *p*, and not the belief that not-*p*, better serves experience in any of a variety of ways. And so we believe that fire is hot because to believe that, and not to believe that fire isn't hot, better serves the broad experiential flow of our lives. Mackie is surely right that in general, a good reason for believing that *X* exists and that *Y* does not, is that we have epistemic support—evidence—for *X* but do not for *Y*. And Mackie is obviously right that we can be fooled. Some people, for example, still believe in ghosts, but we may assume ex hypothesi that something is wrong with that thinking: the evidence has been misunderstood, or bad inferences drawn, or something has been missed. We are in error to believe in ghosts. But on Mackie's view, first-order moral theory is rather like "ghost theory": there just aren't any ghosts, so theorizing about ghosts per se, as opposed to theorizing about our beliefs about ghosts, or about ghosts in English literature or what have you, is misplaced. Just as there are no "ghost properties," there are no moral properties: there is no moral right and wrong.

So as we see it, although Mackie starts out in a proper way—appealing to epistemic considerations to inform his metaphysics—we think that he ends up in the wrong place, in moral skepticism. Specifically, on our view couching the rejection of moral properties on their putative "metaphysical queerness" because they do not comply with the *paradigm of observational properties*, looks very dubious. For as we saw in chapter 2, §2.6 and chapter 3, §3.4 and 3.5, one has a very hard job making the case that all properties are physical properties, if by that one means properties sanctioned by the empirical sciences. After all, contemporary physics—the ne plus ultra of the natural sciences, the science to which some think all natural sciences are reducible, the science that seems to be the final word on the nature of physical reality— cannot do without mathematics. Yet the problems of explaining mathematics in terms of physical cum-observational properties appear overwhelming. So mathematical (i.e., numerical, etc.) properties would seem to be, in Mackian terms, "queer."

Consider, too, that physical states of affairs surely instance more than merely physical properties.[23] Take three apples placed on a chair in a room. Here we have a physical state of affairs which manifests the cardinality of the apples in the room, namely, *three*. However, unlike the properties of "chairhood" and "roomhood" and "applehood," which we may take to be physical properties, and which we may take to be observable in the sense of relying upon observation to confirm or disconfirm their instantiation, we do *not* take the property of the cardinality of the apples to be a physical property. That is a numerical property instantiated by this physical state of affairs. But this property doesn't seem "queer" at all. The mind is perfectly capable of grasping its presence.[24] And we would say the same about *uninstantiated* numerical properties, such as the cardinality of the square of the number of atoms in the universe. We can discuss whether it is a prime number, what its cube root is, etc. Nothing "queer" here. Nor need we be concerned about worries over the causal efficacy of such properties, insofar as "causal" is understood to mean "causal efficacy as manifested in the physical world." For we can, for instance, meaningfully discuss uninstanti*able* properties such as "being a round-square." Again, nothing "queer" in any of this.

The burden of chapter 3 was to argue much the same sort of thing in the case of first-order moral facts, states of affairs, and properties. On our view, the first-order moral supervenes on the physical. Moral properties are not physical properties, not in the same way as are observable properties such a length, color, hardness, etc. This certainly does not mean, however, that they are unknowable. Our challenge to Mackie and other moral nihilists is to show us where our analysis has gone wrong.

Another serious problem for moral nihilism from our point of view, is its overwhelming counterintuitiveness. The proposition 'Coercive sexual intercourse is morally wrong', certainly seems to convey something different in kind from the proposition 'Coercive sexual intercourse is not economically prudent' (or 'sub-optimal' or 'not our custom'). And it certainly seems to convey something far more than a report on our own psychic stance, for example, 'I don't like coercive sexual intercourse', or 'Coercive sexual intercourse isn't cool'. On the contrary, we are wont to say, "Either coercive sexual intercourse is wrong or it is not wrong, perfectly independent of how I feel about it, and perfectly independent of whether it is profit maximizing." But if nihilism is correct, we could rightly say neither of these things—with the result that moral argument per se is rendered nugatory. We would be engaged in arguing over "ghost theory."

We need to think carefully about this. If the moral nihilist is to be taken seriously, moral indignation is groundless: civil rights protesters need to be informed of their misplaced outrage. Moral edification is also groundless: parents and the clergy need to be enlightened on the errors of their ways. You are morally outraged because your child was abused? Very well, you don't like it, and you may understandably be worried about the implications of this abuse for your child's happiness and future emotional stability, but don't attach *moral significance* to what happened. [25] We wish to fire the troops to steadfastness in the face of battle? Fine, but on pain of irrationality, focus on the *practical gains* to be enjoyed, not on the moral righteousness of our cause, our moral duty to our countrymen, our moral obligation to ensure a prosperous future for our children. It is, alas, hard to see how any sensible person could welcome any of this.

In the final analysis, however, successfully rebutting moral nihilism on its own terms requires success in showing that commonsense notions of (first-order) morality do not suffer from presupposition failure, which is to say, requires providing a compelling case that there are moral properties. The nihilist thinks there are none, we have argued that there are: our case rests there. The reader will have to decide for herself which case is more compelling.

*Moral Relativism*: We have already discussed three representative versions of moral relativism in chapter 4, §4.3: sociocultural moral relativism, Gilbert Harman's "implicit agreement" relativism, and conceptual moral relativism. All three comply with the Relativist Evaluation Scheme:

> RES: $x$ (act, policy, judgment, etc.) is morally $y$ (right, wrong, permissible, etc.) relative to $z$.

And all three are, on our view, "skeptical" because they deny that there are any instances of propositions such as

> P1: Chattel slavery, such as was practiced in the southern states of the United States prior to the American Civil War, is morally wrong;

or

> P2: It is prima facie morally praiseworthy to return kindness with kindness,

which are true simpliciter. All are only "true/false relative to ____," and here one fills in the missing variable, according to the version of relativism at issue. All of them, therefore, see first-order moral propositions like these as about something ultimately other than sui generis moral fact.

Think about the implications of this. On the sociocultural relativist model, if predominating sociocultural moral belief is that chattel slavery is morally permissible, then chattel slavery *is* morally permissible. At least morally permissible within the parameters of the applicable sociocultural belief governance, however that is to be determined. And it is not easily determined. What falls under the "morality-determining belief jurisdiction of society *X*," and what does not? What conditions must be fulfilled for an individual to qualify as a member of a society? What if some members of society *X* are also members of society *Y*, but *X*'s moral values are relevantly different than *Y*'s—how then to judge these individuals' actions? What counts as "a society's moral beliefs"? Unanimity? A super-majority? A mere majority?[26]

These are only a few of the well-known problems confronting sociocultural moral relativism: providing *principled* answers is difficult. But suppose they are answered satisfactorily. The fact remains that *if* the society sees chattel slavery as permissible, then it *is* permissible.[27] From our point of view, that is very worrisome. It is worrisome to thoughtful relativists, too. Hence, their efforts to respond to cases like this by pointing out, often quite correctly, that societies/cultures have internal resources—for example, commitment to social equality, human dignity, etc.—adequate to reject such unpalatable consequences. *But none of this is to the point.* The question is, what if the society/culture *did not* have these resources? What if the society in fact endorsed chattel slavery? *What then?* I am not asking a practical question here; I am asking a theoretical question—a question about what moral relativism qua-metaethical theory entails. The relativist can't simply brush such counterfactuals aside and insist that de facto societies have such resources (I very much doubt that some do): the question is how to answer de jure. And as far as I can see, under the conditions of description posed, the relativist is committed to the permissibility of chattel slavery.

As we saw in our earlier discussions of relativism, from the realist's perspective the relativist's central problem is that it runs epistemology together with metaphysics (as is typical of antirealisms). Sociocultural (moral) belief that action *A* is permissible (wrong, etc.) *makes it the case* that *A* is right; implicit moral agreement between parties that *A* is permissible *makes it the case* that *A* is permissible; operative concepts endorsing *A*'s rightness *makes it the case* that *A* is right. The realist thinks that all of this is just wrong: truth and reality are one thing, our epistemic posture is another.

From the realist perspective, this is the central sin of *pragmatism* as well (chapter 4, §4.5): it epistemizes truth by interpreting truth in terms of human activity and interests. That is why we classified it as another form of relativism, and schematized it thus:

> RES$_p$: $x$ (act, policy, judgment, etc.) is morally $y$ (right, wrong, permissible, etc.) relative to the results of inquiry $i$.

No doubt *what* we inquire into and *how* we do so is a function of human interests, purposes, capacities, etc. So much the realist can readily admit. Where the realist jumps ship is when one tries to substitute epistemology for metaphysics. And that is exactly what pragmatism does: truth, which is on our view a metaphysical concept, becomes in the hands of pragmatism an epistemological concept. *Moral* truth, therefore, becomes a function of human purposes and capacities—a matter of the results of epistemic effort. As we have been at pains to argue throughout this book, however, this is a mistake. On our view—on the *commonsense* view—no matter our purposes, no matter our interests or investigative capacities or what have you, some actions are right and others wrong, period. Even in the "indefinitely long run," finite intellects may not get it right—may ever be in error, however unlikely. But further, even if we were dealing with an infinite intellect which never "gets it wrong," truth is conceptually distinct from belief and inquiry. What the finite intellect has over the rest of us is *the capacity to always hit the alethic target*. The infinite intellect, however, does not *determine* the target.[28] Fundamentally, that is where the pragmatist goes wrong, in morality as in other domains of truth.

In chapter 4, §4.3., we also classified radical *moral subjectivism* as a kind of moral relativism, and it will be convenient to do so here as well. For subjectivism holds that moral truth is relative to the dictates of a moral subject: if $S$ declares action $A$ morally wrong, it is. We create moral value and truth by fiat. Like other forms of relativism—sociocultural relativism perhaps most obviously—it collapses the distinction between believing that $p$ is true and $p$'s actually being true, a distinction fundamental to our ordinary thinking about morality. For the subjectivist, then, it would appear that a proposition like

> P8: It is always morally permissible for adults to have coercive sexual intercourse with young children,

is true for $R$ if $R$ says it is, and false for $S$ if $S$ says it is. This is a curious result indeed, if P8 is taken to express the same proposition for both $R$ and $S$; for it would violate the Law of Non-contradiction, according to which, not both $p$ and not-$p$. And as I indicated in effect in chapter 5, §5.2, the Law of Non-contradiction seems a fundamental presupposition of rationality. But perhaps P8 does not express the same proposition for both $R$ and $S$. What then, does it express? Perhaps 'It is *true* that it is always morally permissible for adults to have coercive sexual intercourse with young children *for R*' in one case, and 'It is *false* that it is always morally permissible for adults to have coercive sexual intercourse with young children *for S*' in the other case. Well perhaps . . . but that is not how the proposition is typically interpreted. So it appears that the radical moral subjectivist faces a dilemma: Either (i) moral propositions are such that the very same proposition can simultaneously be true and false, or (ii) moral propositions are unique to each subject's assertorial instantiation, that is, a different proposition is asserted on each occasion of assertion. According to (i), the Law of Non-contradiction is abandoned, with commensurate forfeiture of rationality; and according to (ii), new meaning is created on each occasion of assertion, resulting in it never being the case that the same proposition is asserted on different occasions. But (ii) seems dubious, because it certainly appears to be the case that the inscription 'It is always morally permissible for adults to have coercive sexual intercourse with young children' can express the very same proposition no matter who asserts it. The conditions of understanding are identical, the conditions of communication are the same, the conditions of assessment are the same. In short, it appears to be the very same proposition.[29] Neither horn of the dilemma seems attractive.[30]

Moreover, when subjectivism collapses the distinction between believing that *p* is true and *p*'s being true, the very possibility of error is eliminated. But this seems highly implausible. It certainly isn't how moral discourse typically works. A central point of moral (and other) argumentation is standardly taken to be the avoidance of error. It is an important ground upon which we judge one moral argument superior to another.[31] But all of this is rendered nugatory if subjectivism is correct. Note, too, that other forms of relativism get caught up in the same problem. Sociocultural relativism, for example, must face the consequence that as regards intracultural valuational argument, one argument is better than another either in terms of the greater valuational coherence it preserves, or in terms of the preservation of nonmoral truth which in turn bears on valuational matters. But for the relativist as for the subjectivist, to *be* a value is to *be believed to be* a value; so the efficacy of moral argumentation is problematic.

In any event, our common moral thinking, which seems overwhelming cogent, is that we *can* make moral mistakes, and that in fact we *do* make moral mistakes. Hence, our concern to make "moral progress," which for the subjectivist seems strictly unintelligible, and for other forms of relativism to be cashed out in terms of valuational coherence, or adoption of similar conceptual schemes, or ubiquity of implicit agreement (Harman), or some such thing. Moral progress in terms of "getting closer to truth" is on their view a will-'o-the-wisp. That is why we term them moral skeptics. Again, the reader will have to judge for herself who is on firmer ground, us or them.

*Evolutionary Ethics*: Broadly put, this is the view that moral value is the product of evolutionary processes.[32] In the context of our discussion, we can take this to mean that any proposition of the form, '*X* is morally good (right, permissible, praiseworthy)' is to be understood as asserting that *X* is evolutionarily beneficial, while any proposition of the form, '*X* is morally bad (wrong, impermissible, condemnatory)' is to be understood as asserting that *X* is evolutionarily detrimental. Now what 'evolutionarily beneficial' and 'evolutionarily detrimental' mean is going to vary in detail from one account to another, but most fundamentally, these concepts seem to be explicated in terms of conducing to, or failing to conduce to, an individual's passing on his or her genes to subsequent generations. So '*X* is morally good (etc.)' means that *X* is beneficial (or tends to be beneficial) for passing on one's genes, and '*X* is morally bad (etc.)' means that *X* is detrimental to passing on one's genes. Exponents of evolutionary ethics then typically go on to explain how particular moral values, as embedded in particular sociocultural/environmental milieus, either are or are not evolutionarily beneficial, and therefore either good or bad, right or wrong, or what have you. How convincing these accounts are, for those inclined in principle to views of this type in the first place, will depend on how well they explain the moral dimension of human experience. And I think we can virtually all agree that evolution surely has had a bearing on our moral valuations—on our propensity to value human life, on our valuational averseness to pain, on our pro tanto disposition to value cooperative behavior, etc. That said, however, *if our account of moral properties is correct, any view of this sort must be fundamentally wrong.* For all versions of evolutionary ethics are fundamentally physicalist. That is to say, evolutionary ethics holds that "moral properties," insofar as it is legitimate to speak of them at all, are actually properties of the physical (i.e., "natural") world—properties like "conductivity-to-passing-on-genes," or some such thing. Thus, moral properties are of the same general ontic type as properties such as "physical health" or "proper physiological function" or "aggressiveness." Properties of this type are all describable in physical terms; they all may be empirically identified and measured. But if our analysis in chapters 2 and 3 is correct, moral properties are not physical cum-natural properties: moral properties *supervene* on physical properties, and are insofar sui generis. So if we are right, the evolutionary folks can't be. That is why we call them moral skeptics.

Note, too, how widely the implications of evolutionary ethics diverge from our ordinary moral thinking. Suppose, for example, that it could be established that coercive sexual intercourse with women, that is, the *rape* of women, is, when embedded in such and such a sociocultural/environmental milieu, conducive to passing on one's genes. Do we therefore think that rape thus embedded is right, good, justified? Do we even think it prima facie right, etc.? I think it is clear we do not, evolutionary benefits notwithstanding. On the contrary, we condemn it in terms of its violation of human dignity, or production of suffering, or abrogation of personal autonomy, or something of this ilk. Instead, we counsel respect and self-control—and passing on your genes by securing the willing consent of an appropriate sexual partner. Were we to envision an extreme case (philosophers' forte!) where the very survival of the species was at stake if one's genes were not passed on, the values of respect, autonomy, and bodily integrity—which may or may not be values beneficial to passing on one's genes—would retain their prima facie importance, only to be overridden, *if* they are overridden, by extreme exigency. Simple "conduciveness to passing on one's genes" is not enough, even if deemed relevant. In fact, evolutionary ethics, couched in the terms employed here, looks a lot like a version of naturalistic utilitarianism. One then wonders how compelling such a version of utilitarianism really is—whether a better version is not available—even granting that moral values are properly explicated in terms of physical properties. But if our views on moral properties in chapter 3 are correct, all of this is of course wrong. As we see it, evolutionary ethics' rejection of commonsense morality renders it another version of moral skepticism.

## 6.4. MORAL REALISM

Drawing on earlier chapters, I now want to sketch in summary form a realist conception of morality which not only comports with how we normally see things, morally speaking, but which provides a cogent theoretical underpinning of commonsense moral thought. Moral realism is an important alternative to the metaethical theories discussed and rejected in the previous section. It contrasts perhaps most strongly with moral non-cognitivism, especially in its starker forms such as emotivism, in that realism is staunchly cognitivist: moral locutions are propositional, hence true-bearers. Perhaps next in line is moral nihilism, which although cognitivist, holds that there is no such thing as "morality." First-order moral propositions ascribing rightness and wrongness, and so forth, are false due to presupposition failure. Closer to moral realism, although still incompatible with it, are the various relativisms (including subjectivism). Moral truth for them is epistemic, not metaphysical, as it is for moral realism. Evolutionary ethics, although also cognitivist, construes morality in physical-property terms, not in terms of sui generis moral properties. In short, all of these views contrast with our version of moral realism, which sees morality as cognitivist, non-relative, and non-subjective. Moral values are *objective,* not constructed. Let's see how our realism meets each of these criteria.

It will again be convenient to use a concrete example. Let's take this one[33]—one which harkens back to the very beginning of our study:

P25: It was morally wrong for Adam Lanza to have shot those twenty children
to death at Sandy Hook Elementary School in December 2012.

I assume that P25 is adequately clear for comprehension; and as before, I
assume that we are referring here to a perpetrator who possessed minimal
moral agency. Given these assumptions, P25's plausibility is as uncontroversial as any I can readily think of. If anyone wishes to defend Lanza's actions
*in the context of the situation as we so far know it to be*, then have at it. I
confess that I cannot imagine what such a defense might be without leaving,
as Wilfrid Sellars might put it, "the logical space of reasons."[34]

Now I am not out to provide a full semantic analysis of P25, but to
explicate it in terms endorsed by our version of moral realism. The first thing
to notice, then, is that, as per chapter 2, P25 is *propositional*, hence either
true or false (assuming the Law of Excluded Middle, viz., either $p$ or not-
$p$[35]). Let's assume it is true. On the version of alethic realism we have
developed, P25 is true if and only if it satisfies the T-schema, viz., "the
proposition that $p$ is true *iff $p$*" (§2.2). This means that the proposition 'It was
morally wrong for Adam Lanza to have shot those twenty children to death at
Sandy Hook Elementary School in December 2012' is true if and only if it
was morally wrong for Adam Lanza to have shot those twenty children to
death at Sandy Hook Elementary School in December 2012. This is a realist
interpretation of the proposition because what makes it wrong for Lanza to
have shot those children is that *this is the way the world is, morally speaking*.

In §2.3–2.5, we further developed our conception of first-order moral
truth to say that for a proposition to be true is for it to express a moral fact,
which we understand to be a state of affairs that obtains. Thus, P25's being
true means that it expresses the *moral fact* that it was morally wrong for
Lanza to have shot those children in December 2012. If P25 is false, then it
fails to express this fact. So according to our view, when we assert a moral
proposition to be true, we are asserting that it expresses a moral fact—the
"moral fact of the matter"—in roughly parallel fashion to what we are doing
when we assert the proposition 'The house is painted green': we take it to
express a fact about the color of house's paint, namely, that it is green. If we
are incorrect about the house's paint color, we failed to state the relevant fact
(we got the facts wrong; we asserted a false proposition).

We went on to say (§2.6) that these first-order moral facts—first-order
moral states of affairs that obtain—supervene on physical facts (physical
states of affairs that obtain), and are therefore irreducible to physical facts.
Moral facts are sui generis. So the moral wrongness that P25 expresses is
inextricably linked, although irreducible to, physical states of affairs. Were
there a different physical state of affairs involved, different (types of) moral
facts may well have obtained—assuming that *any* moral facts obtained, for
not all physical states of affairs produce moral states of affairs.

In order for there to be first-order moral facts in our sense of the term, such as the wrongness of Lanza's killing the school children, there must of course be moral properties. Chapter 3 made the case that there are indeed such properties. We understand moral properties to supervene on physical properties (or more strictly, that *instantiated* moral properties supervene on *instantiated* physical properties, which serve as their base): were there no physical properties, there would be no moral properties. And only certain types of physical states of affairs, characterized by a specific (albeit very broad) range of physical properties, ordered in a specific (albeit very broad) range of ways, have the possibility of supporting moral properties. The physical state of affairs of one rock falling upon another rock has no potential to produce moral properties, while the physical state of affairs of one normal human being striking another does.

We further understood properties in general to be platonic universals which are instantiated, *if* they are instantiated, by particulars (e.g., objects or persons or acts) in the case of first-order properties, or by other properties in the case of second-order properties. First-order moral properties were our main focus; and on our analysis of the moral wrongness of the Lanza killings, Lanza' actions were an instantiation of a platonic universal—the platonic universal "moral wrongness." Thus, if doing what Lanza did was morally wrong, it was "really" morally wrong: his act was an actual instantiation of the real property of moral wrongness. There is no matter here of wrongness being "in the eye of the beholder," whether individual or communal. And it is not a matter of how we "feel" about the act, our psychic stance or propositional attitude. It is a matter of *real and genuine fact*, owing to the presence of instantiated moral properties.

Moral realism is a metaphysical thesis, not an epistemological thesis. This is characteristic of any form of realism, applied to any subject matter whatever. Alethic realism, that is, realism regarding truth, sees truth as a matter of the way the world is. Ontic realism, that is, realism regarding entities, sees metaphysical status as a mind-independent. On our view, alethic realism is grounded in ontic realism, because metaphysical (ontic) reality determines truth. Realism keeps metaphysics and epistemology separate, in contrast to antirealisms like sociocultural moral relativism: beliefs do not construct the moral world; moral truth and moral fact are what they are independent of our doxastic stance.[36] This means that there is a gap between reality and our perception of it—and therein the skeptic gets a toe-hold. But moral realism, as we conceive it, is not a theory of moral knowledge; it is a theory having to do with the nature of the possible *objects* of moral knowledge. The attractiveness of moral realism would be gravely diminished, however, if it lands us in skepticism. We think it does not.

Quite the contrary: our study has been staunchly antiskeptical. We think that there certainly is moral knowledge—a lot of it, in fact; and among other things, we are convinced that we know that Lanza shouldn't have killed those children. In chapter 4 we spent quite a bit of time getting clear not only on what alternative theories to moral realism have to say about the nature and possibility of moral knowledge, but also in explaining our realist epistemological views. In brief, we take moral knowledge to be fundamentally propositional, that is, knowing *that* something is the case, and that like other propositional knowledge, moral knowledge is (roughly) justified, true belief—that is, $S$ knows that $p$ if and only if (see chapter 4, §4.1):

(i) $S$ believes that $p$
(ii) $p$ is true
(iii) $S$ is justified in believing that $p$
(iv) $S$'s justification for believing that $p$ does not include relevant falsehood

Some moral propositions may be known only a posterori, but the truth of others—like P25, for example—seem to be knowable simply by understanding them, even though they aren't analytically true. In other words, for us, P25's truth, as with many other first-order moral propositions, is self-evident. It is a synthetic a priori moral proposition.[37]

However, we can of course make mistakes. This is an apparent consequence of realism—the gap between belief/evidence and truth—and one that we, as avowed fallibilists (chapter 5, §5.2), are able to embrace without worries about lapsing into skepticism. For knowing does not require certitude, in any sense of the term. Nevertheless, we hold that we have reason to be very confident of some moral claims—claims such as that Lanza was wrong to have shot those children. Moral intuition is one source of moral belief which may be very secure (chapter 5, §5.3), and one which serves a variety of important epistemic roles. For one, intuition's non-inferentiality serves to stop a vicious infinite regress of justification; for another, intuitions serve as an important check on, and foundation of, moral theory. But moral theory, too, is important (chapter 5, §5.4): intuition cannot do all the work, especially in situations of moral complexity where competing moral considerations are present. What we endorse is a kind of symbiosis between intuition and theory, each reinforcing and correcting the other, resulting in a *reflective equilibrium* where all relevant considerations—including the informed moral testimony of others—are brought into balance. That is the ideal, if only rarely achieved, condition of moral belief.

And so when we claim to know that Adam Lanza was wrong to kill those children (P25), we perceive ourselves to be making a knowledge claim broadly similar to other kinds of propositional knowledge: that Mont Blanc has snow on its summit, that Washington was the first president of the United States, that 3 is a prime number. These claims are not merely about matters of personal perspective, they are about matters of objective fact. That's how the moral realist sees morality.

## 6.5. WHY OUR ORDINARY MORAL THINKING IS FUNDAMENTALLY CORRECT

As we have repeatedly emphasized, our ordinary thinking is that some things are really right and others really wrong, some things really good, and others really bad, etc.—the term 'really' here being used in its metaphysical sense, not as an intensifier. The moral realist certainly thinks that this is correct—that ordinary moral thinking has fundamentally got the nature of morality right. Throughout this study we have made frequent appeal to the power of ordinary moral judgment. Admittedly, and quite properly, most of these appeals have been to paradigm cases of moral agreement—cases in which opinion among informed parties is and has been relatively settled for a substantial time. For by examining such cases, we are able to understand a lot about how morality operates, about its nature and status. And of course there is in fact a great deal of agreement—again, among informed parties—about much of moral life. Many reasons can be adduced for this—sociological, psychological, political, historical, et al.—but as important as these factors surely are, I suggest that another is, as with scientific and prudential affairs, that *we are often able to grasp moral truth.* Can we really imagine, in any robust and plausible way,[38] reversing the general contours of contemporary informed opinion about slavery, about coercive sexuality or racial discrimination or unprovoked brutality? *Of course* not everyone believes, much less abides by these judgments: prisons are full of violators; benighted parts of the world remain wracked by sectarian and religious hatreds seemingly impervious to reason or resolution. But the reader needs to ask herself seriously what she considers to be the moral status of transgressions such as those just mentioned—transgressions which would occasion the most strident cries of injustice and indefensibility were they visited upon her. I am asking a Moorean question here: *there is much room for sophistication and subtlety in philosophy, but none for hypocrisy.*

Our ordinary moral thinking, as endorsed and given theoretical backing by moral realism, best accounts for the confidence and durability that many of our first-order moral views enjoy. This book has been a sustained effort to provide such theoretical backing. The existence of moral facts, such as we have been at pains to develop and defend, not only grounds the evident propositionality of moral discourse, but sanctions the legitimacy of moral argumentation and the standards of truth-conductivity to which it is standardly held. The theoretical and practical advantages of this are incalculable.

But if our ordinary, tutored moral thinking, backed by moral realism, is that some things are really right and others wrong, and that we often know these things to be right or wrong, our ordinary thinking concedes that we are nevertheless liable to error. Moral realism is of course perfectly compatible with this. This is in fact exactly what we would expect if truth is independent of belief: finite intellect, the lot of mankind, can sometimes lead us astray. Yet our commonsense thinking is that, just as with non-moral matters, precautions may be taken to improve our chances of obtaining truth. Moral realism again agrees. Rigor of argument, appreciation of relevant non-moral fact, fairness in assessing evidence—these and similar rational desiderata are just as relevant in the moral sphere as in the non-moral. Not so from the perspective of the non-cognitivist or the nihilist. Even the relativist sits uncomfortably with all of this; for radical external critique, if not totally out of place, is at the very least difficult to accommodate in principle.

A word more about moral realism and moral relativism: one well-known reason why many adopt relativism over realism, and eschew commonsense realist morality, is that relativism purportedly provides a better hedge against the evils of arrogance, intolerance, even violence. Who are we to judge, they ask, when he have so often run amok? Better to admit that all moral judgment is perspectival, a product of time and place, and to remember that what appears odious to you may appear otherwise to those who come from different circumstances. Epistemic humility is much the better path. You live as you deem proper, we shall do the same. To which we realists reply that these sentiments are not without wisdom, and are in many essentials perfectly compatible with our view. As fallibilists, we certainly recognize the possibility of error, and recognize the importance of keeping this recognition front and center while deliberating over acts and policies. Indeed, the realist need have nothing to do with an intolerant absolutism. We are perfectly prepared to allow the relevance of situational detail: what may be wrong in one situation may not in another (as the boxer well understands when he is in the ring versus on the street). But I suggest that moral realism in fact provides a more secure bulwark against abuse than does relativism per se, because there is nothing to guarantee that the operative moral norms prohibit the very things feared. What if the society is intolerant, bigoted, and violent? What if its values endorse, rather than prohibit, imposing its views on other societies? On metaethical relativist principles themselves, external critique is inherently problematic, as noted above, if not otiose. Not for the realist. For the realist may always appeal to the concept of socioculturally transcendent truth, which may serve as a guide for us all. The power of this conception of morality is not to be underestimated, as many advocates of international human rights well recognize.

Epistemic humility, tolerance, fair-mindedness, and other deliberative virtues being as important as they are, morality nevertheless has an ineluctably practical dimension, and therefore must address the need for principled *action*. Commonsense moral thinking fully recognizes this, and moral realism again provides theoretical backing. There is moral truth to be had, and in many cases we are warranted in having great confidence that we possess it. In fact, ordinary thinking counsels the propriety, indeed the necessity for reasoned, defensible resolve in certain situations. Occasions arise when hesitation is a vice, when clarity of judgment condemns to the wastebin of mere "paper doubts"[39] any supposed reservations about action. It is easy to become impatient with the endless fretting and evasions indulged in by those safely ensconced in their armchairs. Not that detached reflection doesn't have its place: we have engaged in many pages of it here! But if one's moral studies lead to the conclusion that morality itself is inherently suspect, that it is unable to muster the conceptual resources requisite to legitimate its raison d'etre, viz., the rational direction and assessment of *human action,* well . . . that is certainly not a happy state of affairs. Our ordinary moral thinking does not accept this, and neither does moral realism.

This book began (chapter 1, §1.1) with an admiring appeal to G. E. Moore's robust respect for common sense. I do not wish to take things quite so far as Moore may have taken them—certainly not so far as some of Moore's critics think he took them[40] —but when it comes to morality—a subject that connects profoundly with our individual and social existence, and with our incliminable need for action—Moore's broad commonsense perspective seems quite right: our ordinary, tutored moral stance deserves a serious attitude of respect. Not an indefeasible respect, but a respect to be relinquished only if shown to be untenable. This book has offered a defense, on metaethical and epistemological grounds, that commonsense morality is actually worthy of that respect.

Adam Lanza really shouldn't have murdered those twenty children at Sandy Hook Elementary School. And that's a *fact*.

## NOTES

1. On the assumption that Lanza possessed moral agency at the time of the killings.

2. Again, as pointed out in chapter 1, §1.5, what I mean here by "ordinary, tutored moral thinking" is the sort of thought that intelligent, informed people, who come from any of a vast array of sociocultural backgrounds, typically have regarding first-order moral matters.

3. The term 'practical' in ethics often connotes action. I use the term more broadly here to refer to matters having to do with *judging* actions, etc., even if not directly entailing overt action. The point is that one may know a lot of abstruse theory, but know little of what to do in practical situations—the typical trope contrasting the cloistered scholar, ill-suited to making practical decisions in life, with the proverbial "man of action."

4. See Alasdair MacIntyre, *After Virtue: A Study in Moral Theory* (Notre Dame, IN: University of Notre Dame Press, 1981); and "Is Patriotism a Virtue?" The Lindley Lecture, University of Kansas, 1984, excerpted in *Morality and Moral Controversies*, 9th ed., edited by Steven Scalet and John Arthur (New York: Pearson, 2014), 405–10.

5. To the extent, however, that MacIntyre's view is a version of moral relativism—*and it is*—we are of course worried about it from the point of view of this study.

6. Probably not "normative theory" as per the Bible or the Koran either, although admittedly in communities heavily influenced by religious tradition, normative systems in the form of authoritative texts, suitably mediated by parents and religious teachers, almost certainly play an early and profound role on value formation.

7. And some of us never get very far in the converse—again, the contrast between the theoretically adept and the practically inept.

8. Dewey discusses this in many places, among others, *How We Think*, in *John Dewey: The Middle Works, 1899–1924*, Volume 6, 1910–1911, edited by Jo Ann Boydston and Bridget W. Graubner (Carbondale and Edwardsville: Southern Illinois University Press, 1978), 177–356. Also see my, *The End of Epistemology: Dewey and His Current Allies on the Spectator Theory of Knowledge* (Westport, CT: Greenwood Press, 1992), chapter 4.

9. I do not intend to suggest that moral nihilists are necessarily bad people: merely misguided. Of course *some* may be bad people, as may some moral realists.

10. I drive home this same point in "Moral Facts and the Centrality of Intuitions," in *The New Intuitionism*, ed. Jill Graper Hernandez (New York & London: Continuum, 2011), 48–66.

11. For a brief but very useful discussion of varieties of moral skepticism, see Walter Sinnott-Armstrong, "Moral Skepticism and Justification," in his *Moral Knowledge? New Readings in Moral Epistemology* (Oxford: Oxford University Press, 1996), 3–48.

12. First, a disclaimer: each of the views discussed below have an enormous literature. I am under no illusion that the remarks to follow are even remotely exhaustive: each view easily deserves book-length treatment. Our project must be much more modest.

13. See A. J. Ayer, *Language, Truth, and Logic* (New York: Dover, 1952).

14. See C. L. Stevenson, *Ethics and Language* (New Haven, CT: Yale University Press, 1944).

15. Ibid, 21; his italics.

16. See my comments on subjunctive conditionals in chapter 2, §2.5, and chapter 3, §3.5.

17. A substantial literature has developed regarding concerns about non-cognitivism's capacity to make sense of moral argumentation. For instance, the "embedding problem," also known as the Frege-Geach objection: If first-order moral discourse is supposed to express a non-cognitive attitude—an emotion, say—what are we to make of moral discourse such as the following? To take a standard form example, suppose *S* asserts the following:

> If chattel slavery is morally wrong, then being a slave owner is morally wrong.
> Chattel slavery is morally wrong.
> Therefore, being a slave owner is morally wrong.

Here, the last locution, 'Being a slave owner is morally wrong' clearly seems to follow from the first two locutions (by *modus ponens*). The non-cognitivist takes *S*'s assertion of the second locution, 'Chattel slavery is morally wrong' to express a (negative) non-cognitive attitude toward slavery, but when the same locution appears as the antecedent of the conditional, it seems that *S* need not there be expressing a non-cognitive attitude of any sort. What then, is the asserter doing? Expressing a propositional attitude? Not according to the non-cognitivist. But how then to make sense of what certainly seems to be a valid deductive argument? My answer: you can't. You need a cognitivist interpretation of moral discourse to do that. Inferential relations between locutions requires propositionality; for inference in general, and validity in particular, is a matter of truth conductivity between evidence and conclusion. But propositions are truth bearers, not emotions or other non-cognitive attitudes. Many, however, would not agree with me. I cannot further pursue this rather specialized matter here.

18. Allan Gibbard, *Wise Choices, Apt Feelings* (Oxford: Oxford University Press, 1990); and *Thinking How to Live* (Cambridge: Harvard University Press, 2003). As in chapter 4, §4.2, I refer here to his earlier text.

19. Gibbard, *Wise Choices, Apt Feelings*, 7. He refines this statement in chapter 2 and following.

20. See R. M. Hare, *The Language of Morals* (Oxford: Oxford University Press, 1952).

21. Friedrich Nietzsche, *The Will to Power*, edited by Walter Kaufman, translated by Walter Kaufman and R. J. Hollingdale (New York: Vintage Books, 1968), sec. 428.

22. See J. L. Mackie, *Ethics: Inventing Right and Wrong* (Viking Press, 1977); also see his "A Refutation of Morals," *Australasian Journal of Philosophy*, 24, nos. 1 and 2 (1946): 77–90.

23. We took up some of these same issues in chapter 2, §2.4. I also discuss them in "Moral Facts and the Centrality of Intuitions."

24. We may say similar things about other properties instanced in the physical state of affairs at issue, for example, the relational property of apple *B* being to the right of apple *A,* and to the left of apple *C*. This looks very much to be a matter of "the way the world is." Are these properties "queer"? Or what about the symmetricality of the property of identity, viz., If (A = B), then (B = A)?

25. And for that matter, what does the term 'abuse' mean, anyway? *Morally* speaking, abusing a child sexually is relevantly similar to "abusing" a car. Counterintuitive, indeed.

26. William H. Shaw makes many of these points in exceedingly accessible and provocative fashion in "Relativism in Ethics," in Steven Scalet and John Arthur, *Morality and Moral Controversies* (New York: Pearson, 2014), 47–50.

27. Harman's relativism and conceptual moral relativism are in essentially in the same boat. If there is no implicit agreement that slavery is impermissible, or if the governing moral concepts do not prohibit slavery, then . . . slavery is permissible.

28. A point that in essence goes back to Plato, where Socrates argues in the *Euthyphro* that the gods loving the holy is not what *makes* the holy in fact holy. See Plato, *Euthyphro*, translated by Lane Cooper, in *Plato: The Collected Dialogues*, edited by Edith Hamilton and Huntington Cairns (Princeton, NJ: Princeton University Press, 1961), 169–85, especially 177–80.

29. Or, more technically, merely different proposition-tokens of the identical proposition-type. The radical subjectivist is committed to there being different proposition-types on each occasion of assertion.

30. Perhaps this same dilemma may be applied mutatis mutandis to sociocultural moral relativism, given that—as we discussed in chapter 4, §4.3—that form of moral relativism shares with radical moral subjectivism commitment to belief being the foundation of moral value and truth, the difference between the two being that sociocultural relativism refers to a collectivity of belief, while subjectivism refers to individual belief. But the collectivity is composed of individuals. We do not appear to commit the Fallacy of Composition if we attribute the property of "value maker" to the individual in both subjectivism and sociocultural relativism. For only if individuals endorse a value is it possible for the collectivity to do so.

31. In fact, argumentation as a truth-governed enterprise is standardly thought to embrace the twin desiderata of maximizing truth and minimizing falsehood; and it is also standardly thought that these desiderata can be in tension with one another. For maximizing truth counsels epistemic risk-taking, therefore exposing one to the possibility of error, while minimizing falsehood counsels epistemic risk-aversion, which does not conduce to maximizing truth. For the moral subjectivist, however, there is no tension here: in fact, you can't go wrong. Surely, this isn't plausible.

32. As noted in chapter 3, §3.4, the spirit of views of this type emanates from Charles Darwin, *The Descent of Man* (London: Penguin, 2004 [1871]), in particular the chapter entitled, "On the Development of the Intellectual and Moral Faculties of Civilized Times of Man."

33. Our last displayed proposition, and very like P24, but modified slightly for even greater explicitness—perhaps unnecessarily.

34. See Wilfrid Sellars, *Science, Perception, and Reality* (London: Routledge and Kegan Paul, 1956), chapter 5.

35. We avoid entanglements with "vague propositions" like 'Smith is bald', where the predicate 'is bald' may not have clear truth conditions.

36. And there is of course a "way the world is" with regard to how we conceive of the world: there are facts of the matter regarding our conceptions.

37. Some first-order moral propositions, however, appear to be analytic such, as 'Murder is pro tanto facie wrong'. Yet it seems that most are synthetic, the most fundamental being synthetic propositions knowable a priori. See chapter 5, §5.1.

38. Yes, cataclysmic social collapse occasioned by, for example, global war may lead to such consequences, but this is the kind of thing I am ruling out by the "robust and plausible" qualifier.

39. See Charles S. Peirce, "Some Consequences of Four Incapacities," *The Collected Papers of Charles Sanders Peirce*, edited by Charles Hartshorne and Paul Weiss (Cambridge, MA: Harvard University Press, 1931–1935), Vol. 5, esp. 264–68; in "How to Make Our Ideas Clear," in *The Collected Papers of Charles Sanders Peirce*, Vol. 5, 388–410.

40. There is dispute over the extent to which Moore privileged common sense. It appears that he may not have been fully consistent on this. See, for example, his comments in "An Autobiography," *The Philosophy of G. E. Moore*, edited by Paul Arthur Schilpp (Chicago: Open Court, 1942), 3–39.

# Works Cited

Alston, William P. *A Realist Conception of Truth*. Ithaca, NY: Cornell University Press, 1996.
———. "Realism and the Tasks of Epistemology." In *Realism/Antirealism and Epistemology*. Edited by Christopher B. Kulp, 53–94. Lanham, MD: Rowman & Littlefield, 1997.
Anscombe, G. E. M. "Modern Moral Philosophy." *Philosophy*, 33 (1958): 1–19.
Aristotle. "Nicomachean Ethics." In *The Basic Works of Aristotle*. Translated by W. D Ross. Edited by Richard McKeon, 935–1112. New York: Random House, 1941.
Armstrong, D. M. "Four Disputes About Properties." *Synthese* (2005): 144, 309–320.
——— *Nominalism and Realism: Universals and Scientific Realism*, Vol. 1, Cambridge: Cambridge University Press, 1978.
Audi, Robert. *Epistemology*, 3rd edition. New York and London: Routledge, 2011.
———. "Intuition and Its Place in Ethics," *Journal of the American Philosophical Association* 1, Issue 1 (2015): 57–77.
———. "Intuitions, Intuitions, and Moral Judgment." In *The New Intuitionism*. Edited by Jill Graper Hernandez, 171–98. London and New York: Continuum: 2011.
———. *The Good in the Right*. Princeton: Princeton University Press, 2004.
Ayer, A. J. *Language, Truth, and Logic*. New York: Dover, 1952.
Blackburn, Simon. *Spreading the Word*. Oxford: Oxford University Press, 1984.
Blanchard, Brand. *The Nature of Thought*, Vol. 2, 264. London: Allen & Unwin, 1939.
BonJour, Lawrence. *The Structure of Empirical Knowledge*. Cambridge, MA: Harvard University Press, 1985.
Bradley, F. H. *Essays on Truth and Reality*. Oxford: Clarendon Press, 1914.
Brink, David. *Moral Realism and the Foundations of Ethics*. Cambridge: Cambridge University Press, 1989.
Chisholm, Roderick. *The Theory of Knowledge*, 1st–3rd editions. Englewood Cliffs, NJ: Prentice Hall, 1966/1977/1989.
Churchland, Paul. *Scientific Realism and the Plasticity of Mind*. Cambridge: Cambridge University Press, 1979.
———. "Some Reductive Strategies in Cognitive Neurobiology." *Mind* 95 (1986): 279–307.
Cornman, James, Keith Lehrer, and George Pappas. *Philosophical Problems and Arguments*. Indianapolis, IN: Hackett Publishing Co., 1992. 43–44.
Darwin, Charles. *The Descent of Man*. London: Penguin, 2004 (1871).
Descartes, Rene. *Meditations on First Philosophy*. Translated by Donald A. Cress. Indianapolis, IN: Hackett Publishing Co., 1993 (1641).
Dewey, John. "How We Think." In *John Dewey: The Middle Works, 1899–1924*, Vol. 6, 1910–1911. Edited by Jo Ann Boydston and Bridget W. Graubner, 177–356. Carbondale and Edwardsville: Southern Illinois University Press, 1978.

————. "Logic: The Theory of Inquiry." In *John Dewey: The Later Works, 1925–1953*, Vol. 12, 1938. Edited by Kathleen E. Poulos, 3–527. Carbondale and Edwardsville: Southern Illinois University Press, 1986.

————. "Reconstruction in Philosophy." In *John Dewey: The Middle Works, 1899–1924*, Vol. 12, 1920. Edited by Bridget A. Walsh, 77–201. Carbondale and Edwardsville: Southern Illinois University Press, 1982.

Enoch, David. *Taking Morality Seriously*. Oxford: Oxford University Press, 2011.

Feldman, Richard. *Epistemology*. Upper Saddle, NJ: Prentice Hall, 2003.

Gettier, Edmund. "Is Justified True Belief Knowledge?" *Analysis* 23 (1963): 121–23.

Gibbard, Allan. *Wise Choices, Apt Feelings*. Oxford: Oxford University Press, 1990.

————. *Thinking How to Live*. Cambridge, MA: Harvard University Press, 2003.

Haack, Susan. *Philosophy of Logics*. Cambridge: Cambridge University Press, 1978.

————, editor. *Pragmatism Old and New*. New York: Prometheus Books, 2006.

Hare, R. M. *The Language of Morals*. Oxford: Oxford University Press, 1952.

Harman, Gilbert. "Moral Relativism Defended." *Philosophical Review* 84 (1975): 3–22.

————. "Moral Relativism." In *Moral Relativism and Moral Objectivity*. Gilbert Harman and Judith Jarvis Thomson, 3–64. Malden, MA: Blackwell, 1996.

————. *The Nature of Morality: An Introduction to Ethics*. Oxford: Oxford University Press, 1977.

Haslanger, Sally. *Resisting Reality: Social Construction and Social Critique*. Oxford: Oxford University Press, 2012.

Hintikka, Jaakko. *Knowledge and Belief: An Introduction to the Logic of the Two Notions*. Ithaca, NY: Cornell University Press, 1962.

Huemer, Michael. *Ethical Intuitionism*. New York: Palgrave MacMillan, 2005.

————. "Three Skeptical Arguments." In *Skepticism and the Veil of Perception*. Lanham, MD: Rowman & Littlefield, 2001: 9–15.

James, William. *Pragmatism and the Meaning of Truth*. Cambridge, MA: Harvard University Press, 1978.

Kagan, Shelly. "Thinking About Cases." In *Moral Knowledge*. Edited by Ellen Frankel Paul, Fred Miller, and Jeffrey Paul, 44–63. Cambridge: Cambridge University Press, 2001.

Kant, Immanuel. *The Critique of Pure Reason*. Translated by Norman Kemp Smith. New York: St. Martin's Press, 1965 (1787).

————. *Fundamental Principles of the Metaphysics of Morals*. Translated by T. K. Abbott. New York: Prometheus Books, 1987 (1785).

Kaspar, David. *Intuitionism*. London and New York: Bloomsbury, 2012.

Kim, Jaegwon. "Concepts of Supervenience." Reprinted in *Supervenience and Mind: Selected Philosophical Essays*. Edited by Jaegwon Kim and Ernest Sosa, 53–78. Cambridge: Cambridge University Press, 1993.

King, Jeffrey C., Scott Soames, and Jeff Speaks. *New Thinking About Propositions*. Oxford: Oxford University Press, 2014.

Kulp, Christopher B. "Disagreement and the Defensibility of Moral Intuitionism." *International Philosophical Quarterly* 56, Issue 224 (December 2016): 487–502.

————. *The End of Epistemology: Dewey and His Current Allies on the Spectator Theory of Knowledge*. Westport, CT: Greenwood Press, 1992.

————. "Moral Facts and the Centrality of Intuitions." In *The New Intuitionism*. Edited by Jill Graper Hernandez, 48–66. New York & London: Continuum, 2011.

————. "The Pre-Theoreticality of Moral Intuitions." *Synthese* 191 (October 2014): 3759–778.

————. *Realism/Antirealism and Epistemology*, editor. Lanham, MD: Rowman & Littlefield, 1997.

Leiter, Brian. "Moral Facts and Best Explanations." In *Moral Knowledge*. Edited by Ellen Frankel Paul, Fred D. Miller, Jr., and Jeffrey Paul: 79–101. Cambridge: Cambridge University Press, 2001.

Lemos, Ramon M. "Bearers of Value." *Philosophy and Phenomenological Research*, Vol. LI, No. 4 (December 1991): 873–89.

————. *Metaphysical Investigations*. London and Toronto: Associated University Presses, 1988.

Lewis, C. I. *An Analysis of Knowledge and Valuation*. La Salle, IL: Open Court, 1946.
———. *Mind and the World Order*. New York: Charles Scribner's Sons, 1929.
Littlejohn, Clayton. "Ethical Intuitionism and Moral Skepticism." In *The New Intuitionism*. Edited by Jill Graper Hernandez, 106–27. New York and London: Continuum, 2011.
MacIntyre, Alasdair. *After Virtue: A Study in Moral Theory* (Notre Dame, IN: University of Notre Dame Press, 1981.
———. "Is Patriotism a Virtue?" The Lindley Lecture, University of Kansas, 1984. Excerpted in *Morality and Moral Controversies*, 9th edition. Edited by Steven Scalet and John Arthur, 405–10. Upper Saddle, NJ: Pearson, 2014.
Mackie, J. L. "A Refutation of Morals." *Australasian Journal of Philosophy* 24, nos. 1 & 2 (1946): 77–90
———. *Ethics: Inventing Right and Wrong*. New York: Viking Press, 1977
McDonald, Fritz J. "A Deflationary Metaphysics of Morality." *Acta Analytica* 25 (2010): 285–98.
McTaggart, J. M. E. "The Unreality of Time." *Mind* 17 (1908): 457–73.
Midgley, Mary. "Trying Out One's New Sword." In *Heart and Mind*. United Kingdom: Harvester Press, 1981. Excerpted in *Morality and Moral Controversies*, 8th edition. Edited by John Arthur and Steven Scalet, 34–37. Upper Saddle River, NJ: Pearson, 2009.
Mill, John Stuart. *An Examination of Sir William Hamilton's Philosophy and of the Principal Philosophical Questions Discussed in His Writings*, Vol. 1. Boston: William Spencer, 1866.
———. *Utilitarianism*. Indianapolis, IN: Hackett Publishing Co., 1979 (1861).
Moore, G. E. "An Autobiography." In *The Philosophy of G. E. Moore*. Edited by Paul Arthur Schilpp, 3–39. La Salle, IL: Open Court, 1942.
———. *Principia Ethica*. Cambridge: Cambridge University Press, 1903.
———. "Proof of an External World." Reprinted in G. E. Moore, *Philosophical Papers*. New York: Collier, 1959.
Moser, Paul K. *Empirical Justification*. Dordrecht, Holland: D. Reidel Publishing Company, 1985.
Moser, Paul K., and Thomas Carson. *Moral Relativism: A Reader*. Oxford: Oxford University Press, 2000.
Nietzsche, Friedrich. *The Will to Power*. Edited by Walter Kaufman. Translated by Walter Kaufman and R. J. Hollingdale. New York: Vintage Books, 1968.
Oliver, Alex. "The Metaphysics of Properties." *Mind*, New Series, 105, no. 417 (January 1996): 1–80.
Peirce, Charles S. "The Fixation of Belief," *The Collected Papers of Charles S. Peirce*. Edited by Charles Hartshorne and Paul Weiss. Cambridge, MA: Harvard University Press, 1913–1935: Vol. 5: paragraph 358–387.
———. "How to Make Our Ideas Clear." *The Collected Papers of Charles Sanders Peirce*, Vol. 5. Edited by Charles Hartshorne and Paul Weiss, paragraphs 388–410. Cambridge, MA: Harvard University Press, 1931–1935.
———. "Some Consequences of Four Incapacities." In *The Collected Papers of Charles S. Peirce*, Vol. 5. Edited by Charles Hartshorne and Paul Weiss, paragraphs 264–317. Cambridge, MA: Harvard University Press, 1913–1935.
———. "What Pragmatism Is," *The Collected Papers of Charles S. Peirce*. Edited by Charles Hartshorne and Paul Weiss. Cambridge, MA: Harvard University Press, 1931–1958), Vol. 5: paragraph 411–415.
Plato. "Euthyphro." Translated by Lane Cooper in *Plato: The Collected Dialogues*. Edited by Edith Hamilton and Huntington Cairns, 169–85. Princeton, NJ: Princeton University Press, 1961.
———. *The Republic*. Translated by Francis MacDonald Cornford. Oxford: Oxford University Press, 1945.
———. "Theaetetus." Translated by Francis McDonald Cornford in *The Collected Dialogues of Plato*. Edited by Edith Hamilton and Huntington Cairns, 845–919. Princeton, NJ: Princeton University Press, 1961.
Popper, Karl. *Conjectures and Refutations: The Growth of Scientific Knowledge*. London: Routledge, 1963.

————. *The Logic of Scientific Discovery*. New York: Harper & Row, 1965 (1959).

Post, John. *Faces of Existence*. Ithaca, NY: Cornell University Press, 1986.

Quine, W. V. "On What There Is." Reprinted in *From a Logical Point of View*, 2nd edition. Cambridge, MA: Harvard University Press, 1961: 1–19.

————. *Philosophy of Logic*. Cambridge, MA: Harvard University Press, 1970.

————. "Two Dogmas of Empiricism." Reprinted in *From A Logical Point of View*, 2nd edition. Cambridge, MA: Harvard University Press, 1961: 20–46.

Rawls, John. *A Theory of Justice*. Cambridge, MA: Harvard University Press, 1971.

Regan, Tom. *Bloomsbury's Prophet: G. E. Moore and the Development of His Moral Philosophy*. Eugene, OR: Wipf and Stock, 1986.

*Report of the State's Attorney for the Judicial District of Danbury on the Shootings at the Sandy Hook Elementary School and 36 Yogananda Street, Newtown, Connecticut on December 14, 2012*, by the Office of the State's Attorney, Judicial District of Danbury, Stephen J. Sedensky III, State's Attorney, November 25, 2013.

Rorty, Richard. *Consequences of Pragmatism: Essays 1972–1980*. Minneapolis: University of Minnesota Press, 1982.

————. *Philosophy and the Mirror of Nature*. Princeton, NJ: Princeton University Press, 1979.

————. "Realism, Antirealism, and Pragmatism: Comments on Alston, Chisholm, Davidson, Harman, and Searle." In *Realism/Antirealism and Epistemology*. Edited by Christopher B. Kulp. Lanham, MD: Rowman & Littlefield, 1997: 149–71.

Ross, W. D. Ross, *The Right and the Good*. Oxford: Oxford University Press, 1930.

Russell, Bertrand. *The Autobiography of Bertrand Russell*, Vol. 1. London: George Allen & Unwin, 1967.

————. *Human Knowledge: Its Scope and Limits*. London: George Allen & Unwin, 1948.

Searle, John. *The Construction of Social Reality*. New York: Free Press, 1995.

————. *Intentionality: An Essay in the Philosophy of Mind*. Cambridge: Cambridge University Press, 1983.

————. "Minds, Brains, and Programs." In *The Behavioral and Brian Sciences*, Vol. 3, Issue 3. Cambridge: Cambridge University Press, 1980. 417–24.

Sellars, Wilfrid. *Science, Perception, and Reality*. London: Routledge and Kegan Paul, 1961.

Shafer-Landau, Russ. *Moral Realism: A Defence*. Oxford: Oxford University Press, 2003.

Shaw, William H. "Relativism in Ethics." *Morality and Moral Controversies*, 9th edition. Edited by Steven Scalet and John Arthur, 47–50. New York: Pearson, 2014.

Shope, Robert K. *The Analysis of Knowing: A Decade of Research*. Princeton, NJ: Princeton University Press, 1983.

Sidgwick, Henry. *The Methods of Ethics*, 7th edition. New York: Dover, 1966 (1907).

Sinnott-Armstrong, Walter. "Moral Perception and Heuristics." *The Modern Schoolman* 86 (2009): 327–47:

————. "Moral Skepticism and Justification." In *Moral Knowledge?: New Readings in Moral Epistemology*. Edited by Walter Sinnott-Armstrong and Mark Timmons: 3–48. Oxford: Oxford University Press, 1996.

————. "Reflections on Reflection in Robert Audi's Moral Intuitionism." In *Rationality and the Good: Critical Essays on the Ethics and Epistemology of Robert Audi*. Edited by Mark Timmons, John Greco, and Alfred R. Mele. Oxford: Oxford University Press, 2007.

Stevenson, C. L. *Ethics and Language*. New Haven, CT: Yale University Press, 1944.

Thagard, Paul. "The Best Explanation: Criteria for Theory Choice." *Journal of Philosophy* 75, no. 2 (1978): 76–92.

Whitehead, Alfred North. *Process and Reality*. New York: Free Press, 1929.

Williams, Bernard. *Ethics and the Limits of Philosophy*. Cambridge, MA: Harvard University Press, 1985.

Wittgenstein, Ludwig. *Philosophical Investigations*, 3rd edition. Translated by G. E. M. Anscombe. New York: Macmillan, 1958.

————. *On Certainty*. Edited by G. E. M. Anscombe and G. H. von Wright. New York: Harper & Row, 1969.

————. *Tractatus Logico-Philosophicus*. Translated by D. F. Pears and B. F. McGuinness. London: Routledge and Kegan Paul, 1961.

# Index

# About the Author

**Christopher B. Kulp** (PhD, philosophy, Vanderbilt University) is associate professor of philosophy at Santa Clara University. His research interests center on epistemology, metaethics, and moral epistemology. In addition to this book, he is also the author of *The End of Epistemology* (Greenwood Press, 1992) and the editor of *Realism/Antirealism and Epistemology* (Rowman & Littlefield, 1997). He is currently writing a book on the metaphysics of morality.